THE ROYAL SCOTS

THE ROYAL SCOTS

1914-1919

BY

MAJOR JOHN EWING, M.C.

WITH A FOREWORD BY

THE RIGHT HON. LORD SALVESEN

EDINBURGH

Published for the Association of Lowland Scots by

OLIVER AND BOYD, TWEEDDALE COURT

LONDON: 33 PATERNOSTER ROW, E.C.

1925

CONTENTS

CHAPTER XXIII

THE EVE OF THE PASSCHENDAELE CAMPAIGN

May to July 1917

CHAPTER XXIV

PASSCHENDAELE

Actions of 31st July and 22nd August 1917

CHAPTER XXV

THE 15TH AND 16TH ROYAL SCOTS AT HARGICOURT

July to September 1917

CHAPTER XXXIV

THE GERMAN OFFENSIVE ON THE LYS

April 1918

CHAPTER XXXV

THE TURN OF THE TIDE

May to August 1918

CHAPTER XXXVI

THE ADVANCE TO VICTORY

August and September 1918

CHAPTER XXXVII

THE COLLAPSE OF BULGARIA

1st Battalion The Royal Scots, 1918

CHAPTER XXXVIII

THE FINAL BLOW

September to November 1918

CHAPTER XXXIX

THE 2/10TH ROYAL SCOTS IN NORTHERN RUSSIA

August 1918 *to May* 1919

CHAPTER XL

THE ROYAL SCOTS MEMORIAL

APPENDICES

LIST OF ILLUSTRATIONS

FULL PAGE

TEXT MAPS.

FOLDING MAPS.

THE ROYAL SCOTS

CHAPTER XXIII

THE EVE OF THE PASSCHENDAELE CAMPAIGN

May to July 1917

Divisions at Rest. Location of Royal Scots Battalions. Pelmanism. Development of offensive methods in the Air. Object of Passchendaele Campaign. How the situation on the Western Front was affected by events in other theatres. Capture of Messines Ridge, June 1917. The German plan of defence in Flanders. Difficulties of the British. Work of 8th Royal Scots.

IN 1917 the British Army reached its greatest strength, and this enabled the High Command to withdraw divisions from the line for longer periods than had hitherto been possible. The normal occupation of a battalion was the holding of a section of trenches, varied periodically by congenial interludes devoted to intensive training and systematic recreation in the back areas, and by brief but hectic spells of fighting in the forefront of an offensive. Trench duty was now regarded not only as a necessary task to be conscientiously performed, but also as a preparation for action, a training for raw soldiers, and raids were encouraged partly to stimulate the offensive spirit, and partly to obtain identifications which would enable the High Command to ascertain the names and the number of the formations with which the enemy was holding his line. The essential obligations of trench duty, however, limited the amount of training that could be performed, and battle-torn divisions were taken from the sound of the guns to the areas in the hinterland, so that they might more quickly recover from their wounds.   Thus many hard-fighting divisions enjoyed interludes of two or three weeks and even longer, during which, free from the necessity of providing working parties or of performing the manifold chores that fell to infantry when in the line, they devoted themselves entirely to training and recreation, and thus rapidly regained confidence and keenness. A strong effort was made to bring the standard of musketry as near as possible to that which had made the original Expeditionary Force the most formidable fighting machine in the world, for the bomb as a weapon of offence had fallen into disfavour, experience having shown that ground was seldom gained by bombing attacks alone.

The veterans among the officers and men formed the vitalising leaven of battalions and divisions, and upon them devolved the arduous duty of assimilating reinforcements and organising the training.   The gigantic scale of the war made the division the natural tactical unit, and owing to this a strong divisional *esprit de corps* was engendered. So much was this the case, that the customary thing to ask a man was to what division, not to what battalion, he belonged. At the same time within every division each battalion flattered itself that it was the pick of its own formation. This co-operative pride was the magic wand that not merely reconciled men to battle, but made them even wish for it, since every additional action, whatever tortures it might hold in store for individuals, brought fresh laurels to the formation to which they were attached. Revived and benefited by a few weeks in the country, a division always returned to the line eager to throw itself into the fray.

All the divisions with which we are concerned appreciated the new policy that secured them long vacations from the line, though the purpose of these was to fit them for another orgy of bloodshed. The Fifteenth Division, after being relieved at Arras, did not return to the line till the beginning of July, when it took over trenches north of the Menin Road. The only thrill experienced by the 13th Royal Scots before the action of the 31st July was an abortive raid by the enemy on the night of the 9th/10th July, when two Germans were captured. The Fifty-first Division, also ear-marked to take part in the first phase of the Third Battle of Ypres, took over its battle-front with one brigade on the night of the 22nd/23rd June. All its units thus had ample time for training save the unfortunate pioneers, the 8th Royal Scots, who were always at work of some description in the obnoxious Salient from the middle of June till the 25th September, a period during which the enemy continuously and violently shelled our battery positions and back areas in a determined effort to regain artillery supremacy.

The 2nd Royal Scots were destined for a quieter region, and after more than a fortnight's rest, during which the battalion football team defeated by three goals to none that of the 16th Royal Scots—the first and only defeat suffered by the latter—they entered trenches in the Louverval sector on the 1st July. The line here consisted of detached posts, and, owing to the nature of the ground, no work could be done in the daytime, but every night the companies laboured hard to improve their defences. A curious incident occurred on the 5th July. At 6 A.M. a German, sheltering in the ruins of the village of Boursies within our lines, was observed to be spying our position through field-glasses and was immediately fired on. Bolting down the Cambrai Road towards the Boche trenches he leaped a barricade across the road, and was fired on by the garrisons of the Royal Scots posts; continuing his flight down the road he disappeared from view, but a small patrol, which went out to search for him, found him lying dead. The battalion remained in the Louverval sector till the 5th September, and though patrols went out nightly there was no contact with the enemy. One raid by "C" Company was planned to take place on the early morning of the 25th August, but the party was discovered before the "Bangalore" torpedoes could be inserted in the hostile wire, and the project had to be abandoned.

The Ninth Division had the good fortune to be kept out of the line for fully six weeks, from the 13th June till the 26th July, and this long spell was thoroughly justified by its tonic effect on the troops. Then followed a sojourn in the line near Havrincourt, where the Ninth Division was on the right of the Third. The 27th Brigade was separated from the enemy's main position by the deep dry channel of the Canal du Nord, and since there was only one hostile outpost, a fortified slag heap on our side of the canal, the possibility of encounters was remote. Patrolling both by day and by night was carried on with great assiduity, and parties from the 11th and the 12th Royal Scots boldly investigated the floor of the canal. This tour of trench duty was chiefly useful in accustoming the new soldiers to the conditions of trench warfare, and at the end of August the Ninth was relieved by the Ulster Division and prepared to move northwards.

The Thirty-fourth Division also went to the south, taking over trenches near Hargicourt at the beginning of July, and an account of its adventures in this area is given in a later chapter. These three divisions, the Third, Ninth, and Thirty-fourth, were within the zone, lying east of Bapaume, which the Germans had laid waste during their retreat to the Hindenburg Line in the early spring of 1917. The enemy had systematically demolished all the villages, leaving no building with a roof to cover it, had blown craters in the roads, and had destroyed the fruit trees, and the indignation of the troops on beholding the general devastation of civilian property waxed high, an indignation all the keener since ruined buildings provided draughty and comfortless billets, while the necessity of tidying up required large working parties from the infantry.

It remains for us to trace the history of the 5/6th and the 17th Royal Scots, the only battalions of the Regiment on the Western front which were not engaged in the Battle of Arras.

The 5/6th Battalion was withdrawn from the line opposite St Quentin on the 15th May, and at the beginning of June was transferred to the far north, where on the 18th it took over the front trenches in the St Georges sector, east of Nieuport. The flat country was intersected and broken by numerous ditches and inundated areas which afforded great scope for amphibian exploits, and on the 4th July 2nd Lieut. Rae of "W" Company had an alarming experience. Early in the morning, when he was walking from a farm to his company H.Q., he was startled on being challenged in German by two men who, appearing over the camouflaged screen on the Nieuport Road, fired at him. He was wounded in the hand, but made his escape to the nearest Royal Scots post. The daring Boches could only have reached the road by crossing in a raft or boat a wide sheet of water in this polder-land. The battalion was not involved in the disaster of the 10th July, when the enemy, by successfully attacking the bridge-head north-east of the Yser between Nieuport and the coast, effectually prevented our Passchendaele campaign from being assisted by the co-operation of the Navy. By this time the battalion under Lieut.-Colonel Fraser was in excellent fighting trim, and later in the year showed great skill in the organisation of a difficult raid.

When Lieut.-Colonel Cheales left the 17th Royal Scots, Major P. S. Hall, on the 16th May, assumed the command of the battalion, which towards the end of the month took over the line near Villers Guislain. On the 7th June, Lieut.-Colonel Heathcote, who had served with the 2nd Royal Scots, arrived to lead the battalion, Lieut.-Colonel Hall being transferred to an English unit. Owing to the activity in Flanders, little occurred to interfere with the daily routine save occasional raids. On the 19th July some Germans attempted a raid which was easily repulsed by rifle and machine-gun fire, but on the 6th August they were more successful, for, though they sustained some losses, they captured two prisoners. The battalion took its revenge on the 16th September, when in a foray on a German trench at least eight of the enemy were killed and two prisoners captured; the only casualty suffered by the 17th Royal Scots in this enterprise was 2nd Lieut. J. Struth, who unfortunately was killed. There were no other incidents of note, and at the beginning of October the battalion packed up and proceeded with the Thirty-fifth Division to the Passchendaele sector.

Two features that affected the Army from 1917 deserve mention. The first was the wave of Pelmanism, which enjoyed an extraordinary vogue during the war. From the testimonials quoted in press advertisements, it appeared that the surest way to obtain promotion was to take up a course of Pelmanism, the wisdom of which

was contained in twelve "little grey books." So potent
were the methods of Pelmanism in promoting efficiency
that the only imaginable reason why we failed to bring the
war to a victorious conclusion sooner than we did must
have been that the Germans were training themselves
in a similar manner. The victims of the epidemic were
legion, and all wore a self-conscious air when they were
discovered in an out-of-the-way corner poring over the
"little grey books," and all tried to convey the impression that the books had come into their hands by
some casual chance.

One story connected with its epidemic was keenly
relished by the Royal Scots of the Ninth Division.
Among the reinforcements that reached the 11th
Royal Scots after the Battle of Arras was Captain
W. Y. Darling who, as a C.Q.M.S. in the 9th Black
Watch, had been wounded at Loos. A born story-
teller with an impressive personality, he became one of
the pillars of the division, and when ill-health rendered
him unfit for front-line service, he was transferred to
the Staff. No company, however august, could awe
him, and shortly after his appointment he was present
at a divisional dinner, when Pelmanism cropped up as
a topic of conversation. One Brig.-General remarked
that he had benefited enormously by a course, having
been promoted to the command of a battalion soon
after he took it up, and to that of a brigade just after
he had concluded it. One or two others were alluding
to instances where similar benefits had followed a course
of study, when Captain Darling broke in : "I can cap
that. I had no sooner written for a prospectus than
I was given a job on the Staff!"

The other feature was the development of offensive
methods in the air. Throughout the war there had
been occasional bombing attacks on infantry and camps

by solitary aeroplanes, but these caused trifling damage and were not taken seriously. It was quite a different matter when squadrons of aircraft were organised to bomb and spray with machine-gun fire infantry, camps, and depots behind our lines. The damage inflicted on camps and transport lines was frequently very heavy, and our troops found that on leaving the front line for the back areas, they could not count on an undisturbed night's rest. So proficient did the hostile aeroplanes become in the use of their machine-guns that our battalions were issued with anti-aircraft mountings for Lewis guns, the fire of which served to keep the enemy's machines from descending to a height where they could be certain of hitting their target. Nowhere was the enemy's activity in the air more marked than in Flanders, where Sir Douglas Haig had planned to launch his main offensive.

Through the subordination of Sir Douglas Haig's schemes to those of the French in the early part of 1917, the development of the Passchendaele campaign was delayed till a season when the prospects of snatching a decisive advantage were remote. The goal of the campaign, the Passchendaele Ridge, was an objective well worth striving for, since by its capture the whole position on the Western front would be altered appreciably in favour of the Allies. It would secure for us the command of the Belgian littoral, enabling us to threaten the communications of the enemy, and would at the same time interfere with his submarine campaign by depriving him of his advanced bases in Belgium, and open the way to a co-operative movement between our naval and military forces.

But the morale of our troops was not as high after the Battle of Arras as it had been at the beginning of the year, and while the morale of the Allies had sunk, that of the enemy had risen. For though they had been driven from the Vimy Ridge, the German forces could plume themselves on having kept a firm hold on Lens and Douai, and they had repulsed with crushing losses to their opponents the grand offensive launched by General Nivelle in May. The effect of the Russian Revolution was to turn the balance temporarily in favour of the enemy, and the Germans, seeking inspiration from history, were roused to optimism by the recollection that in the Seven Years' War Prussia had been saved from extinction by the elimination of Russia as an active foe. It was true that the Allies, while losing Russia, had gained America, but the Germans trusted that they would be able to force a peace before America could throw its weight into the struggle. Left to its own scanty resources, gallant Rumania was driven out of the war, while the scintillating campaign of Sir Stanley Maude in Mesopotamia, which led to the capture of Bagdad in March, could not be turned to its greatest profit without the assistance of Russia. The British offensive in Palestine had been brought to a halt at Gaza, while on the Southern European front, the part played by Italy in the war was almost negligible. The diminution of morale among the Allies chiefly affected the French troops, their despondency being so profound that Sir Douglas Haig was obliged to carry on an offensive in the hope of restoring confidence throughout France.

In spite of every handicap the British made a good start on the 7th June when, by the capture of Messines Ridge, they deprived the adversary of a valuable observation point. The way was now prepared for our attack on Passchendaele Ridge.

The Germans, though disconcerted by the loss of Messines, were confident that they could hold us in check, because they knew that the colossal mining preparations, which had been principally responsible for our triumph on the 7th June, could not be repeated in the course of a few weeks, and because with characteristic thoroughness they had elaborated a system of defence which it would tax all our resources to penetrate. In the swampy soil of Passchendaele ordinary trenches were impossible, so the Germans made use of ruined barns and farms, strongly concreted to an average thickness of 3 feet, which formed insignificant artillery marks and were impervious to all but our weightiest projectiles. These concreted forts, dubbed by our troops "pill-boxes," varied in size according to the extent of the ruins on which they were erected, and were so chosen that each could support its neighbours by cross and enfilade fire. These obstacles were admirably adapted to break up and delay an attack, and even if they were carried, the assailants would have to meet a counter-attack from fresh German reserves in the rear. Distribution in depth and organised counter-attacks formed the basis of the Boche defensive system.

The campaign of 1917 brought Ypres once more into prominence. The vast military importance of that city is easy to comprehend, since practically every highway between northern France and Flanders converged upon it. With their command of the ridge, the Germans, by artillery fire alone, could interfere effectively with our communications, hence an important item in our preparations for the campaign consisted in the construction of subsidiary routes to avoid the city. The maritime plain on which Ypres was situated was overlooked on the north, north-east, east, and south, by low-wooded heights, of which the Passchendaele Ridge was the most important. From his positions the enemy enjoyed a wide view over all our hinterland, and had, therefore, the tremendous advantage of being able to train the fire of his guns by direct observation. It was owing to this that trench duty in the Salient proved more costly to us than in any other sector of our front. The road between Poperinghe and Ypres was one of our main arteries of communication, and as it was constantly subjected to shell fire, movement along it was, as far as possible, carried on after dark. Daylight reliefs were impossible, and the nightly pilgrimages between the reserve areas and the line were in some ways the greatest trials that our men had to endure; they could never be certain when a salvo of shells would drop among them, and they were never free from suspense until they had reached their destination.

In the case of ordinary infantry units the strain was a periodic one, but in the case of the pioneers it was a daily one, and the diary of the 8th Royal Scots for this reason contains brief but significant references to the extreme unpleasantness of conditions in the Salient. It was noted that throughout July the volume of hostile gun fire was perceptibly increasing, and that the vicinity of the Yser Canal banks, where the greater part of the battalion was accommodated, was particularly unsafe. Several men were lost through gas, shells, and bombs, and two officers, Lieut. J. Bremner and 2nd Lieut. Wilson, were wounded before the 31st July. Nevertheless, in spite of interruptions caused by shelling and bombing, all the tasks of the battalion were completed in good time.

Owing to the marshy nature of the country the possibility of a favourable outcome to the campaign depended very largely upon a continuance of dry weather. Even during the height of summer no soil[1]

---

[1] The few places where excavations could be made without the danger of floods were indicated by the Geological Survey of Belgium to the British G.H.Q., and these were used for the construction of battle dug-outs for brigade and divisional H.Q.

could be removed with pick or shovel without the cavity immediately filling with water, and it was quite certain that if there was any prolonged period of rain, the passage of men and animals across the shell-torn swamp would be attended with the greatest difficulty.   As it turned out, the weather after the opening of the battle was unfavourable and ruined our campaign.   All our preparations were completed during July, and on the last day of the month Sir Douglas Haig unleashed his offensive.

CHAPTER XXIV

PASSCHENDAELE

Actions of 31st July and 22nd August 1917

British Offensive begins, 31st July. 13th Royal Scots at Frezenberg. German counter-attack. 15th Royal Scots at Beck House and Square Farm, 1st August. 9th Royal Scots near the Steenbeek. Work of 8th Royal Scots. Campaign interrupted by rain. Fruitless attack by 13th Royal Scots, 22nd August.

THE attack delivered by General Gough's Fifth Army on the 31st July opened so triumphantly that the greater part of the ridge overlooking Ypres from the east was speedily stormed, but Von Armin's system of counter-attack proved very effective, and before the end of the day many of our gains had been recaptured by the enemy. The Germans retained the key of their defence on the Menin Road, but we had at least secured a footing on the ridge, and if the weather during August had been kindly, our attack might have been developed with profit.

The most prominent of the Royal Scots battalions in this action was the 13th, which on the eve of the battle lay in a camp near Ypres. The sector occupied by the Fifteenth Division was immediately north of the Ypres-Roulers Railway, the front line skirting Railway Wood. The main road from Ypres rose slightly after the Menin Gate and then sloped gradually down to "Hell-fire Corner," where it was cut by the railway, whence it again ascended steadily to the remnants of the village of Hooge; just beyond Hooge loomed the ridge which gave the enemy direct observation over the plain of Ypres. The task of the Fifteenth Division was to seize this ridge near

Frezenberg, and then to push on to a slight rise to the north-east of Frezenberg known as Hill 35. The main attack was entrusted to the 44th and 46th Brigades, while the 45th was to go through the other two brigades at the ridge and capture the final objective. The 13th Royal Scots, being in reserve, had no prospect of being involved in the fight unless matters turned out badly.

The sky was dull and cloudy when the battalion set out from the camp at 4.7 A.M., and very little shelling was experienced till the men were passing White Château on the Menin Road. Without any great difficulty, however, the Royal Scots assembled along Cambridge Road, where they remained until word was received that the Frezenberg Ridge had been carried. At 8.50 A.M. the 6th Camerons, the leading battalion of the 45th Brigade, moved forward, the Royal Scots following them at a distance of about 500 yards. Everything at first went well. The Camerons captured Hill 37 and thus occupied a position beyond the division's final objective, while the Royal Scots formed a line east of the fortified farm, known as Beck House, with "A" Company on the right and "C" on the left.

All this was accomplished before midday, but little progress had been made with the work of consolidation, when the counter-attack began. Shortly after noon a large number of Boche aeroplanes flew low over our lines and directed the fire of the German gunners, whose shelling caused many casualties among both the Camerons and the Royal Scots. Lieut.-Colonel Hannay had just reached Beck House, where he established his H.Q., when he learned that an untimely shell had put out of action the whole H.Q. Staff of the Camerons. The hostile pressure increased in fury, and in the afternoon the German infantry kept up a persistent offensive.

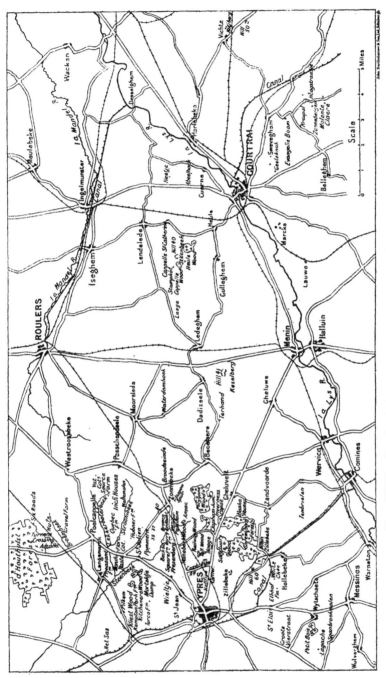

MAP XVIII.—Passchendaele, 1917, and the Offensive in Flanders, 1918.

(*See also* large scale Map at end of volume.)

About 3 P.M. Lieut.-Colonel Hannay noted uneasily that some men belonging to a battalion on the left were retiring, and he correctly conjectured that the Boches were attacking in force along Hills 37 and 35. At once he despatched his front companies, "A" and "C," to assist the Camerons, instructing them particularly to guard the left flank, from which the greatest danger was apprehended. In addition, he sent a platoon from "B" Company to form a defensive flank on Hill 35, with orders to stop all men who were retiring. But the German counter-attack developed more rapidly than Lieut.-Colonel Hannay had anticipated, and before "A" and "C" Companies reached the Camerons, the Highlanders had already begun to withdraw, with the Germans following in close pursuit. All our sacrifices would have been in vain if the ridge were lost, so Lieut.-Colonel Hannay ordered "A" Company to hold on at all costs to its position in front of the Zonnebeke stream, while he directed "C" on its left to throw back its flank and get into touch with the platoon of "B" Company on Hill 35. While this was being done, he sent 2nd Lieuts. J. K. Ogilvie and W. A. Henderson to stop all men who were coming back and rally them along the Frezenberg Line. These adjustments were supervised personally by the C.O., assisted by his Adjutant, Captain A. H. Craig.

At this time the weak point in the position of the 13th Royal Scots was the left flank, where the Germans were doggedly pressing on their attack, and at 4.30 P.M. the fall of their Very lights indicated that they were still making disquieting headway. About 5 P.M. heavy rain, long presaged by the dark moisture-laden clouds that had mustered in the sky, fell and continued without abatement during the night, chilling the men and churning up the broken ground. Meantime 2nd Lieut. Ogilvie, striding through the mud, reached Pommern Redoubt, and rallying, by means of threats and exhortations, some leaderless men of an English battalion, formed them in a line extending from the redoubt southwards. From this position a raking fire from Lewis guns and rifles was directed on the enemy with considerable effect. A heavy attack against "A" Company of the Royal Scots was beaten off by accurate firing, though the men were suffering severely from the pitiless shell fire which the German gunners maintained along our positions. Captain F. J. Turner, whose imperturbability and confidence inspired his men with new courage and self-reliance, was hit in the lung by a bullet, but he refused to withdraw till the counter-attack had been definitely checked.

About 6 P.M. the Germans appeared to relax their pressure, and soon afterwards some of them were seen to be retiring. Patrols were then sent out to follow up the enemy, while every effort was made to strengthen the defence of our position. There could be no reasonable doubt that the Germans would resume the offensive on the following day, and Lieut.-Colonel Hannay, who under orders from brigade withdrew his H.Q. to Square Farm, put Captain Christie in charge of the front line. The 31st July had been a day of mixed fortune, and night closed on a battle the issue of which still hung in the balance. So far, through the dogged resistance of the 13th Royal Scots, the Fifteenth Division had maintained its footing on the precious Frezenberg Ridge, but the hold was far from secure.

During the night the 13th Royal Scots should have been relieved by the 10th Scottish Rifles, but the enemy's deadly shelling and the difficulty of steering men through inky darkness along unfamiliar routes, rendered slippery and treacherous by rain, so delayed the latter that the relief had to be postponed. Seriously weakened in numbers and benumbed by the rain, the Royal Scots were soon called on to meet the assaults of a confident and eager foe, the Germans having sent up fresh troops during the night. The forenoon passed comparatively quietly, but the men had to be careful not to expose themselves on account of persistent sniping. Shortly after 1 P.M. several of the enemy near Hill 35 began to show themselves, and the snipers of the Royal Scots took prompt advantage of their chances. In spite of the restlessness exhibited by the foe, the observers of the 13th Royal Scots at Beck House were convinced that the Germans did not intend to continue their counter-attack.

They were mistaken. At 2.30 P.M. the observers were surprised to see hordes of field-grey figures advancing on the right, and at the same hour hostile guns began to shell the Frezenberg Ridge with terrific violence. Uncertain as to the exact position of the Boches, Captain Christie and 2nd Lieut. Ogilvie crept forward till they saw a group approaching in a south-westerly direction about 500 yards away from Beck House, but no general attack appeared to be in progress. Captain Christie had good reason to feel anxious, since he had no definite knowledge as to the situation on the right of his command. He found that men of the Highland Light Infantry were holding a position south of Beck House, and that the line was continued by Seaforths. The German thrust was now evidently being directed against our defences on the right of the 13th Royal Scots, for about 3.35 P.M. Captain Christie could discern the foe in great strength approaching Borry Farm, which lay to the south of Beck House. He had already taken what precautions he could to guard his right flank, which was in dire peril of being turned by the rapid advance of the enemy, who, by 4 P.M., had swept past Borry Farm. His own men could do little to stem the onset because they were pinned to their positions by a devastating fire which was directed upon them by machine-guns posted on the slopes of Hills 35 and 37, and Captain Christie was soon compelled to withdraw his right flank slightly to the south and west of Beck House. His responsibilities obliged him to run many risks, and he was at length wounded by a machine-gun bullet. The only other senior officer with him, Captain J. H. Logan, had already been killed, and the command of the line now devolved on a young officer, 2nd Lieut. Sandeman of the Camerons. On his passage to the dressing-station, Captain Christie was taken to Square Farm, where he saw Lieut.-Colonel Hannay and informed him that he feared that the Germans had actually penetrated behind the 13th Royal Scots.

His Cassandra forebodings were abundantly justified. At the time that Captain Christie was voicing his apprehensions to his C.O., the front line of the 13th Royal Scots had been cut off and was being attacked from front, flank, and rear. Fully alive to the gravity of the situation, Lieut.-Colonel Hannay petitioned for a barrage to be put down immediately in front of the Frezenberg Ridge. Such news as filtered through from the front was of the most disheartening description. 2nd Lieut. Donaldson of the Camerons reported after 4 P.M. that the Germans, advancing behind a heavy barrage, had fallen on our foremost troops, and after this no further reports were received. Outnumbered and exhausted, the isolated garrisons of the forward positions were swallowed up by the Boche advance, most of our men being either killed or captured.

All that could now be hoped for was that the line

round Square Farm could be held. Beck House was in the enemy's possession and he had won back the crest of the ridge, but beyond this point he made no effort to advance, though Square Farm was relentlessly and continuously shelled. The farm was defended mainly by machine-guns, and the position was further secured after 8 P.M., when a company of the Royal Scots Fusiliers arrived. At 10 P.M. some of the Argylls made a most gallant counter-attack and succeeded in regaining a footing on the crest. The few survivors of "A," "B," and "C" Companies of the Royal Scots were then withdrawn under cloak of darkness to Cambridge Road, where they were joined by "D" Company, which, under Captain J. Kelly, had been engaged in carrying stores for the whole brigade. During these two days of most desperate and exhausting fighting the battalion, in face of more numerous foes, had clung like a limpet to its positions, and the Germans had made their gains only after the resistance of the Royal Scots had been worn down by sheer weight of numbers. The losses were appallingly heavy: thirteen officers[1] and three hundred and fifty-five other ranks formed the total in killed, wounded, and missing.

The 9th Royal Scots with the Fifty-first Division, being in reserve, had no active part in the action of the 31st July. The front line taken over by the division lay due north of Ypres near Turco Farm, and the principal objective of the attack was the line of the Steenbeek. The operation was so decisively carried out by the 152nd and 153rd Brigades that the 9th Royal Scots were not required to move from their

---

[1] In addition to those already mentioned, 2nd Lieut. D. Robertson was killed; 2nd Lieuts. G. M. Kydd, J. R. Gall, and G. E. Curry wounded; Lieut. G. U. Dobbie and 2nd Lieuts. J. S. Aitken, W. T. Low, J. Gibson, and C. W. Gibson (of whom the last named, it was ascertained later, had been killed) and the Medical Officer, Lieut. J. Rickards, missing.

positions at the canal banks. While the battle was
raging, 2nd Lieut. Burnet with some men of "C"
Company of the 8th Royal Scots marked off an over-
land track to Kliest Wood, little more than 1000 yards
from the Steenbeek. There was no lack of work for
any of the pioneers, and before darkness fell a passable
road had been constructed as far as Kempton Park.
At night, under drenching rain, the 9th Royal Scots,
leaving the canal banks, struggled through a sea of
mud and relieved the 6th Gordons and the 6th Seaforths
near the Steenbeek.

In this part of the battlefield, less vital to the enemy
than the Frezenberg Ridge, there was no dangerous
counter-attack, but the new line was an uncomfortable
one to hold. For the most part it consisted of recently
dug posts containing each from three to eight men.
The ceaseless rain caused the Steenbeek to rise in spate,
and the whole country became a gigantic morass through
which the company runners could move only with almost
incredible difficulty. Nevertheless, the terrain in front
of the battalion was thoroughly investigated, and two
reconnaissances made near the Steenbeek by 2nd Lieut.
J. R. Black, under heavy shell fire, yielded valuable
information as to the nature of the ground and the
position of the enemy. Every night the Germans shelled
our approaches, and the 9th Royal Scots had reason to
be grateful to 2nd Lieut. J. S. Thomson, the Transport
Officer, who, with unfailing regularity, brought up the
rations along the muddy tracks under intermittent
gun fire. The 9th continued to hold the line near
the Steenbeek amid these dispiriting conditions till
the 4th August, on which day a Boche was captured
by a patrol, and the battalion on being relieved marched
back to the canal banks. The casualties in this action
consisted of three officers wounded, fifteen other ranks

killed, one hundred and eleven wounded, and four missing.

There was hardly a break in the rainfall from the evening of the 31st July till the last week of August, and the conditions in the Salient became appalling. No one could avoid a sense of depression on viewing a region so foully transmuted by agents of destruction. The sky, as if in sympathy with the wounded earth, was a ceiling of leaden grey, and seldom did a ray of sunshine brighten the landscape, dismal even under the best conditions but infinitely more dreadful under the mournful light of that tragic August. As far as the eye could carry, the pock-marked earth stretched out like a gigantic piece of smutty lattice-work, the deep pools of the shell-holes thinly separated from each other by ridges of mud, while the faint breeze, polluted with the odour of decay and tainted ground, felt damp and musty to the lungs. The sites of the numerous groves, that had once draped with soft greenery the country-side of Flanders, were marked by a naked tangle of unsightly splintered timber. Day and night the region was buffeted by shells till roads and buildings disappeared and the ordinary map no longer performed the office of a guide. Duckboard tracks had to be laid along the inspissated margins of the shell-holes, and the man or animal that deserted them courted death by drowning or suffocation in the mud. These snaky routes were soon discovered by hostile aircraft, and it was seldom that a battalion marched between Ypres and the front line without sustaining several casualties from shell fire on the way. Fleets of Gothas[1] hovered over the camps and more substantial roads near Ypres, discharging their deadly bombs often with dire results. Early in September the

[1] German aeroplanes designed for bombing attacks.

transport lines of the 8th Royal Scots were savagely bombed and forty-nine horses were lost. A new and terrifying form of gas, the mustard variety, was at this time introduced by the Germans and reduced its victims to utter impotence. The eye, the throat, and the skin were affected, and since the gas proved extraordinarily persistent, lingering in the ground and causing casualties many days after it had been used, there was vital need for our men to maintain a high standard of gas discipline, and it was fortunate that our respirators when donned in time proved an effective safeguard.

Under such conditions as these the 8th Royal Scots laboured for weeks in the Salient, and much of their best and most valuable work was performed during this trying period. Several roads across the Steenbeek were constructed, and the battalion had a notable share in the laying of a medium railway from Morteldje Dump through Kitchener's Wood. The pioneers also constructed a light railway from Morteldje through Mintz and Palace Farms and Mon du Rasta to the Langemarck Road, which in the battles of September and October 1917 proved to be of the greatest value. The 9th Royal Scots spent as pleasant a time as men could expect in the Salient, and were engaged in training at various camps in the hinterland till the 6th September.

Owing to the bad weather, operations of any magnitude had to be postponed, but whenever there were any signs of improvement attacks were launched. On the 16th August our position was strengthened when we secured a hold on Langemarck, but after this operation rain again set in. Nevertheless a few minor enterprises were attempted, in one of which the Fifteenth Division was involved. The 13th Royal Scots, after the ordeal of the 31st July, were given a rest till the 20th August, when they took over the front line near Frezenberg, with their right flank on the Ypres-Roulers Railway. "D" and B" were the two front companies, with "C" in support and "A" in reserve. An attack, in which the Fifteenth and Sixty-first Divisions were to co-operate, was arranged for 4.45 A.M. on the 22nd August. The 13th Royal Scots, who went into the action with Major Mitchell in command, formed the right battalion of the division, and their objective was a line extending from south of the railway to Bremen Redoubt, a fortified pill-box, exclusive. In view of the number of formidable pill-boxes to be encountered, special parties furnished by the Royal Scots Fusiliers and "A" and "C" Companies of the Royal Scots were detailed to "mop up" particular points.

Most of the hostile shelling fortunately dropped behind the line of the assembled troops, but the attack, though carried out with the utmost gallantry, made little progress. Numerous Boche aeroplanes audaciously buzzed over our lines and inflicted several casualties on our men, who were met, moreover, by a terrific machine-gun fire, particularly from the large pill-box known as Potsdam. The Royal Scots formed a line in front of Vampir and Potsdam and beat off several counter-attacks, but were unable to make any impression on the enemy's defences. Ultimately Major Mitchell established a new line from the railway, slightly in front of our original position, which the Royal Scots, in spite of a galling shell fire, including "shorts" from our own artillery, maintained without serious difficulty. Heavy losses were inflicted on the Boches by our rifle and Lewis gun fire, on one occasion a party of sixty of the enemy being almost annihilated. Their exertions, however, told heavily on the men, and they were very exhausted when on the night of the 22nd they were relieved and marched to a camp near Ypres. The number of casualties [1] was again alarmingly high, and as a result of the two actions in the Salient practically a new battalion had to be formed. After a brief spell of trench duty from the 26th till the 29th August, the battalion was withdrawn from the Salient, and at the beginning of September returned to familiar and kindlier quarters near Arras.

[1] Two hundred and seventy-six in killed, wounded, and missing, including two officers (2nd Lieuts. W. M. Martin and G. A. F. Renwick), killed.

CHAPTER XXV

THE 15TH AND 16TH ROYAL SCOTS AT HARGICOURT

July to September 1917

Thirty-fourth Division at Hargicourt. Action of 26th August. Attack of 15th and 16th Royal Scots.

DURING the delay in the development of the Passchendaele offensive, minor operations were carried on in other parts of the front, and in Sir Douglas Haig's Despatches it is recorded that "north-country troops (Thirty-fourth Division) attacked on the 26th August east of Hargicourt and captured the enemy's advanced positions on a front of a mile."

The Thirty-fourth Division, when at the beginning of July it took over the line in front of Hargicourt, had the honour of forming the right flank of the whole British Army, the River Omignon being the boundary between it and the Twenty-second Division of the French Army. Its new front was not a homogeneous one; on the left the divisional sector consisted of an almost continuous trench, while from the Quarry east of Hargicourt to the south it consisted of a series of detached posts. The country, in which slag heaps formed the most conspicuous landmarks, was open and rolling, and the enemy had established his front trenches on the western slopes of the loftiest ridge, which completely shut from our gaze the formidable Hindenburg system farther east. The Boches in this region were not disposed to be quarrelsome, but it was obvious that only by expelling them from their ridge could we

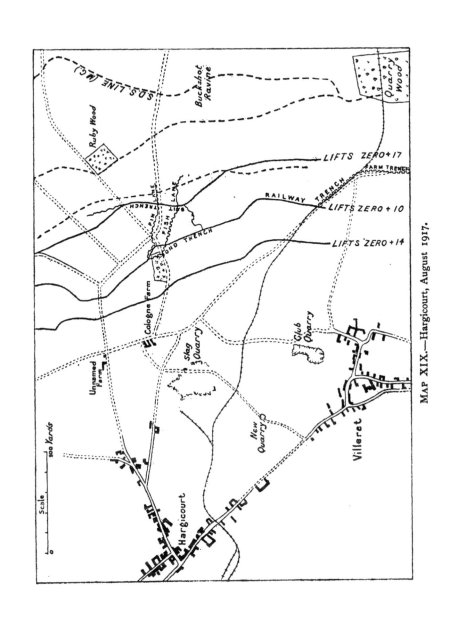

MAP XIX.—Hargicourt, August 1917.

have any satisfactory assurance of safety. This operation was entrusted to the Thirty-fourth Division, but there was no need for precipitate action, and the various battalions were allowed to settle down and become familiar with their new surroundings.

The highest part of the hostile position was almost exactly opposite the village of Hargicourt, and here our line included the ruins of a farm known as the "Unnamed Farm." About this point the opposing lines were comparatively close together, and near the enemy's front were the ruins of Cologne Farm. North and south of this area No-Man's-Land fanned out to a width of several hundred yards, so that there was ample scope for patrolling of an enterprising nature. The battalions quickly grasped the fact that there was business on hand, for those concerned were put through a special course of training, but the men, like true soldiers, did not worry unduly about what was to take place and continued to enjoy the tranquillity of their secluded sector.

Both the 15th and the 16th Royal Scots, when in the line, sent out numerous patrols, but there were seldom any encounters with the enemy. Lieut.-Colonel Lodge, whose health had been undermined by the prolonged stress and strain of the severe fighting at Arras, was invalided home shortly after the division reached Hargicourt, and was succeeded, on the 9th July, by Lieut.-Colonel Guard. Cologne Farm, within the German lines, was twice visited by patrols from the 15th Royal Scots and found to be empty; the enemy, it was discovered, had also deserted a barricade on the Buisson Ridge. The Boches once attempted to raid a post occupied by the 15th near Villeret, but were driven off without any serious fighting. No notable incident marked the end of July, and during August the

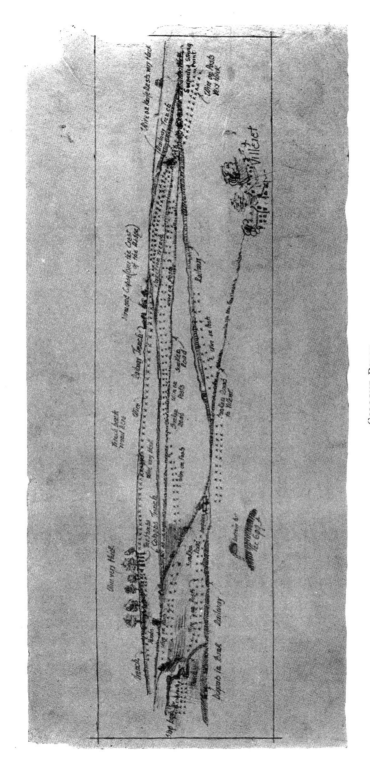

COLOGNE RIDGE.

(Sketch by Major C. H. Dakers, M.C., 15th Royal Scots.)

[To face p. 462.

battalions of the 101st Brigade were busy finishing their preparations for the attack which was to be launched at 4.30 A.M. on the 26th August.

In this affair all the battalions of the brigade were employed, the order from right to left being 15th Royal Scots, 16th Royal Scots, 10th Lincolns, 11th Suffolks. The 16th Royal Scots had Cologne Farm in the centre of their front. The brigade had two objectives: the first, a heavily-wired trench, Railway Trench, on the front of the 15th and Pond Trench on the front of the 16th Royal Scots; the second, a system of dug-outs and short trenches on the front of the 15th and Bait Trench on the front of the 16th Royal Scots. Being a flank battalion, the 15th Royal Scots had a relatively short distance to go, but they had to make their own arrangements for the defence of their right; Lieut.-Colonel Stephenson's men had to advance about 750 yards.

The training for the operation was very thorough, extensive use being made of facsimile spitlocked trenches and aeroplane photographs. On the night of the 23rd / 24th August a company from each of the assaulting battalions took over the front line, and the arrangements for the assembly were rapidly put in order. The 15th Royal Scots had marked their assembly area with pegs, which were joined up by tapes on the eve of the battle, while the other battalions had marked their boundaries with boards, of which one side was luminous. Lieut.-Colonel Guard had three companies, "C" "D," and "A," in line, and these completed their assembly under the protection of a screen thrown out by "B" Company, which was to form the support when the battle opened. "C" Company on the right was the only one to experience any difficulty, a sunken road with a high bank on the south side causing it a little trouble. On the front of the 16th Royal Scots two platoons of "B" Company formed the covering party, and drove in a small patrol of the enemy on the left without raising any suspicion that an attack was imminent. In perfect silence "A" and "D" Companies filed into their positions with "C" Company in support.

The success of the operation largely depended upon the assembly being accomplished without any unusual commotion such as might alarm the enemy. In practice behind the lines there had been a considerable amount of coughing which could be heard a long way off, and, in the hope of checking this, chewing-gum had been issued to the troops. On the critical night there were no unusual sounds, but the credit for the silence with which all arrangements were carried through was probably due more to the discipline of the men than to the chewing-gum.

The Germans, who expected nothing more alarming than raids in this neighbourhood, were taken by surprise, and the brigade obtained all its objectives except the line of dug-outs lying to the east of Railway Trench.

The attack of the 15th Royal Scots was carried out in two waves, each consisting of two lines formed up in lines of sections. Zero was proclaimed by the opening of a machine-gun barrage, followed by the artillery barrage twenty-five seconds later. The hostile counter-barrage was late in falling, and not till six minutes after zero did it come down with any violence. After four minutes the barrage on the first objective lifted, and the men strode forward into the chaos. The German resistance was brushed aside, and by 5.45 A.M. Lieut.-Colonel Guard had received messages from all his companies that both objectives had been carried.

The row of dug-outs, which formed the battalion's final objective, had not been seriously damaged by our gun fire, and was strongly manned by Germans; but, caught unawares by the swiftness of the advance, they were hustled out of their position by the 15th Royal Scots. Less than a minute, however, after our men reached their goal they were furiously counter-attacked, and the enemy succeeded in recapturing the position. In a second rush the Royal Scots regained the dug-outs, but "owing to the darkness, general confusion, and heavy casualties,"[1] they were obliged, except on the left, where "A" Company under Captain Bryson held the line south of Fish Lane, to withdraw to Pond and Railway Trenches, which the men began to consolidate. All the attacking companies had suffered severely, and "B" Company, which had sustained some casualties from the hostile barrage, was called on to send two platoons to the left and the remainder to the right.

The Germans made persistent counter-attacks throughout the day, and succeeded in effecting a lodgment in our trenches on the right by a bombing assault delivered from Farm Trench, which formed the southern continuation of Railway Trench. They thus secured a footing in the latter, but the 15th Royal Scots fighting with great tenacity ultimately stopped their progress and formed a block. During the day the position of the 15th was constantly raked by artillery fire, delivered in fierce gusts chiefly from the south-east. The Boche machine-gunners and snipers were very enterprising, and, shooting down the Villeret valley at everything that moved, they inflicted many casualties on the parties engaged in carrying stores of ammunition and grenades to the front line. So deadly

---

[1] *War Diary*, 15th Battalion.

indeed was the hostile machine-gun fire, that the first carrying party did not arrive at the front line until seven hours after the attack.

In the sector allotted to the 16th Royal Scots the Germans had one communication trench, Hip Lane, running from near Cologne Farm to Square Trench, where it branched into two communication trenches running east into the valley known as "Buckshot Ravine"; these were named Fish Lane and Pin Lane. The formation of the 16th Royal Scots consisted of two waves, each of two lines, with the supporting company in two lines in rear of the last assaulting line.

The leading companies formed up in the sunken road immediately west of Cologne Farm. A heavy barrage was put down by the enemy fifteen minutes before zero, fortunately causing no casualties among our troops. Owing to the fact that only lanes had been cut in the hostile wire, "A" and "D" Companies advanced to the first objective in line of sections in file. The enemy's rifle fire was violent but not skilfully directed, and after some slight resistance "A" and "D" Companies captured Pond Trench. At the second objective, Bait Trench, the Germans were more stout-hearted, and thirty of them fought to the death before "D" Company succeeded in carrying the left portion of the trench.

"C" Company in support had been given the duty, after the capture of Bait Trench, of clearing Pin Lane and Fish Lane down to and including the enemy's company H.Q. on the road. But owing to the strenuous opposition put up by the Germans at Bait Trench, "C" Company had been obliged to assist in the attack, and when the objective was ultimately cleared, it was unable to get forward to the hostile company H.Q. at the east end of Fish Lane. Nevertheless several groups bombed along Fish Lane and Pin Lane for about 100 yards, and established posts from which an accurate fire could be turned on the company H.Q. During their attack the 16th Royal Scots were immensely assisted by several of our aeroplanes which, flying low, inflicted casualties on the Germans and unsteadied their defence. The process of consolidation was interrupted by three counter-attacks, but these were easily repulsed by Lewis gun and rifle fire, the enemy suffering many losses.

Despite the slight check on the right, the 101st Brigade could plume itself on having accomplished a neat and effective piece of work. Several prisoners had been captured, thirty-five by the 16th Royal Scots, and a considerable quantity of war material. Peacefulness inevitably departed from the sector after the 26th August, for the Germans were not disposed tamely to submit to their humiliation, and throughout the night they kept up an incessant fire on our new positions, interfering considerably with the work of consolidation. There was no infantry clash on the front of the 15th and the 16th Royal Scots, and when the 27th August was ushered in the greater part of our new line was already protected with wire.

Much rain fell on the 27th, and in the trenches the men floundered waist-deep in mud and water. The 15th Royal Scots, intent on clearing their right flank, made a bombing attack along Railway Trench with the object of establishing a block at the junction of Railway and Farm Trenches. The goal was almost reached by Lieut. Morton Robertson and three men, but owing to the difficulty of sending reinforcements along the sticky trench, and the fact that rifles and grenades were rendered useless by the mud, the Royal Scots were ultimately forced to abandon the project. The

II   2 G

battalion was exhausted by its strenuous efforts, and on the night of the 27th/28th, after being relieved by the 20th Northumberland Fusiliers, it marched back into brigade support.

The chief trials of the 16th Royal Scots on the 27th were due to the enemy's artillery fire and sniping, for the German infantry made no attempt to attack. The same conditions prevailed on the 28th, on the evening of which date two small parties of Boches approached our trenches but were easily driven off by rifle and Lewis gun fire. Welcome relief came at midnight on the 28th/29th August, when the 9th Northumberland Fusiliers arrived and took over the front trenches.

The main purpose of the 101st Brigade had been brilliantly achieved, for from our new positions we at last secured direct observation over the Hindenburg Line. The casualties[1] of the Royal Scots had not been light, yet they were not out of proportion to the tactical advantage gained. Two of the fallen officers, Lieut. J. R. Devine of the 15th and Lieut. R. C. Lodge of the 16th, had been associated with their battalions for many months before the Thirty-fourth Division proceeded to France, and their loss was widely mourned. The other officers killed were 2nd Lieuts. W. Fyvie and D. R. M. Smith of the 15th, and Lieut. J. S. McHoul of the 16th.

In order to make our position in front of Hargicourt thoroughly secure, it was necessary for us to carry the high ground south of Railway Trench on the Villeret

---

[1] The 15th lost one hundred and ninety-seven and the 16th one hundred and eighty-four other ranks in killed, wounded, and missing. The wounded officers were Captains Brown and Hay and 2nd Lieut. Reid of the 15th, and Captains J. M. Davie, J. Stirling, 2nd Lieuts. J. C. Baird, T. Irvine, Barron, J. A. Gray, C. W. Hodgson, P. Harrower, and J. F. Porter of the 16th.

Col, but this task was entrusted to another brigade and did not directly concern the 15th and the 16th Royal Scots.   Trench routine continued uneventfully till near the end of September, when the Thirty-fourth was relieved by the Twenty-fourth Division, and at the beginning of October moved northwards to the unhealthy environs of the Salient.

CHAPTER XXVI

PASSCHENDAELE

September and October 1917

Action of 20th September. 11th and 12th Royal Scots at Frezenberg. Gallantry of Captain Reynolds. 9th Royal Scots at the Stroombeek. Counter-attack against Fifty-first Division. Attack of 2nd Royal Scots, 26th September. Action of 11th and 12th Royal Scots, 12th October. Action of 15th and 16th Royal Scots, 22nd October. Close of the Passchendaele Offensive. (*See* large scale Map at end of volume.)

THE dry weather which was ushered in with September permitted a resumption of the Passchendaele offensive, but the season was now so far advanced that, except for an unforeseen chance, there remained little prospect of the Allies winning a decisive success. At the best we could only hope to improve our position during the winter by establishing ourselves on the Passchendaele Ridge. While the ground was slowly recovering from the soaking rains of the previous month, Sir Douglas Haig completed his arrangements for an assault to be delivered on a wide front, by the Second and Fifth Armies, on the 20th September. The attack was probably the most successful episode in that strenuous campaign, and as a result "the whole of the high ground crossed by the Menin Road, for which such desperate fighting had taken place during our previous attacks, passed into our possession." [1]

The 11th, 12th, 8th, and 9th were the battalions of the Royal Scots engaged in this affair. The units of the Ninth Division had been able to carry out a

---

[1] Sir Douglas Haig's Despatches, p. 122.

systematic programme of training before they arrived in the hinterland of the Salient at the beginning of September. There was one notable change of command : Lieut.-Colonel Croft of the 11th Royal Scots was promoted to the command of a brigade, and he was succeeded by Lieut.-Colonel Sir John Campbell. Until the 12th September, the division was in camp near Ypres, and on the 16th and 17th it relieved the Forty-second Division on the Frezenberg Ridge, the 27th Brigade taking over the right sector, and the South African Brigade the left. The 11th Royal Scots had a tragic introduction to the new line. Conveyed to the ruins of Ypres by rail, they were in the act of detraining near the Asylum, when a shell burst among them, causing fifty-one casualties in killed and wounded.

The Ninth Division took over the front where the 13th Royal Scots had experienced so much grim fighting on the 31st July and the 22nd August. Our line ran along the Frezenberg Ridge and was cut by the Ypres-Roulers Railway, which formed the most distinguishable landmark in the leprous waste of shell-holes that stretched out on every side. The mellow sunshine of autumn, the silky blue of the sky, seemed to emphasise rather than mitigate the dreary horror of the broken landscape. There were two objectives for the 27th Brigade ; the first was a line extending from Hanebeek Wood to east of a series of strong pill-boxes on and near the railway, including Potsdam, which had held up the 13th Royal Scots on the 22nd August ; the second was along a slight ridge, the Zonnebeke Redoubt.

In order to deal effectively with the pill-boxes, the attack was to be carried out by lines of sections, each section being in file and separated from its neighbours by about 20 yards. Under this system the most suitably placed sections were to deal with the pill-boxes

II   2 G 2

en route, while the others were to go straight on, so that the whole line would not be brought to a halt by the resistance of a single pill-box. Success obviously depended upon the resource and initiative of the section commanders, to the training of whom a great deal of attention had been devoted.

The attack of the brigade was to be delivered by the 6th K.O.S.B., the 9th Scottish Rifles, and two companies of the 12th Royal Scots, the 11th being in support to the K.O.S.B. The 12th Royal Scots were allotted the task of carrying the series of formidable pill-boxes along and near the Ypres-Roulers Railway and were not required to go on to the final objective.

A heavy slanting rain lashed the men on the night of the 19th/20th, and owing to the scarcity of tracks and the insecure footing afforded by the slippery trench boards, the process of forming up proved a lengthy and difficult business. Fortunately the assembly was completed in ample time, so that the men had some leisure to recover from the strain and exhaustion of their anxious night journey. The storm of rain cleared before zero, which was at 5.40 A.M., and feeling that the omens were propitious the brigade swept forward to the attack. The morning sky was overcast with lowering clouds, but the flame of the barrage lit up the country, and the K.O.S.B. on the right pushed on to their objectives without a check, so that the 11th Royal Scots were not required to do any fighting. Since however after the capture of Hanebeek Wood, the K.O.S.B. were obliged to deploy the whole of the battalion in line, two companies of the 11th Royal Scots were sent by Lieut.-Colonel Sir John Campbell to support the assault on the Zonnebeke Redoubt.

On the left of the brigade the enemy fought stubbornly, the 12th Royal Scots encountering strong resistance from the numerous pill-boxes on their front. A row of five, tucked in along the banks of the railway, was flanked on the north by the massive fortifications of Potsdam. "C" Company, on the right of the 12th Royal Scots, was detailed to account for the railway group, but it was beset by machine-gun fire and grenades as soon as it neared the first of the forts. Lieut.-Colonel Ritson, on learning of the check, sent up two platoons from a reserve company to attack the first pill-box from the south, and, when the Germans were dealing with this new menace, "C" Company utilised its opportunity to rush the fort from the front, forty prisoners and three machine-guns being taken. Behind this pill-box the Boches had a machine-gun in action on the top of the railway, but the gunner was sniped, and the remainder of the garrison, about a dozen men, surrendered. From the other pill-boxes on the railway there was no further opposition, since one was totally wrecked by our gun fire and the others were full of water.

The left assaulting company of the 12th Royal Scots, which had for its objective the capture of the pill-box marked on the map as "A" and Potsdam, encountered a very stubborn opposition, and at one time it appeared as if the attack would be broken up by the damaging machine-gun fire directed against the Royal Scots by the garrison of "A." An untimely check was in fact only averted by the pluck and resolution of Captain Reynolds, who, by a noble disregard of personal danger, shored up his company when it seemed on the verge of panic. When the hail of bullets burst upon them the men threw themselves into the muddy sides of the shell-holes for protection, and once they were under cover from the vicious fire, it was no easy matter to induce them to expose themselves again. At this crisis

Captain Reynolds, with six men who were near him, dodging from shell-hole to shell-hole, arrived close under the walls of the pill-box, where they were safe from the enemy's fire, for the sides were so thick that no weapon could be sufficiently depressed to hit men crouching at the base of the pill-box. Taking a grenade from his haversack, Captain Reynolds lobbed it through a loophole, but the Boches fixed a pack in the window, thus preventing the entrance of any more bombs, and kept on firing. Realising that the remainder of his company would not come on as long as the machine-gun continued to function, Captain Reynolds took a desperate risk. Seizing a phosphorous bomb, he raised himself from the ground and squeezed it past the pack into the pill-box. It was only by a miracle that he escaped death. Germans were firing at him from a range that seemed to make a miss absolutely impossible, yet, though his tunic was literally torn into shreds by bullets, Captain Reynolds himself was unscathed. This act of supreme daring brought an immediate reward. The explosion of the grenade set the pill-box ablaze, and on leaving it to escape the suffocating fumes, the Germans walked into the arms of the Royal Scots who lay waiting for them outside the door. Of the garrison three were killed and the other seven surrendered. Hastily re-forming his men, Captain Reynolds led them towards Potsdam, where a lively fight was already in progress. Some South Africans, who had become detached from their own unit, were engaging the garrison from the north, so a number of the Royal Scots attacked the pill-box from the front, while others moved round to the southern flank. This converging onslaught was effective ; Potsdam was rushed, and seventy prisoners and two machine-guns were captured. Thus, principally through the resource and determination of Captain

Captain H. Reynolds, V.C., M.C., 12th Battalion, The Royal Scots.

[To face p. 474.

Reynolds, all the tasks allotted to the 12th Royal Scots were successfully accomplished.

A counter-attack was confidently expected, and the brigade consolidated its position by joining up the shell-holes into short lengths of trench to form the new front line.   Two terrific barrages put down by the enemy in the course of the day were taken as the prelude of a counter-stroke, and the men seizing their rifles awaited with assurance the onset of the German infantry.   But, to the disappointment of the troops, no foemen appeared, the enemy taking revenge for his discomfiture by savagely bombarding our positions.

Equally successful was the action of the 9th Royal Scots on the 20th September.   Owing to the un-remitting labours of the 8th Royal Scots, the 9th, when they returned to the line on the 6th September, found that the communications had been vastly improved. The front of the battalion lay north of St Julien near the Lekkerboterbeek, but in order to complete its final preparations for the battle it was relieved on the 9th September, and lay at Siege Camp till the eve of the attack.   The ground which the Fifty-first Division was asked to carry was about 1500 yards in depth. From the Steenbeek, which now lay behind the divisional front, the land rose gradually, cut by the shallow ditch of the Lekkerboterbeek, till it reached a slight ridge near Pheasant Farm, from which direct observation over Poelcapelle could be obtained.   South of the Lekker-boterbeek, the country formed a slight depression, marking the tiny water-course of the Stroombeek, and rose again to a gentle ridge near Quebec Farm.   The attack was to be carried out by the 154th Brigade, with the 9th Royal Scots on the right and the 4th Seaforths on the left.   There were two objectives : the first being the line of the Stroombeek, which was to be carried by the leading battalions; the second, a line through Quebec Farm, which was to be taken by the 7th Argylls and the 4th Gordons, who were to pass through the Royal Scots and the Seaforths on the first objective. The Boche defences consisted chiefly of concreted fortifications, and in addition there lay about 150 yards from our front a fairly well-defined trench line (Pheasant Trench). Lieut.-Colonel Green chose this as the first objective for his battalion, the second, the line of the Stroombeek, being the first objective of the division.

Over the ploughed-up ground the march from Siege Camp to the assembly area was an arduous undertaking, but with few casualties, the 9th Royal Scots took up their allotted positions with "A" and "B" in front, supported by "C" and "D" Companies. The left flank of the battalion was clearly marked by the Lekkerboterbeek, and when our barrage dropped at 5.40 A.M. the men followed behind it. On the right the Germans were strongly posted in pill-boxes close to our front line, but "A" Company, led by Captain W. M. Urquhart, who had been slightly wounded during the march to the assembly area, with fine dash rushed these fortifications before the Germans had time to make their fire effective. On the swampy soil near the Lekkerboterbeek, the left company, "B," came under ravaging machine-gun fire and some of the men retreated to our front line, but the company commander, Lieut. F. M. Scott, ably assisted by 2nd Lieut. J. R. Black, and by an artillery liaison officer, Lieut. L. F. Fairlie, speedily rallied them and led them forward again. Anxious to make amends for their momentary unsteadiness, the men advanced in a most resolute fashion under the enemy's machine-gun fire, and their attack was magnificently supported by some of the company who had succeeded in entering Pheasant

Trench on the right. Corporal A. Horne, with two men, worked his way along the trench from the south and succeeded in putting out of action the machine-gun which had been chiefly responsible for holding up the advance. The combined flank and frontal attack over-powered the hostile resistance, and the whole of Pheasant Trench passed into the hands of the Royal Scots.

After these initial adventures the other two com-panies passed through " A " and " B," and by skilful manœuvring reached the line of the Stroombeek. " C " Company, on the right, had a brisk contest near Flora Cot, where Private James Flynn led the attack, and here fifteen Germans were killed. The company sustained several casualties from enfilade fire by Germans posted in Hubner Farm, a strong pill-box in the area of the 2/8th London Regiment on the right of the Royal Scots. Two Lewis gun teams and two rifle sections engaged the farm with fire, and inflicted such losses on the garrison that the 2/8th London Regiment was able to carry the pill-box by a direct assault. " D " Company, on the left, though much reduced in strength as a result of the *mêlée* near Pheasant Trench, succeeded in reaching the objective, having encountered little opposition.

The battalion thus secured all its objectives, and at the Stroombeek the 7th Argylls passed through and advanced the line about 500 yards east of that stream. The Germans lost no time in delivering their counter-stroke. Thousands of shells were thrown into the Stroombeek valley, and under cover of a series of violent bombardments, the Boche infantry bore down on the left flank of the division. The line was kept intact until the afternoon when, most of the rifle ammunition being exhausted, the 4th Gordons were forced to retire. The Royal Scots sent a Lewis gun team to reinforce the Argylls, while "B" Company threw out a defensive flank to the left. From our posts near the junction of the Stroombeek and the Lekkerboterbeek our men had splendid targets, and inflicted enormous losses on the compact masses of field-grey figures attacking on the northern side of the Lekkerboterbeek. It was by no means pleasant for the troops on the left wing to see the Germans pressing past them, but they kept their heads and used their rifles and Lewis guns with deadly effect. The Boche artillery fire could not silence our flank posts, and though one was so thickly plastered with shells that the whole garrison was buried, when the men were dug out the post commander, Lance-Corporal G. Fernie, with the most admirable nonchalance, promptly reorganised them and set them to work to clear out the post. Our battalions on the left counter-attacked in the late evening, but did not quite succeed in getting up in line with the 7th Argylls. Thus the 9th Royal Scots spent a troubled night, "D" Company picketing the ground between the left of the Argylls and the Germans by posts along the line of the Lekkerboterbeek.

Nothing untoward occurred during the hours of darkness on the front of the 27th Brigade, against which the Germans did not attempt a counter-attack. On the 21st the whole brigade was thrown into mourning when the sorrowful news was received that Brig.-General Frank Maxwell had been killed by a sniper. A man of graceful figure, whose every movement revealed the control of the athlete, there was that distinctive quality about him which instantly swept up the loyalty and love of those who came into contact with him. The death of one so honoured and esteemed robbed the victory of its glamour, and it was with an oppressive sense of gloom that the 11th and the 12th

Royal Scots returned to the back areas of the Salient on the 24th, when the Ninth was relieved by the Third Division. Their casualties were remarkably low, the 11th losing about one hundred other ranks in killed and wounded and the 12th one hundred and sixty-two. Only one officer, 2nd Lieut. J. M. Reilly of the 12th, was killed, and one, 2nd Lieut. Kingan also of the 12th, was wounded. The new commander of the 27th Brigade proved to be an old friend, Brig.-General Croft, and there was none more likely than he to maintain the lofty standard which his predecessor had set.

On the 21st September the Germans continued their counter-attacks on the front of the Fifty-first Division. After a day of heavy shell fire, the infantry attack developed about 6.30 P.M., but our men were ready for it, and our shell, rifle, and machine-gun fire availed to prevent the Boches from reaching assaulting distance. On the night of the 21st/22nd September the 9th Royal Scots were relieved and marched to Siege Camp. The officers killed during the fighting were 2nd Lieuts. J. K. Alexander, J. Allison, and C. J. McLean; two[1] were wounded, and the losses in other ranks were thirty-one killed, one hundred and sixty-three wounded, and twenty-seven missing. The whole division was now transferred to the south, where it took over, at the beginning of October, trenches in the Heninel-Wancourt sector.

The gratifying nature of our success on the 20th September rekindled the hope that the resistance of the enemy was on the wane, but the Germans, who required a mere sprinkling of troops on the Russian front, could fling reinforcements into Flanders as the situation demanded, and as the campaign progressed

[1] 2nd Lieuts. J. M. Irvine and R. P. Fraser.

the opposition of the enemy, so far from diminishing, appreciably increased. The next phase of the attack was planned for the 26th September, and on this occasion the only Royal Scots battalion engaged was the 2nd.

The battalion had come up from the south to a camp near Poperinghe on the 19th, and on the 24th moved to a position in support near Square Farm. In the forthcoming battle it was required to continue the advance begun by the Ninth Division on the 20th. On a two-company front, with the Ypres-Roulers Railway as the right boundary, the 2nd Royal Scots were to carry a line extending from the railway to west of Hill 40; on the left of the battalion were the 8th East Yorks, and south of the railway was the 76th Brigade.

Immediately after dusk, on the 25th, the battalion marched up to its assembly area, "C" Company being on the right and "D" on the left, supported by "A" and "B" respectively. Everything was ready by 11 P.M., and Lieut.-Colonel Lumsden established his H.Q. in a pill-box beside the Zonnebeke Road.

At zero hour, 5.30 A.M., when the attack began, a grey mist hung over the ground, so dense that even the outline of the railway embankment could not be distinguished, and when the men plunged forward into the sticky gloom they had great difficulty in preserving direction. The German barrage, late in coming down, passed over the attacking troops and fell heavily in the valley behind our old front line and around battalion H.Q. A capital start was made. "C" and "D" Companies, pushing on rapidly, captured some prisoners and gained the objective by 8 A.M. There they began to consolidate, while the Royal Scots Fusiliers prepared to pass through and attack Hill 40. But the success was not maintained, for the battalions on the flanks had lost direction in the obscuring mist, and the Royal Scots Fusiliers were unsupported when they began their attack on the hill. The defenders were vigilant, and by accurate fire pinned the Royal Scots Fusiliers to the ground, where they held a line of shell-holes nearly 250 yards short of the brigade's objective.

About noon the 12th West Yorks of the 9th Brigade, which was in support, took over the old front line, and at 5.30 P.M. Lieut.-Colonel Lumsden received orders that the whole brigade, supported by the West Yorks, would carry out a further attack at 6.30 P.M. There was no time to issue more than verbal instructions, and these reached only a few officers, who had no opportunity to communicate them to any but the men in their neighbourhood. Accordingly, when the hour for attack arrived, just a mere handful of men and officers went forward, and at the same time the Boches began a counter-attack from Hill 40. Both sides wavered, and our men, seeing that the majority of their comrades had not left the shelter of their shell-holes, turned to go back to the position that they had left. This unfortunate, though natural, retrograde movement caused a momentary panic, and men began to dribble backwards from the centre of the line. But the flanks stood firm, and before their unflagging resistance the Boche counter-attack collapsed. On learning from Lieut. Grossman that some men were retiring, Lieut.-Colonel Lumsden and Captain the Hon. J. Stuart, assisted by the other H.Q. officers, stopped the retreating troops and re-formed them along our original front line. Strong patrols were then sent out to ascertain the position in front, and when this was made known two companies of the West Yorks moved up to strengthen the line there. No attack was made on the 27th, and on the night of the 28th/29th the 2nd Royal

Scots were drawn back to the vicinity of Square Farm. During the next night the division was relieved by the Third Australian Division, and by easy stages proceeded to a sector of the line south of Arras.

The casualties of the 2nd Royal Scots in this engagement were very high, and included, among the killed, Captain D. D. A. Berry and 2nd Lieut. E. G. Elmslie; six officers were wounded and two missing[1]; while forty-five other ranks were killed, two hundred and seventy-eight wounded and sixty-six missing.

On the whole Sir Douglas Haig was satisfied with the results of the fighting on the 26th, and preparations were soon put in hand for a renewal of the attack on the 4th October, when the British forces wrested still more of the ridge from the tenacious foe in spite of a complete breakdown in the weather. Further successes were won on the 9th, and there seemed a fair possibility of the enemy being pushed down the far side of the ridge before the end of the year, but the weather steadily worsened, and this even more than the stout opposition of the Germans, was the reason for our slow progress after the 9th October.

For a time our attacks were pressed on regardless of the heavy rains, and a new onslaught was arranged for the 12th October. The Ninth Division, which since the 21st September had been reorganising and training in the back areas, was again brought into action. On the night of the 9th October, under a stinging downpour of rain, the battalions of the 27th Brigade arrived at Brake Camp, where the men snatched what sleep they could under the flimsy cover of bivouacs, hastily erected on the sodden ground.

[1] Wounded, 2nd Lieuts. Mackay, Peacock, Honeyman, Yuille, Purves, and Richards; missing, Captain Thomson and 2nd Lieut. W. A. McIntosh (later it was ascertained that they had been killed).

The sector in which the brigade was to operate was near the place where the 9th Royal Scots had been fighting on the 20th September. The left boundary of the division was the Lekkerboterbeek, and though the whole area was studded with fortified farms and houses, there were no clear landmarks. The first stage of the attack was to be carried out by the 26th Brigade, which was to advance the line to a point beyond Source Farm, when the 27th Brigade, led by the 12th and the 11th Royal Scots, was to carry on the line to Vat Cottages.

On the night of the 10th/11th the Highland Brigade took over the divisional front. The 27th Brigade, lying in reserve, was instructed to move forward to the assembly positions by two duckboard tracks. About midnight, on the 11th, the sky discharged itself in torrential floods, and no garment fashioned by mortals could have kept a man dry. In inky darkness the troops groped their way along the slippery and treacherous tracks, and after they crossed the St Julien Road they came under a heavy barrage of gas and H.E. shells. The men dared not don their masks, since they could not possibly have seen where they were going, and trusting that their eyes would not be affected, they put the tubes between their lips to keep the gas from their lungs and carried on. The shelling along the assembly line was ferocious, and both Highlanders and Lowlanders suffered grievously before the battle began at 5.35 A.M.

The unpropitious start was the prelude to a disastrous battle. On the right, small parties of Highlanders made some progress, but the line as a whole was broken up and the 12th Royal Scots were involved in the struggle long before the first objective of the 26th Brigade was reached. They co-operated with the Seaforths in charging and capturing Inch Houses, and a mixed

II   2 H

group of Black Watch, Seaforths, and 12th Royal Scots pressed on as far as the eastern fringes of Wallemolen, but being attacked from both flanks was forced to return to a line running from the Cemetery to Inch Houses.

On the left, where the ground formed an almost impassable swamp, here and there intersected by a few strips of mud capable of bearing a man's weight, practically no progress was made. As Lieut.-Colonel Sir John Campbell of the 11th Royal Scots floundered in the mire he remarked gloomily to Major Innes Browne of the 6th K.O.S.B., "Only people with webbed feet could fight with comfort here." Wallowing waist-deep and often neck-deep in the liquid slime, our men were helpless and at the mercy of the Boche marksmen and machine-gunners, and the garrison of a pill-box near the front line fired with such accuracy that it held up the whole advance. Manœuvring being out of the question, a body composed of Camerons, K.O.S.B., and 11th Royal Scots went bald-headed for the pill-box, and, undeterred by losses, forced an entrance and slaughtered the occupants. By this time the barrage had been irretrievably lost; the various units were so mixed up that it was impossible to sort them out, and the men were so exhausted that they were unable to carry on the amphibious warfare. A line was formed in front of the captured pill-box, and no further attempt was made to advance. The penalty of failure is generally a lengthy casualty list, and both the Royal Scots battalions were sadly crippled by the action. Of the 11th Royal Scots, five officers [1] were killed and three wounded; twenty-one other ranks killed, one hundred and sixty wounded, and thirty missing; the 12th lost

[1] Captains C. W. Grant and A. A. Stuart, 2nd Lieuts. A. J. Fernie, C. W. Johnston, and W. Moncur.

eight officers,[1] and two hundred and twenty-seven other ranks in killed, wounded, and missing.

Along the whole British front the dreadful conditions of soil and weather had caused the battle to be broken off at an early stage, and the amount of ground gained was negligible. Winter was in firm alliance with the enemy, and it was obvious that there was no longer any hope of driving him off the ridge before the end of the year. The campaign however was still carried on, with lessening effort, while Sir Douglas Haig prepared for a new stroke in the south.

The 11th and the 12th Royal Scots remained in the Salient till the 24th October, and during this period hostile artillery and aeroplanes shelled and bombed the back areas and approaches, causing many casualties to reliefs and working parties between St Julien and the front. On one occasion the 12th Royal Scots lost nearly one hundred men through air bombs. The greatest safety was possibly to be found in the front line, where by skilful patrolling a few more pill-boxes came into our possession. On the night of the 24th, a patrol of the 11th Royal Scots lurking near Inch Houses took prisoner two Prussians. The division was relieved on the night of the 24th/25th, and the various units after a brief sojourn in the Salient hinterland proceeded to the quieter regions of the northern coast.

There now entered the battle area the 15th and the 16th Battalions, fresh from their triumph at Hargicourt, and the 17th Battalion. After the usual dreary sojourn in the depressing camps near Ypres, the 15th and the 16th Royal Scots, on the night of the 20th/21st October, went into the front line, just to the north of Poelcapelle. Both battalions were buffeted by shell fire on the way

---

[1] Of these, Captain J. McMurray and 2nd Lieuts. D. C. Kerr and D. M. McBlane were killed.

to their new positions and lost their commanding officers, who were gassed during the morning while reconnoitring the line. Lieut.-Colonel Guard was succeeded by Major Selby, and Lieut.-Colonel Stephenson by Captain P. Russell. The 15th Royal Scots held the front line, consisting of shell-holes, from Gravel Farm to Turenne Crossing, the line being continued by the 16th to. Aden House.

The attack of the division was to be delivered by the 102nd and 101st Brigades on the 22nd October, at 5.35 A.M., with a brigade of the Thirty-fifth Division on their left flank. The 15th and the 16th Royal Scots were the leading battalions of the 101st Brigade, each on a two-company front, and their final objective was a line running from Gravel Farm to Six Roads Cross Roads at the outskirts of the Forest of Houthulst. The task allotted to the battalions was difficult and complicated. For some reason, never explained to the infantry, the barrage line did not correspond with the front line, and at one point actually fell behind it, so that the left company of the 15th and the right company of the 16th were obliged to go back for some distance in order to form up. The attack was to pivot on the right wing of the 15th Royal Scots, while the left company of the 16th was to advance in conformity with the 23rd Manchesters of the Thirty-fifth Division as far as the Six Roads.

The water-logged nature of the country rendered the punctual assembly of the troops a very anxious business. The men could scarcely drag themselves through the mud, and the Boches added to their misery by putting down a savage barrage along the assembly positions, causing many casualties and throwing the troops into confusion. But the excellent leadership of the officers and N.C.Os., and the discipline of the men, triumphed over all the difficulties, and the assembly was completed in time.

"A" Company of the 15th Royal Scots, operating south of the Broembeek, had the shortest distance to cover, and making magnificent progress over the spongy surface, reached its objective. But "B" Company on the left, which had as its first objective a block of huts near the Ypres-Staden Railway, had a stormy passage. A message from it was received to the effect that it had reached its goal, and was suffering terribly from machine-gun fire from concreted huts on its left, but when the second wave followed up, it saw no trace of any living man of the leading line, and it was with great difficulty that its own survivors, only fourteen all told, returned to our original front. "C" Company was ordered to support the attack on the left, but it was unable to cross the flooded Broembeek, which was being violently shelled, and was compelled to return. These misfortunes rendered the position of "A" Company south of the Broembeek untenable, and it also withdrew to its original position. Shortly after our attack opened, the Germans began a counter-movement, and about 100 of them advanced against a group of "A" Company, their officer calling on it to surrender. He was answered by a shot from the officer in command (probably 2nd Lieut. Simpson) and fell dead. The Boches made a very feeble effort to revenge the death of their leader, and were dispersed with surprising ease by the thirteen men who constituted the group. At noon the Boches again formed up about 200 yards from our line, but our Lewis-gun fire deterred them from attempting a charge.

The original plan of the 16th Royal Scots had been to attack the first objective with two companies in lines of sections, while the others were to pass through and take the final objective. So many officers and men, however, became casualties through the hostile shelling during the assembly that barely a sufficient number remained to form one wave, which advanced at zero in line with the Manchesters. "A" and "B" Companies on the right suffered grievously from the enemy posted in the huts who had played such havoc with "B" Company of the 15th Battalion. The hostile machine-gun fire was so intense and accurate that the men were forced to embed themselves in the mud, without stirring a limb above the surface, and in this uncomfortable posture they remained till 7 A.M., when a Boche counter-attack gave them the opportunity to retire to their original line. 2nd Lieut. J. A. Hope and about twenty men refused to retire and were killed by the enemy.

Considering all the difficulties, the progress made by "C" and "D" Companies on the left flank was extremely creditable. The natural tendency was to veer towards the railway, which formed a convenient guiding mark, enabling the Royal Scots to keep in close touch with the Manchesters. Along with these, "C" and "D" Companies reached their final objective, a group of pill-boxes near Six Roads within the shelter of the grubby trees of Houthulst Forest. While the Royal Scots kept the pill-boxes under fire, the Manchesters entered the forest and attacked them in flank. A Lewis gun section of the Royal Scots penetrated the wire and captured a pill-box containing six Germans, but the bold adventurers were trapped when the Boches counter-attacked. The Manchesters were actually scraping a passage through the wire guarding these concreted forts, when the foe suddenly fell upon them about 7 A.M. and drove them back to their starting-point.

The situation was changed with dramatic suddenness. The assailants were now the defenders, and with difficulty kept the Germans at bay. With the tenacity of their race the Royal Scots clung grimly to their gains, and their vicious fire caused numerous losses among the Boches who, darting from shell-hole to shell-hole, strove to isolate our men and force them to surrender. The enemy in the pill-boxes kept up a fire so galling and ruthless that a man who made the slightest movement was almost certain to be hit. Captain D. M. Sutherland received a bullet in the elbow when he raised himself to study the situation, and 2nd Lieut. A. Baxter was shot through the chest. Three possible courses were open to Captain Sutherland and his men ; to allow themselves to be captured, to wait till they were all shot down, to endeavour to crawl back. The last course was clearly the soldierly thing to attempt, and, with a fervent hope that luck would befriend them, the Royal Scots set off. Fortunately, the Germans at this moment were mainly concerned with the retreating Manchesters, so that Captain Sutherland and his men were able to crawl and roll painfully back to a less perilous spot, and ultimately the majority of the party reached the old front line.

The 22nd October was probably the most ghastly day experienced by the 15th and the 16th Royal Scots. The former lost seven officers[1] and two hundred and twenty-eight other ranks, and the latter twelve officers[1] and two hundred and forty-four other ranks in killed, wounded, and missing. All day the Germans continued to shell our positions without mercy, and both battalions were sadly depleted and disorganised. During the tempestuous night the Lincolns and the Suffolks moved up in spite of wretched weather and pitiless

[1] The officers killed were 2nd Lieut. G. D. Simpson of the 15th, and 2nd Lieuts. G. Adam, J. A. Hope, N. S. Honeyman, P. Linn, and D. F. Low of the 16th.

shelling and relieved the remnants of the 15th and the
16th Royal Scots. For their failure the Royal Scots
were in no sense to blame; the conditions which they
had to endure were such that it was not in mortals
to command success. The considered verdict of Brig.-
General Gore may stand as a fair appreciation of their
achievement. "In view of the enormous difficulties
encountered it is greatly to the credit of the attacking
battalions that they succeeded in forming up, though
in greatly diminished numbers, and in making so gallant
an attempt to carry out the task allotted to them, and
it was no fault on their part that they were unable to
hold what they had gained."

The Thirty-fourth Division was relieved on the
night of the 23rd/24th October, and after a short rest
to train and refit moved south to a less foul sector
near Fontaine les Croisilles.

The 17th Royal Scots entered the Ypres area on
the 17th October, but though the Thirty-fifth Division
was engaged in the battle of the 22nd October, the
battalion was in reserve and had no active part in the
struggle. It had the misfortune to be stationed in the
Salient throughout the winter, remaining there till the
German offensive in March caused it to be hurriedly
transferred to the Somme area. The Passchendaele
offensive dragged on till November and secured us a
few more yards of muddy war-scarred territory, but
before the year closed the main interest was suddenly
shifted to the south.

CHAPTER XXVII

CAMBRAI

November to December 1917

British preparations for attack at Cambrai. Work of 8th Royal Scots. The German defences. Task of Fifty-first Division. Result of the attack, 20th and 21st November. German counter-attack, 22nd November. Operations of 23rd November. German counter-thrust near Gouzeaucourt and Gonnelieu. 9th Royal Scots at Mœuvres.

THE offensive which opened the Battle of Cambrai on the 20th November 1917, when at a low cost we secured a large strip of territory, much war material, and many prisoners, was distinguished by an unexpected subtlety in conception and a boldness in execution which contrasted sharply with the bludgeon methods employed by us at Passchendaele. Yet when the commotion stirred up by our diversion subsided, it remained a matter of doubt whether or not we had derived any advantage from our efforts.

One of the fundamental principles of military science is to take the enemy unawares, but with the opposing armies facing each other in continuous lines extending from the Channel to the Alps, it was by no means as easy to effect a surprise as it was in the days when armies had flanks. Generally an offensive betrayed itself weeks, if not months, before the date of its execution by the thick mustering of men and batteries in the selected area, by the accumulation of munition and other depots, by the registration of guns and a systematic programme of wire-cutting, and by a series of bombardments. The only point about which the enemy might be uncertain was the precise time at which the blow would fall.

All the obvious signs of an offensive were avoided in November 1917. Gaps in the hostile wire had to be cut to allow our infantry to penetrate the German defences, but with the improvement and development of the tanks, this work no longer required to be done by artillery and trench-mortars. Tanks, provided they reached the enemy's front without being detected, could crush lanes in the wire for the infantry. It was upon this idea that the Cambrai stroke was planned. The close packing of troops, British and German, in the Salient was an assurance that other parts of the front would be thinly garrisoned. Every effort was made to take advantage of this in the Cambrai sector. Fresh batteries were brought up and installed in carefully concealed positions, and were not to open fire until the hour of zero, while precautions were taken to prevent the Germans from detecting the arrival of new divisions.

The Fifty-first Highland Division was one of the formations chosen to engage in the enterprise, fixed to take place at 6.20 A.M. on the 20th November. It had, as we have seen, taken over the Heninel-Wancourt front at the beginning of October, and its tour of duty there was marked by no unusual incidents. The 9th Royal Scots had one encounter with the enemy on the night of the 11th/12th, when a hostile raiding party was beaten off, leaving three dead in front of their wire. On the 28th October the battalion was moved to Izel le Hameau, where, in conjunction with tanks, a course of training for the projected operations was carried through. In order not to raise the suspicions of the Germans, the battalion was not sent

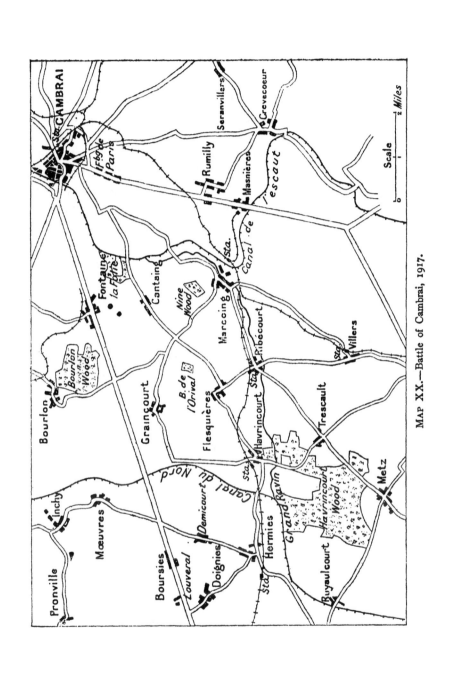

MAP XX.—Battle of Cambrai, 1917.

to the battle area until the eve of the attack, and only parties of officers and N.C.Os., clad in breeches and trousers, were sent to make preliminary reconnaissances. It was of course desirable that the assaulting troops should be within easy reach of their assembly positions, and the 8th Royal Scots with the sappers of the Fifty-first Division were industriously employed in constructing hidden shelters, where the infantry could be accommodated for some forty-eight hours prior to the battle. Under the very eyes of the enemy, but without his knowledge, the pioneers and sappers so transformed the village of Metz-en-Couture and Havrincourt Wood that the whole division was comfortably and secretly housed there from the 18th November. Entraining for Bapaume on the 17th November, the 9th Royal Scots arrived at Metz on the following day.

The German defences, consisting of the famous Hindenburg system, were so enormously strong that they did not seem to require a large garrison. From the assembly trenches of the Fifty-first Division, situated on a spur near Trescault, the ground sloped down to the valley of the Grand Ravin which meandered in an easterly direction towards the village of Marcoing, then rose swiftly to a ridge crowned by the ruins of Flesquières. From this point the land gradually dropped into the flat basin of the St Quentin Canal, except on the north, where it rose abruptly to the lofty upland over which like a dark shadow brooded Bourlon Wood.

The Fifty-first Division, with the 152nd and 153rd Brigades in front, was required to advance to a line extending approximately from Bourlon Wood, through the hamlet of Cantaing, to Nine Wood. To achieve this, three systems of hostile trenches had to be carried.

The front system, thickly wired, consisted of three lines of trenches with numerous saps and communication trenches; behind it, to the south of Flesquières, was the Hindenburg support system with two lines of densely wired deep trenches; and some 4000 yards in rear of this lay another double line of trenches south-west of the village of Cantaing.

All the preliminaries were completed without a hitch, and with the Sixth Division on the right and the Sixty-second on the left, the 152nd and 153rd Brigades began their advance at 6.20 A.M. The Germans were utterly surprised, and the initial signs of resistance came when the Highlanders began to swarm up the ridge towards Flesquières. The fighting there was of the sternest character, and sheltered by a strong brick wall surrounding a château on the southern outskirts of the village, the Boches made a most gallant stand and for a time checked all progress. Tanks attempted to come to the rescue, but many of them were knocked out by direct hits from field-guns firing at close range from a position behind the ridge, and, in spite of the utmost efforts on the part of the Highlanders, the village was still in the enemy's hands when darkness fell. The 9th Royal Scots, in reserve with the 154th Brigade, had yet to enter the fray, and after assembling near Trescault returned to Metz in the afternoon.

On the 21st November the tide of success flowed strongly in our favour, and the Fifty-first Division, after carrying the village of Flesquières, entered Cantaing early in the afternoon. Just before dusk the 4th Gordons and the 7th Argylls of the 154th Brigade, assisted by tanks, captured the village of Fontaine, but the attack on Bourlon Wood lying to the north-west of Fontaine was repulsed. Moving up from Metz, the 9th Royal Scots, soon after 9 A.M., concentrated on the Havrincourt-Marcoing Railway directly south of Flesquières, and at 10.15 A.M., in two lines of company columns at 200 yards interval and 200 yards distance, the battalion again advanced and took up a position astride the Flesquières-Cantaing Road to the east of Orival Wood. Shortly after noon, while the battalion was still in this position, Lieut.-Colonel Green, fearing that our forward troops on the Graincourt Road were about to retire, despatched a company to this point to make the flank secure, but fortunately it was not required. About 1.30 P.M. the battalion moved back 500 yards to a position where it remained for three hours in brigade reserve. Then Lieut.-Colonel Green was ordered to take his men up and relieve the 4th Gordons in the line near the eastern outskirts of Cantaing; after the company commanders had reconnoitred the position, the relief was carried through by 3.45 A.M. on the 22nd.

Up to this point the sudden assault planned by the Third Army had been brilliantly successful, and the Germans had been badly shaken; the losses inflicted on the enemy were considerably higher than those sustained by our men. At this stage Sir Douglas Haig had to make a momentous decision. The position reached by our troops on the evening of the 21st was not a satisfactory one, for, overlooked from Bourlon Wood, it could not be held throughout the winter without a heavy drain in casualties; hence it was necessary for us either to withdraw to the Flesquières Ridge or to push on and occupy Bourlon Ridge. If the key-point at Bourlon could be captured, the position of the Germans in Cambrai would be rendered very precarious, and the enemy might even be obliged to abandon that important railway centre. An advance, therefore, offered a prize worth striving for, and as

Sir Douglas Haig reckoned that the enemy had not had time to send up more reinforcements than would serve merely to make good his wastage, he decided to press on the attack, and the 22nd was spent in making the necessary arrangements.

The events of the 22nd November furnished disquieting proof that the German resistance was stiffening, the left flank of the 9th Royal Scots being tested by a series of vigorous counter-strokes. The battalion's front was held by all four companies, the right occupying the sunken road leading from Cantaing along the eastern margin of Nine Wood, and the left being posted along another sunken road running in a north - north - west direction to Fontaine. The efforts of the Germans were concentrated on Fontaine, garrisoned by the 4th Seaforths, against whom a converging attack was delivered from Bourlon Wood, the north, and the Cambrai-Bapaume Road. " B " Company under Captain A. D. Maxwell, on the left of the 9th Royal Scots, was favourably posted to assist the defence of the village and by a raking fire exacted a heavy toll from the Boches. Five times the Germans, massing near a road running south-east from Fontaine, roughly parallel to the line of the Royal Scots, endeavoured to cross the country between Fontaine and La Folie Wood, but on each occasion they wilted before the blasting fire of " B " Company, and ultimately were forced to dig in behind a low ridge. The left centre company also had good targets and inflicted considerable casualties on Germans mustered in Folie Wood. Eventually however the weight of the hostile attack proved too strong for our defence, and the Seaforths after a desperate resistance were driven from La Fontaine and fell back on the left of the 9th Royal Scots. Captain Maxwell assisted by Corporal G. Leighton, who was in charge of the extreme left post of the company, rendered yeoman service in reorganising the new line, and the Seaforths and the Royal Scots acting in co-operation prevented the Germans from exploiting their success by breaking through on the left flank of the division. The battle died away on the approach of night, during which several readjustments of our line were made. The right company of the Royal Scots was brought back to a position in reserve, while " B " Company extended its front to the north along the sunken road.

In the operations of the 23rd November the task allotted to the Fifty-first Division was to capture Fontaine, while the Fortieth attacked Bourlon Wood. The assault of the Highlanders was delivered by the 152nd Brigade, but though the troops advanced with the utmost gallantry it failed to clear the village. " B " Company of the Royal Scots assisted the attack with rifle and Lewis-gun fire which caused many casualties among the Boches, and if the Fortieth Division had been able to maintain its hold on Bourlon Wood, the village would probably have been captured. But a hostile counter-attack, by regaining a portion of the wood, uncovered the left flank of the 152nd Brigade and rendered all the efforts of the Highlanders unavailing. The Germans, as on the previous day, tried to follow up their success by breaking through our line, but our front held firm. During the momentary confusion consequent on the repulse of our attack, Sergeant J. R. Jamieson of the Royal Scots distinguished himself by the initiative and power of control that he displayed in reorganising some leaderless troops of the 152nd Brigade. No further change in the situation took place, and late in the evening the division was relieved, the 9th Royal Scots returning to Metz. Though the whole battlefield had been savagely shelled by the enemy, the losses of the 9th were few, three killed and seventeen wounded, and they had the satisfaction of having caused a much greater wastage among the enemy.

The battalion had just reason to be proud of the efficiency of its signal service during this action. There was no signalling officer, but Sergeant A. C. Mitchell, who was in command of the signallers, performed his duties with such thoroughness that, in spite of the severity of the German shell fire, telephone communication between battalion H.Q. and the companies was maintained intact throughout the battle.

The 8th Royal Scots were extremely fortunate in escaping losses, for they were constantly employed in constructing roads from Trescault up to Flesquières Ridge while the division was in the line.

In spite of heavy fighting, extending over several days, we never succeeded in making our position on Bourlon Ridge secure. The village of Fontaine again passed into our hands, but was recaptured by a German counter-attack. Numerous prisoners and a vast quantity of war material had come into our possession in the course of the operations, but strong-points near Bourlon Wood, as well as the village of Fontaine, required to be carried before our general position could be considered as satisfactory.

The last word was with the enemy. A German counter-stroke was delivered on the 30th November and, though it had been expected, it reaped a greater measure of success than our attack had done. After a brief but ferocious preliminary bombardment the enemy attacked, and his infantry advanced with such speed that parts of our line fell without any resistance, and an awkward fissure was created in our entrenchments near Gouzeaucourt and Gonnelieu. Only by immediate counter-attacks was a serious disaster averted, and when the fighting ceased in this sector, the Boches retained much of the ground that they had overrun. At Bourlon Wood itself, where the main counter-thrust was expected, the progress of the enemy was fiercely contested, and the withdrawal of our line to Flesquières Ridge on the morning of the 7th December gave us a sound defensive position.

The rest which the Highlanders had amply earned by their exertions was rudely interrupted by the commotion arising from the Boche counter-attack, and the Fifty-first Division was hurriedly sent at the beginning of December to take over the line in the Mœuvres area from the Fifty-sixth Division, which had been one of the victims of the German drive. On the 2nd December, while the 9th Royal Scots were relieving the 2nd Highland Light Infantry, the enemy made a bombing attack, but was defeated after some brisk fighting. The new line was a most precarious one, and, being exposed on the left, encouraged the Germans to attempt enterprises against it. Two raids were delivered against the 9th Royal Scots on the 4th. The first, directed against a sap in the sector of "A" Company, was frustrated by the gallant defence of a platoon commanded by Sergeant T. Smith, the enemy suffering at least two casualties and leaving nine rifles in our hands. In their second effort, the Germans tried to rush a sap held by "B" Company, but after a bombing fight that lasted nearly an hour, they were compelled to retire, having sustained several losses. These forays were an indication of what might be expected in a line with an exposed flank, and a feeling of relief spread through the division when it was informed that the position was to be evacuated. This was done on the evening of the 4th, and after the movement was accomplished, the 9th Royal Scots proceeded to a camp in Fremicourt. In the new line taken over the trenches consisted of little more than scrapings, and the division was required to construct, before the worst of the winter weather came, a totally new system of trenches. Immediate protection was furnished by the indefatigable labours of the 8th Royal Scots, who performed the highly creditable feat of wiring in one night the whole of the new divisional front.

CHAPTER XXVIII

THE STRUMA VALLEY, 1917

Events in the East. The 1st Royal Scots at the Struma. Raid on Homondos by 1st Royal Scots, 22nd July. Operation against Homondos, October. Training and sport. (*See* Map XIV.)

IN 1917, while the rapid succession of murderous conflicts on the Western front appeared to produce no radical alteration in the relative position of the antagonists, events in the East brought a happy change in the fortunes of the Allies. Our operations in Palestine, brilliantly conducted, broke down the defence of the Turks, and while in the Balkans the Allies had little success in offensive enterprises, our position in that region was made tolerably secure. German intrigue was divested of power for harm by the compulsory abdication of King Constantine in June, and by the establishment of the pro-ally Venizelos as head of the Government of Greece. Gossip about the Greek Court was eagerly discussed by our troops, who were unfeignedly pleased when they heard that King Constantine had been expelled from Athens, for they all knew that no active assistance would be forthcoming from Greece till Venizelos was put in charge of Greek affairs. So it proved. The Allies removed the naval blockade, thus conciliating the people, and Greece instead of being an unfriendly neutral became a useful ally.

There was no marked change in the military situation in the Balkans during 1917. Garrison duty and patrolling formed the staple of life for the 1st Royal

Scots in the Struma Valley till the spring of the year. In that season of hope the Royal Scots and the other battalions of the 81st Brigade dug and occupied a new line on the Struma plain in preparation for a grand offensive, but this was cancelled. With the lengthening of the days and the approach of summer, an ineffectual struggle was waged against the mosquito, and so many men were stricken down by malaria that it became clear that the unhealthy valley of the Struma was rapidly becoming a graveyard. Accordingly, our forward positions in the plain were evacuated in June, and our line was established along the foothills with only a few posts on the right bank of the river. At the time of the evacuation the Royal Scots were holding Homondos, but they had no difficulty in achieving their retirement from the village, the rearguard company alone being slightly engaged with the enemy. Few men were required for the bridge-heads at the Struma, and consequently it was possible to withdraw the bulk of our forces to summer camps on the slopes of the Krisha Balkans, where intensive training and recreation were carried out daily. The troops benefited enormously in health, and they became keen to take part in enterprises against the enemy, who had not been slow to occupy the positions that we had vacated.

The possibility of an offensive by the Allies in the Balkans was sadly affected by the collapse of discipline in Russia and the total defeat of Rumania, and it is surprising that General Sarrail decided to make any attack at all. With exuberant optimism he had planned to make a general advance in the first week of April, but he was forced to restrict his schemes on account of the Russian revolution. After that event he would have been wise to remain on the defensive, but in the hope of assisting the arms of the Allies in

France, he ultimately determined to launch an assault on the Doiran front. This was carried out by British troops on the 28th April and the 8th May, a small strip of territory being gained, which was poor value for the serious losses incurred. This campaign in no way affected the troops in the Struma region, and after May the whole front became stabilised.

The yearning of the keen soldier for adventure could be partly gratified by patrolling and raids. The troops of the 81st Brigade, although they appreciated the advantage of living on the salubrious slopes of the hills, were far from being pleased at seeing their former positions on the plain pass into the hands of the enemy, and they particularly resented his reoccupation of Homondos, which the brigade had come to regard as its own property. The Bulgarians were occupying it in some strength, for they had established two mountain guns there. It was decided to make a raid on the village, and the honour of carrying it out fell to the Royal Scots.

The objects of the enterprise, which was arranged to begin at 5 A.M. on the 22nd July, were to kill or capture as many Bulgarians as possible and to bring back the mountain guns; all details connected with the operations were left to Lieut.-Colonel Forbes. A preliminary reconnaissance by Corps Cavalry revealed the fact that none of the approaches to Homondos from the Struma were guarded by the enemy, and that the garrison of the village was very lax indeed. Lieut.-Colonel Forbes arranged to strike his blow from Komarjan with three companies, "B" and "D" in line supported by "A" Company, and owing to the enemy's lack of vigilance, he was able to move his whole force under cover of night close to its objective by way of the sunken roads that abounded on our

side of Homondos.   "C" Company was in reserve.
Lieut.-Colonel Forbes established his H.Q. near Blicks
Drift, named after Lieut. S. Blyth, the energetic Scout
Officer who came from South Africa to join the battalion.
The Bulgarians were severely punished for their un-
soldier-like carelessness.   "B" and "D" Companies
were within 20 or 30 yards of the opposing trenches
before the defenders opened a wild and scattered fire.
The Homondos garrison was taken completely unawares,
many Bulgarians being only partially clothed when the
Royal Scots appeared among them.   Not a single round
was fired by the hostile artillery, and within a few
minutes the Royal Scots had killed sixty of the enemy
and taken thirty prisoners.   One of the mountain guns
was discovered, and since it was impossible to take it
away, it was dismantled.

The 1st Royal Scots remained for half an hour in
Homondos, and withdrew before the Bulgarians had
time to deliver a counter-attack.   Only one man was
killed in this neat exploit, and a few, including Lieut.
G. A. King and 2nd Lieut. T. Rogers, were wounded.
Valuable help was received from a contact aeroplane,
which co-operated in the attack by firing with a machine-
gun on the Bulgarian trenches, and through its timely
assistance Lieut. King was saved from falling into the
clutches of the enemy.

The Royal Scots were by no means surprised to
learn from prisoners that the commander of Homondos
had been dismissed on account of slackness, but his
successor had not had sufficient time to reorganise the
defences before the 22nd July.   This splendidly executed
raid was followed by continual patrolling of No-Man's-
Land, culminating in the operations from the 13th till
the 23rd October, the aim of which was to re-establish
our front on the line that we had held prior to the

evacuation in June.   These were carried out principally by the Scottish Horse (10th Black Watch)[1] and the 2nd Camerons, who experienced little trouble in driving the Bulgarians from Homondos, which was then occupied and fortified by the Royal Scots.   A period of aggressive patrolling then ensued, and ultimately the salient at Homondos was flattened out, our line of defence being advanced east and west of the village.   Our front in the Struma Valley having been thus solidly established, the units of the Twenty-seventh Division settled down during the winter to trench routine, varied by patrols towards the foothills on the north of the Salonika-Constantinople Railway, where the Bulgarian trenches were situated.

No accounts of the skilfully conducted operations near Homondos appeared in the British Press, but the action of the 81st Brigade made a great impression on the foe.   When the Bulgarians ultimately capitulated in 1918, one of the two officers whom they sent to arrange terms confessed to a British general that they were more harassed in the part of the line opposite the 81st Brigade than anywhere else.   With the detached candour that marks the professional soldier, he spoke in terms of high praise of our enterprises in the vicinity of Homondos as models of a night attack, and admitted that the morale of the Bulgarians was sapped by the patrolling and raiding, which frequently resulted in the surprise and consequent destruction of their outposts.

Thus the work of the units of the Twenty-seventh Division was not without avail, for long before the end of 1917, though there appeared to be no appreciable difference in the general situation, a clear moral ascendancy had been gained over the enemy.

[1] By the inclusion of this battalion, which in November 1916 took the place of the Gloucestershire Regiment, the 81st Brigade was composed entirely of Scottish units.

The routine arranged by Brig.-General Widdrington in the Struma Valley provided for the units of the 81st Brigade the greatest possible facilities for recreation and variety. A battalion spent three weeks in the front line and one in support, each battalion going back to a different front in rotation. Thus no unit was allowed to take root in any one spot, and each became intimate with the whole brigade front.

A comprehensive programme of recreation was carried out, the chief games and pastimes being football, hockey, athletic sports, boxing, all types of race-meetings, lawn tennis, and even golf. Two golf courses were laid out with the help of the brigade Padre, the Rev. Professor D. M. Kay of St Andrews, and Lieut. R. L. Gorrie of the Royal Scots, and they were at least as good as the more celebrated one near Salonika, which received some notice in the Press. Officers enjoyed a greater variety of sport than in any other theatre of the war. Game was plentiful, and although no large "bags" were made, the pot of most messes was kept fairly well supplied. Lieut.-Colonel Railston of the Scottish Horse, assisted by professional whips from his battalion, ran a "bobbery" pack with great success, and gave the officers of the brigade many a good gallop after hares and occasionally after foxes. The brigade took especial pride in its polo team, which never sustained a defeat.

This record of sport and recreation would seem to indicate that more time was devoted to play than to work, but this was far from being the case. Opportunities for recreation came only when a battalion was away from the front line, and even the unit in support had many duties to perform. In all kinds of weather eight hours a day were given to solid work, and it was merely in their scanty leisure that officers and men could turn to sport.

CHAPTER XXIX

THE FALL OF GAZA

November 1917

Preparations for Attack on Gaza. Patrol adventures. The Turkish positions. The Terrain. Sir Edmund Allenby's plans. Attack on Umbrella Hill. 4th Royal Scots at El Arish Redoubt. Turks evacuate Gaza. Beginning of the pursuit, 8th November 1917. (*See* Map XVI.)

PALESTINE, where in the Middle Ages Christendom had experienced so many reverses, was the scene of one of the most conspicuous victories of the Allies in 1917. When our advance from Egypt was checked by the Turkish resistance at Gaza in April, a lull in the operations followed, during which new plans were excogitated and the necessary preparations were carried through for the resumption of the offensive. At this period Sir Archibald Murray relinquished the command and was succeeded by Sir Edmund Allenby, who had been in command of the Third Army in France during the Battle of Arras. Communication between our forces in front of Gaza and Egypt was insured by road and rail on land and also by sea ; by these routes, stores and reinforcements could be sent without molestation to our battle front. Not the least important part of our preparations consisted in the provision of a reliable supply of water, and the sappers rendered magnificent service by laying pipe lines from Egypt to Palestine. Thus was fulfilled "a saying current in Palestine, that the Turks would not leave that country until the waters

of the Nile flowed into its borders"[1]; it was the story
of Birnam Wood in a modern setting.

The lull, while bringing a cessation of fighting,
imposed many labours on the troops of the Fifty-second
Division, who, in addition to working on railways and
roads, constructed a strong system of trenches and
defences facing Gaza. Our line ran approximately
from Sheikh Ajlin on the beach along Samson's Ridge,
Lees Hill, Mansura and Sheikh Abbas Ridges to the
point known as Abbas Apex, where our position formed
a pronounced salient. Thence it was extended in a
south-westerly direction to Dumb-bell Hill. From this
position to Shellal the line was guarded by cavalry.

The soil was infested with insects of every description,
and in the numerous trenches and hollows the troops
found unpleasant companions in snakes, flies, tarantulas,
scorpions, and centipedes. During the hot and dry
weather the atmosphere was thick with dust so that
even the tiniest scratch tended to become a septic sore.
The health of the men was best preserved by sea-bathing,
but this was possible only for battalions stationed near
the beach. Even in bathing there was danger; two
men of the 4th Royal Scots while out for a dip suddenly
sank, and though they were brought to the beach
through the plucky efforts of 2nd Lieuts. G. Monks
and W. H. Robertson, they could not be revived.

The equipment of the force was at this period
brought up to date, the men being issued in June with
the short-service instead of the long-service rifle, and
in October, when the weather was becoming cool, with
steel helmets. The 4th Royal Scots experienced another
change of command, when Lieut.-Colonel Goldthorpe,
who left the battalion on the 4th June, was succeeded
by Lieut.-Colonel A. M. Mitchell from the 7th Battalion.

[1] *History of the Fifty-second (Lowland) Division*, p. 354.

In the line the efforts of our troops were devoted to securing the control of No-Man's-Land, and in a series of encounters previous to the resumption of the offensive, they established a marked superiority over the enemy. In some sectors No-Man's-Land extended to a width of nearly 3 miles, and in these places, owing to the long stretches of broken and difficult ground to be covered, patrols consisted of at least a platoon. Most of the aggressive work was done by our men, the Turks, as a rule, contenting themselves with lying in ambush in the hope of taking our patrols by surprise. These adventures were the particular province of junior officers, the jauntiness of whose bearing disguised the tension which these nightly explorations imposed on all concerned. Only once, on the 31st July, did the Turks succeed in ambushing a patrol of the Royal Scots. On that occasion a party of the 4th Battalion, consisting of three officers and twenty-nine men, ran into a hostile patrol at least one hundred strong, and sustained several casualties. The Royal Scots, taken unawares, put up a good fight, but their Lewis gun jammed and when they extricated themselves 2nd Lieuts. J. Wallace and J. M. Brunton and three men were missing. A favourite device frequently employed with success by Lieut.-Colonel Mitchell was to send out a patrol, equipped with a telephone, to locate a Turkish standing patrol, and if this object were achieved, the position of the enemy was telephoned to our gunners who would then direct a sudden burst of shells on the Turkish lair.

Indications were not wanting that the Turks were growing tired of the war and resented the overbearing manner of their German supervisors. Many deserters came into our lines. On the 31st August a major (a battalion commander), a lieutenant, and two privates surrendered to the 7th Royal Scots, and from their accounts it was clear that the Turks were suffering from shortage of food as well as war weariness. Thus our superiority in patrolling, and the knowledge that the morale of the enemy was low greatly increased the confidence of our men. In one sphere only had the Turks the ascendancy. Their aeroplanes were much faster than ours, and it was not till the end of summer, when new machines were brought for our airmen, that the balance was redressed.

With the collapse of Russia a new store of strength, the Turkish Caucasian army, became available for the enemy ; but, owing to disagreements between the Turks and Germans, there was considerable delay before a decision was reached as to how these reinforcements could be most profitably employed. Ultimately the enemy decided to use them for an attack on Sir Edmund Allenby's army, but the delay proved disastrous, for our stroke was launched before the Turks were ready. The foe, trusting to the natural strength of his position, was convinced that his defence would prove impregnable. His fortifications ran from the beach at Gaza to Beersheba, 30 miles away, east and south of which the country was so broken and the water-supply so poor that the Turks regarded an outflanking move-ment by our cavalry as impossible. So confident were the Turks in the impregnability of their entrenchments that they had even neglected to prepare a second-line system along the Wadi Hesi. From Gaza to Beersheba the hostile line consisted of a series of strongly fortified localities and trench systems with good lateral communi-cations, so that any threatened point could be quickly reinforced.

It is not surprising that the Turks thought that we were bound to advance along the coast, thus committing ourselves to a succession of frontal attacks, for the terrain offered enormous difficulties to an invading host. The salient feature of the land is the spine of mountain range, over 3000 feet at its highest point, running parallel to the sea-board from Mount Carmel in the north to Beersheba in the south. It stands between the coastal plain, about 20 miles in width, on the west and the deep valley of the Jordan on the east, and consists chiefly of boulder-strewn barren moorland. Valleys, fissures, and hollows, bearing olives, figs, and vines, vary the arid mountain mass ; the scattered villages, squalid and poor, are usually perched on the summits of hills and protected by thick cactus enclosures. Deficient in water and practically devoid of tolerable paths, this mountainous country seemed adapted by nature for a protracted defence. There were only two passable roads to ease the communications of a large army, one stretching from the port of Jaffa to Jerusalem and Jericho, the other leading down the spine from Nablus in the north through Jerusalem to Beersheba.

The difficulties of transportation in these rugged highlands would naturally predispose an invader to take the easier route along the coastal plain, where in the enclosed hamlets and among the low hills and ridges that abounded on it, the Turks had a bountiful choice of convenient places for defence. From Beersheba, a railway ran north through Junction Station, which was connected by branch lines with Gaza and Jerusalem, to Damascus.

A frontal assault on Gaza, even if successful, was bound to be costly, so Sir Edmund Allenby turned his attention to the idea of compelling the Turks to evacuate the city by a flanking attack on Beersheba. In this project, regarded by the Turks as impracticable, the tremendous problem was how to provide the troops with an adequate supply of water. The difficulty was met by the organisation of a camel transport. The enterprise against the Turkish left was entrusted to the cavalry, assisted by four divisions of the XX. Corps, and for the infantry alone 6000 camels were employed in carrying water. After the capture of Beersheba, a containing attack on Gaza was to be made by the XXI. Corps and then our main assault was to be launched against Hareira, which if successful would enable us to roll up the Turkish line from east to west, piling the Turks up against the coast and leaving an opening for our cavalry to move up and seize Junction Station, thus severing the railway communications of Jerusalem. A vigorous bombardment of the defences of Gaza, in which the navy co-operated, was opened on the 27th October and kept the enemy's attention fixed on the right of his line.

The Fifty-second and Fifty-fourth Divisions were detailed to carry out the assault on Gaza which was to begin on the 1st November. The two objectives of the 156th Brigade were the elaborate earthworks in front of the city, Umbrella Hill and El Arish Redoubt. The former was an advanced position, situated on a sand-hill overgrown with bushes and trees. "It took its name from one of the latter, which from a distance looked like a 'Sairey Gamp' umbrella."[1] Since it protruded like an arrow-point into No-Man's-Land, its garrison could sweep with fire the ground on either flank, so it was decided that it should be captured before the assault on El Arish took place. The 7th Scottish Rifles were to attack Umbrella Hill, their right flank being covered by No. 3 Company of the 7th Royal Scots, and the 4th Royal Scots were to attack El Arish Redoubt. Many of the preparations were similar to those which had preceded the Battle of Arras in April,

[1] *History of the Fifty-second (Lowland) Division*, p. 340.

and the units of the 156th Brigade had carefully studied models of the positions that they were to storm.

The bold strategy of Sir Edmund Allenby achieved a signal success. On the 31st October Beersheba fell, and the time was ripe for the attack on Gaza. For days and nights the air had been vibrant with the shriek of shells, and heartened by a heavier artillery support than any they had hitherto experienced, the battalions of the 156th Brigade quickly concluded their preparations for the battle.

The 7th Cameronians commenced to deploy for the attack on Umbrella Hill shortly before 11 P.M. on the 1st November, and No. 3 Company of the 7th Royal Scots under Captain J. B. Greenshields followed when they moved forward to the assault. The Cameronians made excellent progress, and the Royal Scots, in spite of fierce Turkish shelling, advanced without a hitch to their objective between the south-east corner of Umbrella Hill and the Cairo Road. Captain Greenshields was hit by a fragment of shell during the advance, but he remained with his company. Before 11.30 P.M. the hill was in our possession, and the work of consolidation proceeded apace. An excellent line was prepared and wired by No. 3 Company of the 7th, and it was found when daylight came that it could not have been improved upon; this position was held by the company till the 5th November. A faint-hearted counter-attack against Umbrella Hill was smartly repulsed, and the time soon drew nigh for the second and more important phase of the battle.

The 4th Royal Scots, supported by two companies of the 8th Cameronians, had as their objective El Arish Redoubt, including a maze of short trenches on its right, rejoicing in the forbidding name of " Little Devil," and they could count on assistance from a company of the 7th Royal Scots if necessity arose. The Turks, thoroughly scared by the loss of Umbrella Hill, sent gusts of shells over our lines, but the 4th Royal Scots had suffered just four casualties, when they began to deploy along tapes that had been laid out about 500 yards from the objective. The movement was detected by the enemy who opened machine-gun fire, but the assembly was completed without confusion. The battalion was drawn up in four waves on a two-company front, "A" and "B" leading. Two tanks accompanied the Royal Scots and advanced before zero, which was 3 A.M.; one was put out of action before it reached the hostile wire, but the other had succeeded in crossing the first two lines of trenches, when it was hit and set on fire.

The hostile machine-guns were droning angrily when the 4th Royal Scots jumped off at 3 A.M., but the leading waves without faltering swept right through to the Turkish third and fourth lines. When the fourth wave was nearing the opposing front line, it was momentarily staggered by a terrific crash, while stones and earth hurtled through the air and the ground seemed to rise in eruption; it had arrived at the front line just as two land mines exploded. The wave sagged for an instant, but, rallied by the officers and N.C.Os., recovered its cohesion and pushed on towards its objective. "C" Company, wheeling with marvellous precision in the darkness, turned into the "Little Devil" trenches where a desperate fight was waged. With bomb and bayonet the Royal Scots gradually drove the Turks from saps and dug-outs and gained the trenches. "B" Company, on the left, went past its objective and had to return in order to maintain touch with the unit of the Fifty-fourth Division that was attacking along the coast. Consolidation was repeatedly interrupted by counter-thrusts, which were most vicious on the right, and the captured trenches were deluged by a deadly fire from a building in rear of the Redoubt. On locating the chief source of annoyance, 2nd Lieut. Dalgleish with a small group of men darted through our protective barrage, and, storming the building, killed the defenders and destroyed their machine-gun. After this the work of consolidating the trenches was carried on with less disturbance.

Before daylight most of the necessary work had been accomplished, and the line was strengthened by a company of the 8th Scottish Rifles. No. 1 Company of the 7th Royal Scots also proceeded to El Arish Redoubt and arrived there in time to give valuable assistance to the 4th Royal Scots, when the situation on the right had become critical.

The most vulnerable part of our line was at the "Little Devil" trenches, against which the Turks, fighting at the top of their form, delivered a tempestuous attack about 6.30 A.M. "C" Company of the 4th resisted with true Lowland stubbornness, but Captain Macrorie was killed, all his officers and senior N.C.Os. were wounded, and by the sheer fury of their assault the Turks established a footing in our trenches. Lieut. Winchester with a platoon of "D" Company at once moved up to the threatened point and rallied the survivors of "C" Company, while two platoons of No. 1 Company of the 7th also joined in the fray. A combined assault ejected the enemy from his gains, but consolidation under the circumstances was almost impossible, for the shallow trenches were exposed to enfilade fire from Mazar and Romani trenches, which were both held by the Turks.

From daylight until late in the afternoon, the captured Redoubt was systematically swept by shell and machine-gun fire, but all the efforts of the Turks did not avail to shake the defenders. The last serious attempt by the foe took place at night, but his concentration was observed and was smashed by our artillery fire. The 4th Royal Scots, who had undergone a severe strain and had sustained many casualties, were relieved on the night of the 2nd/3rd November by the remainder of the 7th Royal Scots and went back into reserve.

Brig.-General A. H. Leggett was greatly impressed by the determination with which the 4th Royal Scots carried out their task. While they were still in action he heartened them enormously by the brief message : " Well done, 4th Royal Scots ! Hold on for all you are worth. Your battalion has covered itself with glory." And after they had shown how well they could hold on, Lieut.-Colonel Mitchell received the following letter : " I particularly desire to thank you and every officer, N.C.O., and man of your gallant battalion for their magnificent services and unequalled dash and bravery in the attack, capture, and consolidation of El Arish Redoubt. The task was a very formidable one, but nothing could or ever will be able to stand against the gallantry and iron determination, you, one and all, so recently displayed. I hope to see you all soon and thank you all personally for all you have done, but in the meantime I should much like you to make it known to all ranks how grateful I am and how intensely proud I am of the Queen's Edinburgh Rifles."

Our action had been highly successful, and we were now in secure possession of the outworks of Gaza, though the city itself still remained in the hands of the enemy. Unfortunately the plans of Sir Edmund Allenby were to some extent upset by the fact that the water-supply at Beersheba was less than had been expected, and the cavalry had in consequence to be withdrawn. This inevitably hampered the preparations for the grand attack by the cavalry and the XX. Corps on Hareira, which was arranged to take place on the 6th November. Meantime there was a tremendous artillery duel at Gaza. El Arish Redoubt, occupied by the 7th Royal Scots, was one of the principal targets of the Turkish guns, and tons of steel and shrapnel descended upon it. Among the killed was the R.S.M., T. Simpson, a soldier of great experience and efficiency, and his death was a sad blow to battalion H.Q. On the night of the 3rd/4th November Lieut. C. L. M. Marburg was wounded. On the 6th November our lines were subjected to the most violent bombardment that they had yet endured, and it is probable that the Turks, having decided to retire, fired off as much as possible of their ammunition before evacuating the city. One shell burst on the regimental aid post of the 7th Royal Scots and killed or wounded all the inmates except Private J. Mackay, who, with admirable coolness, stuck pluckily to his task of dressing the wounds of injured men. The sector of No. 2 Company also seemed to receive undue attention, and among the wounded was Captain McGeachin.

After continuing for six hours the cannonade died away at 5.30 P.M., and a patrol of the 7th Royal Scots, on going out at 11 P.M., found the nearest hostile trenches untenanted. Other patrols were then pushed forward, and their reports confirmed the suspicion that the foe had decamped. Gaza had fallen. The Turks, utterly disheartened by the loss of their strong earthworks on the 1st and 2nd November, and demoralised by our pitiless shelling, had silently departed from the city which they had arrogantly deemed to be impregnable.

One of our most substantial victories in the war had been gained at a cost that could not be regarded as excessive. The 4th Royal Scots, who had borne the brunt of the fighting on the 2nd November, had naturally the most casualties. Besides Captain Macrorie, Lieut. E. Dawes and fifty-six other ranks were killed, while twelve officers [1] and one hundred and seventy-four other ranks were wounded. In the 7th Royal Scots eight other ranks were killed and four officers [2] and seventy-nine other ranks wounded.

On the 6th November, while the Turks were completing their preparations for the evacuation of Gaza, the XX. Corps broke through the hostile trench systems near Sharia and occupied the railway station. But the Turkish resistance had not been sufficiently undermined to permit the use of cavalry, and the water-supply was inadequate to meet the barest needs of men and horses, so Sir Edmund Allenby rapidly readjusted his plans. It was imperative to prevent the enemy from making a stand along the line of the Wadi Hesi, and since the difficulties in the way of an immediate pursuit by the cavalry and XX. Corps appeared to be insuperable, Sir Edmund Allenby instructed the XXI. Corps to press with the utmost speed along the coast. Most of the camels and other transport were transferred from Sharia to Gaza, and on the 8th November the pursuit of the Turks began.

[1] Captain D. M. Stewart, Lieuts. Carmichael, McEwen, W. R. McNiven, C. Minks, P. Souter, R. B. Wallace, Winchester, L. Young, and 2nd Lieuts. R. Davie, J. Halley, and H. J. Jones.

[2] Besides those already named, Lieut. J. K. Stewart was hit, and later died from the effects of his wounds.

CHAPTER XXX

THE 4TH AND 7TH ROYAL SCOTS IN PALESTINE

November 1917 *to April* 1918

Burkah and Brown Hill. Advance into the Judean Mountains. Nebi Samwil. Turkish counter-attack, 27th November. Fifty-second Division at the Auja. Preparations for Attack. The crossing of the Auja, 20th/21st December. Advance continued, 22nd December. Fifty-second Division transferred to France, April 1918.

THE 157th Brigade led the chase, and in co-operation with the 155th captured the line of the Wadi Hesi, thus breaking up the Turkish right wing. By the 10th November the enemy had been driven beyond Mejdel. The 156th Brigade up to this time was in reserve, and at 2 P.M. bivouacked near the north-east of Mejdel. With every man heavily laden, each carrying a blanket in addition to his ordinary equipment, the march of the brigade on the 11th, a day of oppressive warmth, to Esdud and Kummam, where it relieved the 157th Brigade in the outpost line, was most exhausting. Over two miles off were the Turks, gathered at the village of Burkah and a conical-shaped hill, which, rising coffee-coloured above the greenery of the plain, was fitly named Brown Hill. Burkah, with its mud huts and cactus enclosures, formed the front system of the enemy's defence. In the village were two lines of entrenchments, which were continued along ridges to the west and north-west, and to the rear of Burkah was a third line also sited on a ridge. Brown Hill, which lay a mile to the east from Burkah, was the

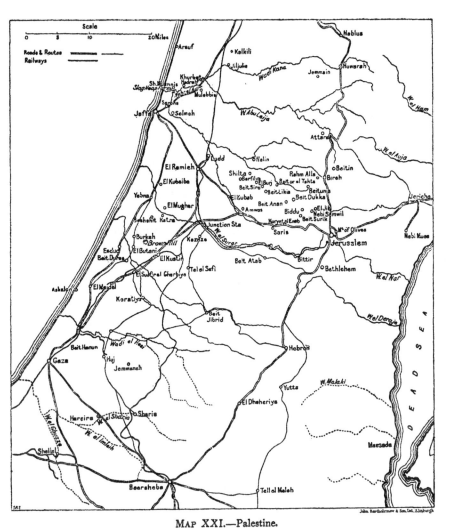

MAP XXI.—Palestine.

:(*See also* large scale Map at end of volume.)

most prominent height in the landscape and was also entrenched. These places were believed to be only lightly held by the Turks, but a reconnaissance at daybreak on the 12th November by a party of yeomanry established the fact that Burkah and Brown Hill were both strongly manned.

Simultaneous attacks against these places were to be delivered by the 156th Brigade on the 12th. For the thrust on Burkah the infantry consisted of the 7th Royal Scots, the 7th Cameronians, and three companies of the 8th Cameronians, supported by two sixty-pounders, a battery of R.F.A., and three sections of machine-guns. The whole of this force was under the command of Lieut.-Colonel Peebles, the 7th Royal Scots being led by Major Ewing. Against Brown Hill the assaulting detachment consisted of the 4th Royal Scots under Captain J. Gray, a company of the 8th Cameronians, two batteries of R.F.A., a mountain battery, a section of machine-guns, and a squadron (less one troop) of yeomanry, the whole under the command of Lieut.-Colonel Mitchell. The former force was to operate from Esdud, and the latter from Kummam.

The flat plain stretching from Esdud to the slight ridge where Burkah stood was almost destitute of cover except for two wadis, and when the force of Lieut.-Colonel Peebles began its advance at 11 A.M. hostile batteries immediately sprayed the plain with shrapnel. In artillery formation the 7th Royal Scots led the way, with No. 2 and No. 3 Companies in front. The first wadi was reached with scarcely any loss, but, on advancing from this point, the Royal Scots came under rifle and machine-gun as well as shell fire. By skilful use of open warfare tactics they reached the second wadi, a shallow water-course about 400 yards from the enemy's front trenches. Under cover of this nullah a firing-line was built up, and by superior accuracy and control the rifle and machine-gun fire of the Royal Scots soon began to prevail over that of the Turks. About 2 A.M. No. 2 Company on the right of the Royal Scots, taking advantage of tiny folds in the ground, pushed forward for 150 yards. Our fire was now growing too hot for the Turks, groups of them being seen to bolt to the rear, and at 3 P.M. a general advance carried Burkah and the enemy's first two lines of entrenchments. A few snipers remained in the cactus gardens and buildings of the village, but these were systematically dealt with by No. 1 Company. The men dug themselves in near the crest of Burkah Ridge, and preparations were made for the attack on the enemy's third line, situated on a higher ridge about 800 yards away. With the Cameronians on the right a general advance was directed against this height, which, despite a very gallant resistance by the Turks, was captured at 6 P.M., just as darkness fell. A vast quantity of miscellaneous war material and several prisoners were taken, while the battle-ground was strewn with Turkish corpses. Arrangements were promptly made to meet a counter-attack, but they proved to be unnecessary, for the discomfited Moslems were in full retreat. A cold night followed a hot day, and the thin drill garb of the troops gave such meagre protection against the chilly air that few could snatch more than a moment or two of sleep.

The attack on Brown Hill, after a stiff struggle, was also successful. With their right flank covered by yeomanry, the 4th Royal Scots left Kummam in artillery formation at 11 A.M., passing the village of El Butani on the left, and for the first hour were little inconvenienced by the Turkish artillery fire. But after the battalion, at noon, had cleared a wadi north of Butani, it came under an accurate and heavy fire. With three companies in front, "A" "B" and "D," the Royal Scots advanced by section rushes, while "C" Company moved out to attack the hill from the left, and the whole pressed on with such skill and persistence that the foe became nervous, and a general charge by the Royal Scots gained them the crest of the hill about 4 P.M. But beyond the crest the Turks had a second trench, where they resisted with fanatical tenacity. The enemy's reserves temporarily tilted the balance against us, and in a determined counter-stroke the Turks, by sheer weight of numbers, pushed the Royal Scots off the crest.

It seemed that all our efforts had been unavailing. Casualties had been serious, the only unwounded officers being Captain Bolton and 2nd Lieut. Smith. Nothing daunted, however, the Royal Scots fell back to a wadi about 300 yards from the summit of Brown Hill and prepared to launch another attack.

Meantime, Lieut.-Colonel Mitchell had sent forward Major Slater to ascertain the situation, and the latter arrived just as the battalion was driven from the hill. At this juncture the 2/3rd Gurkhas of the Seventy-fifth Division chanced to be passing the H.Q. of Lieut.-Colonel Mitchell, who appealed to them to assist the Royal Scots with one or two companies in a second assault on Brown Hill. An invitation to fight was a temptation that the Gurkhas never tried to resist, and they promptly despatched two companies to aid the Royal Scots, but when they reached the wadi, where they were greeted with tremendous cheering, it was found that they had no English-speaking officer with them. It chanced, however, that Captain Bolton belonged to the I.C.S., and with his assistance the

Gurkhas and the Royal Scots were formed up for the attack. Led by Captain Bolton, the advance proved irresistible, and speedily swept the Turks off the hill. The enemy sustained numerous casualties and did not again venture to counter-attack, for by this time the Seventy-fifth Division was coming up on the right of the 156th Brigade.

The capture of Burkah and Brown Hill was a skilful action in which the 7th and the 4th Royal Scots proved themselves to be fully versed in the art of soldiery. The section rushes were admirably conducted, and the discipline and training of the men were testified by the manner in which they established superiority in the fire-fight prior to the assault on the village. The operation, too, had notable consequences, for the right wing of the Turkish forces was now crumpled up, and the foe was compelled to draw back his right flank from the coast until his line ran almost north and south. Our cavalry were able to send patrols as far north as Beshit, while the 155th Brigade pursued the enemy up to his last line of defence for the all-important railway, which was the immediate objective of General Allenby.

The losses of the Royal Scots were much lighter than those they inflicted on the Turks. The casualties of the 4th Battalion consisted of three officers and forty-nine other ranks killed, four officers[1] and one hundred and fifty-seven other ranks wounded; those of the 7th Battalion were thirty-two other ranks killed, six officers[2] and eighty-six other ranks wounded. The dead officers were Captain G. M. Clark, the commander of "C" Company, a gallant and experienced leader, and Lieuts. W. Dalgleish and W. R. Robertson.

---

[1] Major J. O. Taylor, Captains Gray and Bolton, and Lieut. Waterston.
[2] Lieuts. R. Cairns and R. Waterston, 2nd Lieuts. L. R. Binnie, R. P. Innes, J. S. Weir, and J. West.

No respite was given to the enemy. On the 13th November the Fifty-second Division continued its advance, the 155th Brigade leading the way, and in one of the critical actions of the campaign the Turks were driven from the villages of Mughar and Katrah. The 156th Brigade followed in reserve, and was approaching Beshit while the action was in progress. After the defeat of the enemy the 4th Royal Scots moved on to Katrah, the 7th to Beshit, and on the 14th both battalions proceeded to El Mughar.

A worthy prize was the reward of our victory on the 13th November. The Turks on the northern wing of the battle were disheartened and disorganised, and their humiliation reacted disastrously on their line to the south. The loss of the railway, including Junction Station, was not the only result of their rout, for in their flight their army had split into two groups, one retiring north to the River Auja and the other making east for the shelter of the mountains. The pursuit was taken up by our cavalry, and by the 16th November we had secured Jaffa, Ludd, and Ramleh. It was absolutely essential to prevent the Turkish forces from reuniting, and Sir Edmund Allenby decided to advance eastwards into the massive mountain system of Judea, and thus sever the communications between Jerusalem and the north, before the Turks had time to recover from their demoralisation.

While the preparations for this risky and audacious drive were being made, the Fifty-second Division enjoyed a comparatively tranquil time. It was a necessary precaution to disarm the inhabitants of the district now in British hands, but as a rule the only weapons surrendered at the various depots appointed for the purpose were of an obsolete type. The advance was begun on the 18th November, and the difficulties that beset the campaign were prodigious. The physical strain of manœuvring in mountainous regions is always colossal, and no troops could relish the prospect of campaigning in a country which was more wildly rugged and desolate than the Grampian plateau of Scotland. In the district to be traversed there were no decent paths, so that it was almost impossible to send up artillery to support the infantry. Wheeled vehicles had to be left behind, and supplies for the troops were conveyed by camels. Thus there was a deficiency in stores of all kinds, and the troops had to resign themselves to a course of very frugal fare; the menu contained only half-rations of bully beef and biscuits, and even the most urgent necessities as regards equipment could not be supplied. The tunics and shorts of the Royal Scots were already showing signs of wear, but most distressing of all was the condition of the footgear; even before the tramp into the highlands commenced, many of our men were almost bootless, and it speaks volumes for their discipline and powers of endurance that remarkably few succumbed to the rigours of the march over jagged rock and crumbling shingle. Before the campaign ended, scores of the men had stripped the puttees from their legs and wound them round their feet as a guard against the hard flinty mountain tracks.

On the morning of the 18th November the 156th Brigade marched to Ramleh, and after a brief stay there went on to Ludd, where the brigade halted and lay overnight by the roadside. The weather had become bitterly cold and a drenching rain soaked through the flimsy tunics of the troops; all packs and greatcoats were left behind at Ludd, and the only protection a man had against the bite in the air was a woollen cardigan. The brigade was now in the foothills of the Judean plateau, and the route assigned to it led over the hills by the old Roman Road to Berfilya, thence to Beit Likia, where an outpost line was formed on the mountain tops. The Roman Road was a name rather than a road ; in most places it was no better than "a mountain pass over rocks and boulders covered with loose stones, so that the going was very heavy and in many places single file was the only possible formation." [1] The first few nights were miserably cold and wet.

The Fifty-second Division in its march had to exercise unrelaxed vigilance ; it had to watch not merely its front but the northern flank, from which the Turks might launch a sudden counter-attack and turn our victory into disaster by destroying all our troops entangled in the Judean Highlands. Leading the division, the 157th Brigade experienced hard and strenuous fighting on the 20th, but broke down the enemy's resistance at Beit Anan and Beit Dukka. Progress continued to be made on the 21st, and the Seventy-fifth Division, veering to the left, gained a footing on the Nebi Samwil Ridge, reputed to be the burying-place of the prophet Samuel, a point of considerable tactical importance, from which in the twelfth century the Crusaders of Richard I. caught their first glimpse of Jerusalem, about $4\frac{1}{2}$ miles to the south-east. In the higher altitudes now reached, the cold was intense, and only during the day, when the sun was high in the heavens, did the men feel comfortably warm. All units not engaged in fighting laboured strenuously with blasting charges, picks, and crowbars, to form a track for the guns, and by the 23rd November it was possible for the heavy artillery to go as far as Biddu. But despite unflagging effort only a few guns could be got up to support the infantry, and the supply of ammunition for these was very limited.

[1] *History of the 7th Royal Scots.*

NEBI SAMWIL.

JUDÆAN HILLS.

[To face p. 528.

A desperate struggle was waged for the possession of Nebi Samwil, the key to Jerusalem. After their surprise by the Seventy-fifth Division, the Turks delivered a furious assault, which nearly succeeded in driving us from the western part of the ridge, but a timely counter-thrust by the 7th Scottish Rifles restored the situation, and we retained all our gains intact. On the 22nd November the battalions of the 156th Brigade were ordered to relieve the 234th Brigade in the forward positions. The 4th Royal Scots accordingly marched up to Beit Surik and the 7th Royal Scots to Biddu. From both these places a view of the outskirts of the Holy City could be obtained, and the fact is recorded in the war diaries of the battalions.

Nebi Samwil, upon the possession of which the Turks rightly set great store, was a lofty ridge extending to the north-east for nearly a mile. Its highest point, nearly 3000 feet above sea-level, was at the western end, where stood a small village with orchards and gardens enclosed by stone walls. Close behind our front line, a mosque, with its tapering minaret rising gracefully into the sky, formed a startling contrast to the wild grandeur of the landscape. In the immediate vicinity of the mosque a network of stone walls and enclosures furnished the Turks with priceless facilities for shooting their assailants at point-blank range without receiving a shot in return. When these enclosures were stormed, the victors would have before them the long summit of the ridge, almost destitute of cover, stretching to the north-east, and would be troubled throughout their advance by the fire which the Turks could direct upon them from the bold promontory of El Jib, cutting into the earth like the prow of a ship.

On the night of the 23rd/24th November the

156th Brigade concentrated behind the mosque as a preliminary to an attack by the division, the object of which was to cut the communications of Jerusalem with the north by an advance across the Jerusalem-Nablous Road. The 7th Royal Scots reached their position before dawn, but when the 4th Royal Scots were relieved at Beit Surik the sun was shining brightly, and they had to cross the valley leading to Nebi Samwil in small groups, several casualties being sustained from the Turkish fire. The attack was arranged for noon on the 24th. The task of the 7th Royal Scots was first to clear the enclosures and orchards in front of the mosque, and then to sweep the Turks off the remainder of the ridge. The 4th were to support the 7th Royal Scots in the first phase of the action and, on the final objective being reached, to prolong the line of the 7th to the right.

With the enemy holding every point of vantage, and with a totally inadequate artillery support for the infantry, our only hope of success was that the Turks were yet too cowed by their series of defeats to be capable of offering a determined resistance. But those now opposed to the Fifty-second Division were mainly fresh troops; they possessed the advantage in numbers as well as in position, and on the 24th November they revealed no symptoms of demoralisation. Our push was checked, and the small amount of ground that we gained cost us many lives.

For the attack on the enclosures Lieut.-Colonel Peebles detailed his No. 1 and No. 4 Companies. During the whole forenoon the mosque and its neighbourhood were kept under fire by the enemy, and when the 7th Royal Scots began their advance the hostile bombardment became intense. No. 1 Company, under Captain Bell, passing on the right of the mosque, after advancing about 100 yards, found it impossible to proceed any farther owing to the fury of the Turkish fire, which raked the ranks of the Royal Scots from the flanks as well as from the front. There was a bare chance that by creeping round the eastern slopes of the ridge the men might avoid the fire-beaten zone, but the Turks had anticipated this manœuvre, and all who attempted it were hit. In No. 1 platoon there were only three survivors, and two officers, 2nd Lieuts. J. W. Hutchison and J. MacNab, were wounded. The company stuck pluckily to its gains, but suffered serious losses from the enemy's shell fire during the afternoon.

On the left, No. 4 Company under Captain A. H. Rogers at the outset met with better fortune. After passing the left side of the mosque, it reached a court-yard, in front of which stood a long, flat-roofed shed. This courtyard suddenly became a scene of extra-ordinary turbulence, bombs and bullets coming among the Royal Scots apparently from all directions. With quick decision Captain Rogers led his men to the shed, cleared it, and placed some of them on the roof to fire down on the Turks in the walled gardens and orchards. But the enemy countered this move by concentrating his fire on the roof of the shed, and Captain Rogers and several of his men were killed. Captain Malcolm Smith, upon whom the command of the company devolved, seeing that a frontal assault was doomed to failure, decided to make an attempt to turn the enemy's right flank by taking his men along the left slopes of the ridge. The only suitable exit from the courtyard was by a gap in the wall, but this was taped off by a Turkish machine-gun, and the first men of the Royal Scots who daringly plunged through it were shot down. Captain Smith then endeavoured to set up a Lewis gun to deal with the Turkish gun, but

the enemy's fire was accurate and deadly, and those
men who bravely essayed to bring the Lewis gun into
action were either killed or wounded, and the gun itself
was irreparably damaged.

The enemy's gun unfortunately was beyond the
range of our grenades, and in the indiscriminate bomb
fight that was waged around the courtyard the Turks
had a huge advantage, since their stick grenades could
be thrown farther than our Mills bombs. The Royal
Scots established a bombing post to guard their left
flank, and by a sudden rush some bombers, riflemen,
and a Lewis gun section got through the breach in
the wall, though not without losses, and cleared the
Turks from the first wall, which became our line of
defence and a jumping-off point for the next assault.
The Turkish frontal fire from the wall beyond was
speedily beaten down, but the position of the Royal
Scots soon became uncomfortable owing to the severity
and accuracy of the enemy's enfilade fire, and when the
Lewis gun was blown up, retirement became imperative.
The dead and wounded were collected and carried behind
the gap, which was again held, and a convenient loophole was bored through the wall. After two other
fruitless attempts to advance, the company was ordered
to hold on to the ground that it had won, and for this
purpose was reinforced by two platoons from No. 3
Company.

The 4th Royal Scots, owing to the collapse of
the attack, were not involved in the fray, and though
exposed to the hostile shell fire they did not sustain
many casualties. The Fifty-second Division had been
set to accomplish a task which without strong artillery
support was beyond the power of mortal men, and the
engagement was broken off before nightfall. Just at
dusk, No. 4 Company of the 7th Royal Scots observed

parties of Turks creeping towards our lines for the purpose of rifling the dead; at least three different groups attempted this, but they were dispersed by the vengeful fire of the Royal Scots. About 8 P.M. the sorely battered battalion[1] was relieved, and moved back to the outpost line at Biddu.

The action of the 24th November, despite the fact that it failed to achieve its object, was far from being futile. The position of our troops, now faced by strong forces of Turks in the Judean Highlands, was a most precarious one, and a resolute counter-attack from the north might have easily upset all the plans of Sir Edmund Allenby. Under these circumstances a persistent offensive was probably our safest policy, and the vigour and enterprise shown by the Fifty-second Division on the 24th November must have bewildered the Turks, and caused them to estimate our strength as being greater than it really was. They delayed their blow and gave Sir Edmund Allenby time to send up fresh troops.

With the Sixtieth Division now available, it was possible to relieve the tired and war-weary units of the Fifty-second Division, and on the 26th November the 4th and the 7th Royal Scots with their faces to the coast began their march from the plateau, but, before they had gone far, the Turks delivered a critical counter-attack, and the Royal Scots had to bear their share of the defence. The British front at this time touched the coast at the mouth of the River Auja, and was continued into the Judean plateau to the north of Nebi Samwil. The protection of the important flank in the mountains rested upon the yeomanry and the

---

[1] Captain A. N. Rogers was killed, 2nd Lieut. J. W. Hutchison died of wounds, 2nd Lieuts. J. MacNab and R. Burns were wounded; the casualties in other ranks were seventeen killed, eighty-nine wounded.

Fifty-fourth Division, but even with all their men strung out in a series of posts, there was a gap of 5 miles, stretching from Beit Ur El Tahta to Shilta, between the two. A sally through this opening would enable the Turks to reach the Ludd-Nebi Samwil Road and sever the communication of our troops in the vicinity of the Nebi Samwil Ridge. As it happened, the Turks dealt their blow on the 27th November, just as the nearest troops of the Fifty-second Division (155th Brigade) were approaching the unguarded space.

The units of the 156th Brigade were thrown into the line wherever reinforcements were necessary. On the 28th the 4th Royal Scots were detached from their brigade and sent to help the 155th Brigade, which was heavily engaged defending the gap. The battalion had just accomplished an 8 miles' march when it was ordered to storm Abu Fureij, a commanding promontory immediately north-west of El Burj. Fortunately no fighting was necessary, for the 5th Royal Scots Fusiliers had never lost their grip on the place, and a relief was all that was required. For some time matters here were very critical, and the Turks were deterred from advancing only by the accuracy of our rifle and machine-gun fire, but by the 29th November the situation at El Burj was well in hand. On this front the Turks were utterly discomfited by their warm reception, and as a result of the opportune arrival and stubborn resistance of the 155th Brigade the fissure between Shilta and Tahta was closed.

The other units of the 156th Brigade were marching from Beit Annan to Beit Likia, when the Turks commenced their attack by pressing in our line on the north, and opening fire on the road which our men were traversing. The fire was most concentrated on a pass two miles to the east of Beit Likia, and while the 7th

Royal Scots were passing through it, Captain Kermack and three men were wounded. About 3 P.M. the battalion was diverted to hold the outpost line north of Beit Sira, on the right of the 155th Brigade. Every attempt of the Turks to pierce the line was mercilessly broken up by well-controlled fire, and during the 29th the enemy was satisfied with engaging the 156th Brigade with rifle and artillery fire. The hostile demonstrations continued with lessening fury up to the 1st December and then died away. The 156th Brigade, which the 4th Royal Scots rejoined on the night of the 29th November, was relieved on the 1st December and proceeded to bivouacs about 4½ miles south-west of Beit Sira.

The work of the division had been fruitful in result. It had crossed the mountains to the key of the Holy City, and had played no small part in staving off the great attack with which the Turks endeavoured to retrieve the fortunes of the campaign. Repulsed at every point, the foe lost heart, and early in December the whole of the Nebi Samwil Ridge passed into our hands. On the same day, the 9th December, Jerusalem itself was captured, and this happy consummation was hailed with delight by the units of the Fifty-second Division, without whose efforts it could never have been achieved.

Marching to El Kubah on the 2nd December, the 4th and the 7th Royal Scots on the following day proceeded to a camping area near Ramleh, where for three days, in the more genial air of the plain, they were given a much-needed rest. The next move of the brigade was to Selmeh, 3½ miles east of Jaffa, but the Ramleh-Jaffa Road was under range of the Turkish guns, so that the march had to be made after sundown on the 7th December. The night was one of the worst ever endured by the 4th and the 7th Royal Scots. A terrific rainstorm flooded the ground, which became a welter of oozy mud, and in the pitch darkness animals and men found it difficult to keep their footing. A deep and treacherous wadi caused enormous trouble to the transport. "The rain had made the surface of the ground so slippery that the camels could hardly stand, and more than one toppled over and rolled down the banks of the wadi, baggage and all."[1] The trials and difficulties of the march may be faintly gauged from the fact that the men required more than nine hours to cover less than 8 miles. The transport took an even longer period, for it had to make a wide detour to cross the wadi at a convenient point, and it did not reach the battalions till the early hours of the 8th December.

Scarcely recovered from the miseries of this terrible march, the 4th and the 7th Royal Scots, on the night of the 8th December, took over a portion of the outpost line at the River Auja, "the first perennial river after the Nile which we had met during our months of trekking."[1] Happily the rigours of war in this district were appreciably less than in the mountains, and the troops were rendered more comfortable by the issue of new clothing and equipment. Reinforcements were received, and the units quickly showed evidence of being battalions in strength as well as in name. Most congenial of all were the billets at Sarona, where a man could revel in some of the cherished luxuries of civilisation, especially a hot bath. Bully beef and biscuits still formed the staple food, but the orange groves near Jaffa provided an abundant store of juicy fruit, which not only added variety to the diet but greatly improved the health of the men.

The drawback of our position on the coast was that Jaffa, now our chief port of supply, lay within easy

[1] *History of the 7th Royal Scots.*

range of the Turkish guns on the northern bank of the Auja. It was therefore desirable for our comfort, if not for our safety, that the Turks should be driven so far to the north that they could not interfere with the shipping at the port. But the position of the enemy was unusually strong, being protected by the winding waters of the Auja. In ordinary conditions the width of the river varied from 35 to 40 yards, and its depth from 10 to 12 feet, while the normal speed of the current was from 2 to 3 miles per hour. The river was quickly affected by rain, after forty-eight hours of which it would rise a fathom in depth and become a raging torrent. On the north bank the enemy had the benefit of two dominating positions at Sheikh Muannis and Khurbet Hadrah, situated on ridges, from which he commanded an extensive field of fire. Except for these places the ground on both flanks of the Auja was almost a dead level, with practically no cover for assailing troops. The immediate vicinity of the river was composed of rich black soil, admirable for the growth of cotton but unstable for marching, and in the damp weather, prevalent at this season, it softened into an agglutinative stretch of mire. The general conditions were such that if the Turks put up a serious resistance, a crossing during the day could be effected only at a gigantic cost in lives.

The plan of the XXI. Corps was to force a crossing by the methods of the "set" battle, the infantry advancing on limited objectives, supported by the greatest possible weight of artillery; but Major-General Hill of the Fifty-second Division suggested that our object might be secured at a small cost by a surprise crossing during the hours of darkness. After some hesitation he was given permission to carry out his plan, and the whole division braced itself up for a supreme effort, for it felt that its reputation was at stake.

Reconnaissances of the banks had revealed the disquieting fact that there was only one practicable crossing, a ford near the mouth, "which was liable to shift with the strength of the stream and in flood-time to disappear altogether."[1] Appliances for crossing, therefore, had to be constructed by the sappers, and the possibility of using these without alarming the Turks depended partly upon the quietness with which our troops did their work, and partly upon the degree of vigilance maintained by the enemy. On so many occasions had the Turks been surprised since the opening of the operations, that it might be supposed that they would have adopted adequate measures to patrol the river bank. But in this respect they were incorrigible, and their indolence was largely responsible for the disaster that soon overtook them.

The enemy's negligence was first detected by a very daring patrol carried out by a small party of the 4th Royal Scots on the night of the 13th/14th December. At 8 P.M., Lieut. G. S. Smith with Lance-Corporal McGregor and Privates Horsburgh, Liddell, and Newton embarked on a light boat, specially constructed for the purpose by sappers, and crossed to the Turkish side of the Auja. Though the night was exceptionally clear and the boat formed a dark shadow on the silvery ribbon of water, the nocturnal adventurers were not observed. The northern bank was thoroughly explored, and for 200 yards on either side of the landing-place there was no indication of any hostile sentry or patrol. On the Turkish side the grass was long and gave cover from view, while the ground furnished a tolerable footing for infantry and was easy to dig. Having collected a vast quantity of

---

[1] *History of the Fifty-second (Lowland) Division*, p. 479.

useful information, the patrol then returned to our side of the river.

Since judged by the slackness of his watch, the enemy apparently did not anticipate a nocturnal attack it was important not to disturb his sense of security. He had to be kept in ignorance of the preparations being made by our sappers, so all the appliances for crossing the river were manufactured under cover. Most difficult of all was the problem of storing the bridging apparatus in a place screened from the prying gaze of Turkish observers and at the same time accessible for speedy transport to the river. By infinite care every obstacle was surmounted. The crossing-place for the 156th Brigade was fixed at a point about 2500 yards west of Jerisheh Mill, where there was a grove in which all the bridging material could be conveniently concealed. Two bridges were prepared for the units of the brigade, and these were spread with thick carpets, taken from houses in Sarona, to dull the sound of marching feet. In addition there were several light canvas boats and rafts, each capable of carrying fifteen men, which were to assist in conveying the troops across the river.

For several nights before the enterprise our guns bombarded the Turkish positions, so that the suspicions of the enemy would not be unduly excited by the barrage which was to support our troops on the eventful night. The infantry carried through a programme of training behind the lines. A pond at Sarona gave suitable facilities for practising the men in embarking and disembarking from the canvas boats, and exercises in marching by compass were undertaken nightly.

The date fixed for the crossing was the night of the 20th December, but three days before this, the river became a raging flood as the result of a heavy and prolonged rainstorm. The Auja spread over its banks, and all the ground in its neighbourhood became a vast swamp. In order to ease the passage of the troops and the carriage of the bridging apparatus, fascines were laid and covered with canvas to form routes down to the crossing-points. One redeeming feature of the bad weather was that the hostile trenches on the river bank were flooded, and after the rain had persisted for three days, Major-General Hill hoped that it would continue till the enterprise was launched, for a wet night gave the best chance of effecting a surprise. "What did it matter if we got wetter than we had been for the past three days? But what happened? After raining all the night before and up to midday it began to clear up, and when the time you were going to attempt your crossing and surprise arrived, there was hardly a cloud in the sky and a half-moon." [1]

All three brigades of the division were required for the operation and all were to cross simultaneously. At 10.30 P.M. the artillery was to open fire, and the assaulting units, having reached the far bank of the river, were to move forward. Every officer and man knew that the success of the attack depended upon the strictest silence being observed, and all were keyed up to prove to the Corps that Major-General Hill had not underrated the discipline and skill of his division. There was to be no indiscriminate rifle fire, for to ensure surprise the attack had to be carried out at close quarters with bomb and bayonet.

The objective of the 4th Royal Scots was Slag Heap Farm, to the south-west of Sheikh Muannis village, the capture of which was the task of the 7th Royal Scots. With every tool and even their steel helmets muffled, the troops, about 7 P.M., began to file down the appointed

[1] From Major-General Hill's New Year message to the Division.

routes to the crossing-place. The start was unlucky, for owing to the strength of the current the bridge could not easily be fixed in position, and for a considerable period the men had to be ferried across in the canvas boats. By 10.30 P.M., of the 4th Royal Scots, the first unit of the brigade to advance, only "C" Company and a platoon of "D" Company were on the northern bank. Fortunately the attack was postponed for half an hour, by which time the whole of the battalion had reached the other side.

Only one company of the 7th Royal Scots was across at 11 P.M. when the 4th Royal Scots began their advance on Slag Heap Farm, which lay some 2000 yards to the north of the Auja. "C" and "D" Companies led the way, with "A" on their left in support. At 2 A.M., Lieut.-Colonel Mitchell, having received no information from these companies, sent forward "B" Company to establish touch with them. Then, while he was moving towards the farm, the welcome news reached him that the objective had been captured without serious opposition. Two wounded prisoners and one machine-gun with other war material were captured, and the battalion set to work to consolidate the farm.

Before midnight all the 7th Royal Scots had reached the far side of the river, in time to escape the shells which the Turks belatedly poured on the banks. The battalion advanced side by side with the 8th Cameronians for three-quarters of a mile, when the latter turned east to attack the right rear of the hostile system of redoubts protecting Sheikh Muannis. The 7th Royal Scots held straight on to storm the rear and eastern defences of the village and prevent any attempt by the Turks to retreat. It was anxious work marching over unknown ground in the dark, but not a hitch occurred, and the

7th Royal Scots fell upon a bewildered foe, hardly awake to the fact that an onslaught was in progress. Sheikh Muannis was easily captured, and by dawn the 7th Royal Scots had formed an outpost line beyond the village ready for any counter-attack. Many Turks were killed and wounded, and twenty-seven (including two officers) were taken prisoners. Machine-guns during the campaign were common trophies, but one seized by the 7th Royal Scots excited particular notice, for it was engraved with the Ottoman arms and was believed to have been sent as a gift to the Turks from the Kaiser.

By 6 A.M., on the 21st, the 156th Brigade had consolidated its objectives, and the triumph of the other brigades was equally complete. The confidence of Major-General Hill in his division had been splendidly vindicated, and the discipline and control shown by all the units during this difficult night operation were such as would have filled well-trained professional soldiers with justifiable pride. At a cost of less than one hundred casualties, the Fifty-second Division had forced back the right wing of the enemy for nearly 2½ miles on a front of 3 miles.

Jaffa was now reasonably secure from effective artillery fire, but it was advisable to drive the enemy still farther back in order to disengage the Auja bridges from Turkish gun fire. On the 21st the Turks contented themselves with shelling their lost positions, to little purpose, and our troops spent the day in making preparations for another advance at 9 A.M. on the 22nd. The object of the division was to push forward its front for 3½ miles. Supported by the guns, the three brigades advanced in artillery formation and made rapid progress ; there was no fighting worth the name, for the Turks had been utterly demoralised by the crossing of the Auja. The plain was dotted with numerous clusters of our troops, and they moved forward with such steadiness that a spectator might well have imagined that they were engaged in peace-time manœuvres rather than in an actual combat. The new line, reached and consolidated, extended from Arsuf on the coast to Ferrekhujeh on the Auja; it gave Jaffa an insurance against even long-range gun fire, and secured us the advantage as regards both the lie of the ground and observation.

The casualties sustained by the 4th and the 7th Royal Scots during the whole of these operations were almost incredibly low. The former lost only twenty-seven in all, five men killed, and one officer and twenty-one men wounded; the latter had one officer (Captain M. Smith) and one man wounded.

There now ensued a long lull in fighting which was not unwelcome to the troops. In turn the brigades relieved each other in the line, and the rest billets were at the German-Jewish village of Sarona. The garrisoning of the line involved few hardships; indeed the right sector on the Auja with its orange groves was an ideal haunt for troops who had been in the desert for a year. The fruit itself made existence more than tolerable. "One at least of the three sandbags carried by each man was employed as a pillow—not stuffed with eider-down but with his own private supply of oranges. On our right flank there stretched to the Judean Hills the wide flat plain where Richard Cœur de Lion tried his famous manœuvre to smash Saladin's army—only foiled by the jealousies and disobedience of his allies in arms. Less than a mile out on this plain was the fortress which he built and which certain of our officers visited. It brought the Crusades near and made us feel that the Crusaders were not so much historical figures as brothers-in-arms."[1]

[1] *History of 4th Royal Scots.*

The work of the 4th and the 7th Royal Scots in the East was now accomplished. They had borne themselves valiantly in Gallipoli and had played a noble part in the wonderful campaign across the Sinai desert into Palestine, which brought the Turk to his knees. At the Auja they had rounded off two months of glorious achievement by one of the neatest and most difficult feats in the whole of the campaign, and it was small wonder that Major-General Hill in his admiration for the exploits of his troops ended his New Year's message to the Fifty-second Division with: "Here's tae us! Wha's like us!"

The great crisis of the war had occurred in France. The Germans launching a desperate offensive in March won many acres of ground and captured numerous prisoners and guns. Our position on the Western front was sorely taxed, and there was urgent need for reinforcements. Thus, at the end of March, the Fifty-second Division received word that it was to be transferred to France. On the 28th March the units of the 156th Brigade assembled at Surafend, and on the 3rd April entrained at Ludd for Alexandria, "passing in a few hours the long weary miles which we had but lately conquered wholly on 'Shanks Mare' after a year's plodding."[1] Embarkation commenced on the 8th April, the 4th and the 7th Royal Scots being conveyed on the *Leasowe Castle*, which arrived at Marseilles on the 17th April. The voyage was, fortunately, devoid of alarming incidents, and the men were pleased with the change, partly because France seemed so near home, and partly because they were anxious to strike a blow in the biggest of all the theatres of the war.

[1] *History of 4th Royal Scots.*

CHAPTER XXXI

EVE OF THE GREAT GERMAN OFFENSIVE

September 1917 *to March* 1918

Situation on the Western Front. British Brigades reduced to three
Battalions. Defensive arrangements of Sir Douglas Haig. 5/6th
Battalion at Nieuport and Houthulst Forest. Movements of 2nd,
8th, 9th, 11th, 12th, 13th, 15th, 16th, and 17th Battalions. German
plan of attack.

At the close of 1917 there was no counterpart on the
Western front to the elation that buoyed up our warriors
in Palestine. The reason for pessimism lay on the
surface. In France and Flanders we had made our
most conscious and resolute efforts to force a decision,
but after perhaps the most strenuous campaign in the
history of the world, we seemed further off from a
decision than when the year opened. Indeed we appeared
to have lost rather than gained; for after the events of
November it could not be disguised that the initiative
had passed into the hands of the enemy.

Other factors contributed to the general despondency.
Our position at sea was not entirely satisfactory, since,
though the German navy had been reduced to impotence
by the Battle of Jutland in 1916, the submarines of the
enemy had played such havoc with our merchant shipping
that in Britain a serious stringency in the food supply
had been created and a system of rationing adopted.
Ireland was seething with disaffection, and ate up
garrisons that could ill be spared from the battle-front.
Generally, there was a gloomy impression throughout

the country that our maximum effort had been made to no purpose and that our power was on the wane. The Germans controlled the Balkans except for Greece, Russia had reverted to barbarism, and the military pretensions of Italy had been ignominiously laid low by the German-Austrian drive in October which forced her armies back to the line of the Piave. Against the want of success in the main theatre of the war, the victories of General Marshall in Mesopotamia and of General Allenby in Palestine appeared mere bagatelles, little likely to affect the result of the war.

The few, however, who refused to allow themselves to be unduly influenced by the menace of immediate peril discerned that a decision was nearer at hand than was generally thought. The campaign of 1917 had been a great drain on our man-power, but it had also eaten into the strength of Germany. The entrance of America into the war had provided us with a source of reserves, infinitely larger than that at the command of Germany, which except for some dramatic catastrophe was bound ultimately to give us the victory. The one hope of the enemy rested on the fact that American forces would not be available in large numbers until 1918 was well advanced, and he realised that, unless he could extort a peace before the balance tilted against him, his doom was assured. Although in the field Germany had the initiative, she was on the defensive as regards the general position; the desperate offensive that she was on the point of launching had been forced on her by circumstances over which she had no control. If the hostile attack were repulsed, then our brilliant victories in the East would contribute to a speedy collapse of the foe.

Thus the immediate object of the Allied commanders in the West was to weather the storm that would inevitably burst on them in the early months of 1918, and in the preparations for that purpose all their thoughts and activities were engrossed. The difficulties which confronted Sir Douglas Haig were enormous. The sanguinary battles of 1917 had cost the British Army numerous casualties, and Sir Douglas Haig, in February 1918, was obliged to reorganise his divisions by placing all his infantry brigades on a three instead of a four-battalion basis. He was further handicapped by having to take over an additional 28 miles of front in deference to a decision of the Versailles Council. The whole front for which the British Commander was responsible stretched virtually from the sea to the south of the River Oise, and it was by no means an easy matter to settle how his forces should be disposed for the protection of this long line. All the vital sectors, especially those that screened the Channel ports, had to be adequately furnished with reserves, and it was only to the south of Arras that much ground could be yielded under pressure without entailing serious consequences. It was anticipated that the blow would fall on the Third and Fifth Armies. The former was responsible for the protection of Arras, and was more generously provided with reserves than the latter, which had in its rear the vast tract of country devastated in the Battle of the Somme and during the German retreat in the spring of 1917.

While despondency was general, there was no thought of admitting defeat among the regimental officers and the rank and file engaged in active service. These were too much concerned about the matters of the moment to speculate on the future ; they were so busily employed in training or in work that they had no leisure to worry unduly about the situation. No suggestion of hopelessness or despair appears in the diaries of the Royal Scots battalions, and all the

II   2 M

preparations for the ineluctable crisis are recorded in a matter-of-fact fashion.

Two battalions, the 5/6th and the 17th, had been practically immune from battle during 1917. The latter, we have seen, had been condemned to spend the winter in the Salient, and for the 5/6th time had on the whole jogged along quietly; it had not been caught in the vortex of any of the titanic struggles, and under the skilful guidance of Lieut.-Colonel Fraser it had developed into a very formidable and efficient unit. It squatted on the coastal sector near Nieuport from July till the beginning of November 1917. The terrain, intersected with bogs, ditches, and streams, seemed to offer little scope for enterprises, but the 5/6th Royal Scots in September contrived to carry out a smart operation. An ambitious raid was planned for the night of the 11th/12th September. The objective was Groote Bamburgh Farm, lying to the north of a broad canal, and the raiding party consisted of 2nd Lieuts. R. A. Jones, W. O. Steuart, W. K. Good, and forty other ranks. Tapes for the assembly were laid and ditches bridged by 2nd Lieut. R. A. Jones and Lance-Corporal Doughty; this preliminary work was extraordinarily well done and reflected great credit on those engaged in it.

The raiders assembled to the north of the canal, their movements being covered by a small forward party under 2nd Lieut. R. A. Nairne. At 11 P.M. they advanced on the farm, and without being detected got into the Boche trenches, which were found to be badly damaged and in places water-logged. The party now split into five groups. One under 2nd Lieut. Jones went behind the trench towards the farm and came on a concrete dug-out, from which a sentry suddenly opened fire with a revolver. A rush was immediately made on the dug-out; it was full of Germans, but many of these had just been roused from slumber and were without equipment. While 2nd Lieut. Jones and his men were engaged in clearing the place, some Germans from a trench in the rear began a counter-attack, but were held at bay by a second group of the Royal Scots which, under C.S.M. Primrose, had passed the first party and formed a block.

Meanwhile, 2nd Lieut Good with a third group had gone about 40 yards to the left, and entering a trench which was flooded almost to the brim, formed a block to guard the operations on the right. Six Germans, who had been engaged in wiring about 150 yards from the point of entry, on hearing the sound of bombing, walked down the outside of the trench and were bombed by 2nd Lieut. Good and his men. All this time a confused fight was going on at the dug-out, where the Boches, though taken by surprise, resisted pluckily. More Germans appeared and began to attack the party of 2nd Lieut. Jones from the right, but fortunately the fourth group of the Royal Scots, under 2nd Lieut. W. O. Steuart, arrived and held these in check until the dug-out was ultimately cleared. There remained only one unwounded German, and he was handed over to an escort. No machine-gun was found in the dug-out, but one was discovered about 15 yards in front of the trench; this was bombed and destroyed. The fifth group of the raiders, veering to the right, had encountered some Germans who were making for the farm, and with these an indecisive bombing fight was waged until the signal to withdraw was received by the Royal Scots.

When the raiders had been in the hostile trenches for fifteen minutes, a strong force of Germans, led by an officer, advanced from the rear, and the Royal Scots just had time to extricate themselves. All the wounded were carried away, and the triumphant raiders started back to their lines with two prisoners, the second having been taken by C.S.M. Primrose. The return journey was conducted with a speed suggestive of nervousness, and the excuses given by the party for killing the two Boches who had been captured were not convincing; on reaching the limit of the hostile wire one refused to move and was shot, and the other slipping in a shell-hole sprained his ankle, then resisted the proddings of his captors, and he also was killed. Thus the raiders who had cleverly carried out a difficult operation across the treacherous polder-land nullified all their good work by returning without an identification. At least eight Boches were known to have been killed during the raid and several more were wounded; of the raiders two were killed and three wounded. Unfortunately Major Stewart, the Second-in-Command of the battalion, while directing the men back to our lines, was killed by shell fire.

At the beginning of November the unit was transferred to the northern part of the Salient. Prior to this move the general system of numbering the companies was adopted: since the amalgamation they had been known as "W," "X," "Y," and "Z," but they were now known as "A," "B," "C," and "D." During September two officers were wounded, and a plucky but unsuccessful raid under Lieut. G. Denholm was balanced by the repulse of a strong German patrol. For sheer misery the conditions near Houthulst Forest could hardly be surpassed, but the men were never in better fighting trim than at this stage. For the second time since the battalion's entrance into the Salient, Captain J. W. K. Darling was wounded, and another victim of the hostile shell fire was Lieut. T. D. Burt, wounded on the 10th February.

On the 27th February, the 5/6th Royal Scots with

the other units of the 14th Brigade carried out a most successful enterprise against the German positions on the south-west margin of Houthulst Forest.   Practically the whole battalion was employed in this operation, and each company had assigned to it a definite series of objectives, consisting chiefly of pill-boxes.   Each company, on a two-platoon front, was formed up in two lines, each line consisting of two waves.   Supported by a violent barrage, the battalion advanced at 7.52 P.M. and accomplished all its tasks.   Numerous Germans were killed and many prisoners taken, while the losses of the Royal Scots were very light, two men being killed and thirty-four wounded.   Of the officers 2nd Lieut. W. K. Good was killed and three[1] were wounded.

The next thrill occurred in the early morning of the 8th March, when the battalion was in brigade support. The Germans made a violent attack and broke into the outpost line of the brigade on the right of the 14th. At 9 A.M. two companies of the 5/6th Royal Scots were detailed to support a counter-attack by the 2nd King's Own Yorkshire Light Infantry, and, moving forward over the open under a raking shell fire, they reached their allotted positions and established touch with the English battalion.   The attack of the latter was a brilliant success and the outpost line was restored. The losses of the Royal Scots in this affair were not heavy, five men being killed and fourteen wounded, but they included some of the most experienced officers in the unit: Lieut.-Colonel Fraser, Captain A. H. S. Paterson, and Lieut. A. M. Macdonald were all wounded, and the command of the battalion passed for a time to Lieut.-Colonel G. D. A. Fletcher.   A few days later all interest was suddenly diverted to the south, where the great German offensive swept down our defences,

---

[1] Lieuts. D. S. Stevens, P. Walker, and L. Westwater.

and it came as no surprise when, towards the end of March, the battalion was hastily sent southwards to take part in the struggle.

The 2nd Royal Scots when transferred from Passchendaele to the neighbourhood of Bapaume must have regarded themselves as fortunate during the month of October. Officers and men had no dearth of work or training, but they had a long respite from trench duty and found time for sport and recreation. In November the battalion occupied trenches in the Noreuil sector. On the 15th, Lieut. Lyell and 2nd Lieut. Murchison with two men crawled across No-Man's-Land and reconnoitred the German positions. They were discovered and fired at by the enemy, and one of the men, Private Watson, accidentally slipping, toppled over into the trench and was taken prisoner. There was some turbulence on the 20th when the 9th Brigade raided a hostile trench, and during the fight one of our aeroplanes was forced to come down in No-Man's-Land. 2nd Lieut. A. M. Scott and C.S.M. Burnett pluckily dashed out and rescued the pilot, who was found to be wounded in four places. As a result of the German retaliatory barrage, two officers and several men were wounded. For the 24th, "C" Company arranged a raid on the Boche trenches, but owing to some misunderstanding our barrage did not lift, and the men had to return without having had a chance to accomplish their object. December was an uneasy month on account of the liveliness of the enemy, who attacked trenches held by the Third Division on the 12th and 13th, and though the battalion was not involved in any contest it had always to be on the *qui vive*. In January the 2nd Royal Scots were out of the line for the greater part of the month, and on their return in February found the situation fairly quiet. Lieut.-Colonel Lumsden at this time left the unit to command the 46th Brigade of the Fifteenth Division.   Never was promotion better earned, and the new Brig.-General carried with him the best wishes of the battalion which he had commanded with such conspicuous skill and success.   The new C.O. was Lieut.-Colonel J. M. Gillatt, who had previously been in command of the 5/6th Battalion.   At the beginning of March the 2nd Royal Scots were transferred to the Heninel area, where no incident of note occurred up to the opening of the German offensive.

All units in the Third and Fifth Armies had to work hard in the preparation of the defences, but none more so than the 8th Royal Scots, who, from December to March, laboured at high pressure without any of the relaxation afforded by the interludes of training that ordinary infantry units enjoyed.   The battalion constructed the major part of the defences in the Louverval-Boursies-Demicourt sector, and put up miles of wire entanglement on a pattern invented by General Harper.   Much of its work was done under shell fire, and the Royal Scots were fortunate in losing only one officer, 2nd Lieut. Taylor of "C" Company, who was killed on the 8th February.   Difficulties with respect to man-power affected the battalion, which, like all other pioneer units, was reduced to three companies, the officers and men of "B" Company being absorbed into the other three companies.

The 9th was the only battalion of the Regiment affected by the general reorganisation of brigades which was carried out early in February 1918.   This unit had played a noble part in building up the great reputation which the Fifty-first Division had won for itself during the war, and it was with natural regret that they left to join another formation, the Sixty-first Division.   It was some consolation to the battalion, however, that it was brigaded with the 5th Gordons and the 8th Argylls, who had also been detached from the Fifty-first Division. In consequence of this transference the 9th Royal Scots came into a sector almost directly opposite St Quentin, and experienced an unusually tranquil time until active fighting began on the 21st March.

The 11th and the 12th Royal Scots had left Passchendaele, elated with the prospect of spending a few weeks at the seaside, and they had just begun to enjoy the quietness of the coast sector, when their future was suddenly darkened by the successful counter-stroke of the Germans near Gouzeaucourt at the end of November. Nursing a feeling of implacable resentment against the Boches, the two battalions, with the other units of the Ninth Division, were hastily conveyed by rail to Peronne. The whole division was hurried to the line, and on the night of the 5th/6th December the 27th Brigade relieved the 3rd Cavalry Brigade near Heudicourt. By this time the German thrust had exhausted itself, but anxious and busy weeks followed till the trenches were strengthened and abundantly protected with wire. Time during the winter seemed to move on crutches, weary days being spent in the maintenance and improvement of the trenches and uneasy nights in patrolling. The Germans also were active in patrolling, and encounters in No-Man's-Land were not infrequent. In the early hours of the 23rd January a large hostile patrol, consisting of three parties, attempted to rush a post held by the 11th Royal Scots, but it was beaten off after a sharp fire-fight. On the night of the 25th/26th January a Lewis gun section of the 12th Royal Scots detected a small group of Germans and opened fire; one of the Boches was killed and another captured. In February the whole division benefited enormously by nearly six weeks of training, and the 11th and the 12th

Royal Scots were at the top of their form when they returned to the line at the beginning of March.

The sector occupied by the Fifteenth Division during the winter was in front of Arras. The diary of the 13th Royal Scots for the first few months contains scarcely a reference to the great storm that was brewing, and regales us chiefly with details of working parties. In two raids during November patrols of the battalion entered the German lines, but secured no identifications, because the enemy's front trenches were unoccupied. A curious incident occurred on the 18th January, when before dawn four Boches approached the trenches of the Royal Scots, one waving a white paper and the others making signs and shouting, "Scots! Saxons! Come over." They vanished almost as suddenly as they had appeared, and the Royal Scots were left in doubt as to whether this party had offered to surrender or had invited them to surrender. The disquieting month of March duly arrived, and on the 19th the 13th Royal Scots were in support.

The front of the Thirty-fourth Division, which extended from opposite Fontaine les Croisilles on the right to the Arras-Cambrai Road on the north, was at first held by two brigades, the third being in reserve. Near the end of the year the divisions holding the VI. Corps front were reduced from three to two, so that all three brigades of the Thirty-fourth Division had to be put into the line. The conditions during the first weeks of 1918 were most disagreeable, and on the 16th January a company of the 16th Royal Scots after being relieved became bogged in a communication trench, where it had to remain till darkness fell, when the men, weary and exhausted, scrambled on to the parapets and strode over the open to their quarters. February brought a welcome spell of training, and in such time as could be devoted to sport, the 16th Royal Scots upheld their supremacy in football by winning the divisional league competition. At the beginning of March the 15th and the 16th Royal Scots returned to the line.

The 17th Battalion found trench duty in the salient an irksome and dangerous task. In October Captain J. Mitchell was mortally injured, and three officers[1] were wounded, while the casualties in other ranks during the month totalled one hundred and forty-three. In November the tally was not quite so alarming, one officer, 2nd Lieut. J. V. Wilson, being killed, and the losses in other ranks amounting to fifty-three. The fighting in the vicinity of Cambrai brought relief to our troops near Ypres, and from December time crept on monotonously.

In March all the battalions of the Royal Scots, except the 5/6th and the 17th, were with the Fifth and Third Armies; in the former, from south to north, were the 9th, 11th, and 12th Battalions, and in the latter were the 8th, 15th, 16th, 2nd, and 13th Battalions. The units under the command of General Gough were far apart, there being four divisions between the Sixty-first and the Ninth, which formed the left formation of the Fifth Army. The Royal Scots battalions under General Byng were more closely grouped; two divisions intervened between the Fifty-first and the Thirty-fourth, but the latter, the Third, and the Fifteenth, lay side by side.

Our first concern was to push on our defensive arrangements before the season became propitious for campaigning. Since 1916 our troops had been accustomed to an offensive rôle, and consequently they had not devoted the same attention to the construction of defensive

[1] Lieut. W. D. Sym, 2nd Lieuts. D. G. Ednie and C. T. Thornton.

systems as had the Germans.   The leeway could not be made up in the course of a few weeks, and as in many cases the tasks allotted to the troops were performed in a shockingly leisurely fashion, our preparations were far from being completed by March.   The general principle adopted throughout the army was the distribution of our troops in depth.   "With this object three defensive belts, sited at considerable distances from each other, had been constructed or were approaching completion in the forward area, the most advanced of which was in the nature of a lightly-held outpost screen covering our main positions."[1]

The Germans possessed an accurate knowledge of our dispositions and arrangements, and the plans of Ludendorff were skilfully devised to take advantage of our weakness.   He was well aware that the front of the Fifth Army was but thinly covered, and against it his principal stroke was directed.   The Germans had two fronts of attack, a northern extending from Croisilles to Mœuvres, and a southern from Villers-Guislain to a point on the River Oise near the junction of the French and British Armies.   The gap between these two thrusts was filled by the Flesquières salient, and the Germans hoped that by attacking both north and south of it, they would be able to pinch off and destroy the divisions which garrisoned it.   The main object of Ludendorff, however, was to drive a wedge between the British and French Armies, and this he expected to effect by the capture of Amiens.   He planned also to force a breach between the armies of General Gough and of General Byng, and annihilate that of the former before Sir Douglas Haig had time to send reserves to its assistance.

The whole of the German arrangements were drawn up with characteristic attention to detail, all the troops

[1] Sir Douglas Haig's Despatches, p. 184.

earmarked to take part in the attack receiving an extensive and thorough training. Ludendorff was favoured by fortune. An unusually dry spring hardened the ground and even made passable the normally marshy district near Moy, so that the Germans were enabled to launch "the most formidable offensive in the history of the world"[1] before our defensive arrangements were completed.

From the beginning of the month our troops lived in a state of continual suspense, and the strain of unremitting vigilance which reduced their hours of sleep was beginning to tell on them. Statements from prisoners gave us the information that the enemy's effort would be made in March, and after several alarms the tidings spread round the Fifth and Third Armies that the battle would probably open on the 20th or 21st March.

[1] *A Short History of the Great War* (A. F. Pollard), p. 325.

CHAPTER XXXII

THE GREAT GERMAN OFFENSIVE (PART I.)

March 1918

Opening of great German Offensive, 21st March. Retreat of Fifth and Third Armies. Failure of Germans to achieve their objective. 9th Battalion near St Quentin. Its movements from 21st March to 3rd April. 11th and 12th Battalions near Gouzeaucourt. Their movements from the 21st to the 27th March. Arrival of 17th Battalion in the Battle Area. Its movements from 24th to the 29th March.

> "Sad tidings bring I to you out of France,
> Of loss, of slaughter, and discomfiture."

THE fateful battle opened on the 21st March under conditions that at the outset favoured the enemy. A spring mist, shutting in the area of the battlefield, blinded and thus disorganised our defence and enabled the Boche storm-troops to muster for the onslaught without being detected. Shortly before 5 A.M. the German guns opened a savage bombardment along our front, and the air became crepitant with the rush of thousands of shells. Then the field-grey infantry surged forward and overwhelmed many of our forward garrisons before these had realised that the conflict had begun. In many cases our infantry had no time to signal the S.O.S., and even when it was possible to do this, the mist was so dense that the signals were not observed by our gunners, with the result that the Germans suffered less castigation and made more rapid progress than we had anticipated.

The method of the enemy was to advance swiftly through such fissures as he cleft in our lines, and by

thus threatening their communications, to compel our
units which had clung to their ground to retreat.
Several critical points of entry were made in our
positions on the 21st March. In the south the
Germans broke through our forward defensive zone
near La Fère and at Ronssoy, and between these two
points pertinaciously developed their success. Along
the major part of the Fifth Army front our forward
zone was captured, and at several points, notably south
of St Quentin, the foe even won a footing in our second
defensive system, the battle zone, which had been
intended to form our main line of resistance. In the
northern attack the Germans made some notable gains
at the expense of the Third Army by seizing Lagnicourt
and reaching the outskirts of St Leger.

The positions held by the Fifth and Third Armies
at the close of the 21st were by no means satisfactory,
and during the night several readjustments, including a
partial evacuation of the Flesquières salient, were made.
On the 22nd March the Boches continued to make
disquieting progress, especially in the area of General
Gough's army; by nightfall in the southern part of
the battle they had penetrated our third defensive zone
and compelled a further retirement. Our defensive
measures for a bridge-head at the Somme at Peronne
were so far from completion that General Gough decided
to reorganise his line along the western bank of the
Somme; but even this plan could not be adhered to,
for on the 23rd the Germans succeeded in crossing the
Somme at Ham, thus imperilling the right wing of
General Gough's army. Moreover, a new danger had
arisen. During the retreat of the right flank of the
Third Army, in conformity with the movement of the
Fifth, a gap had developed between the two forces.
The situation, fortunately, was considerably eased by

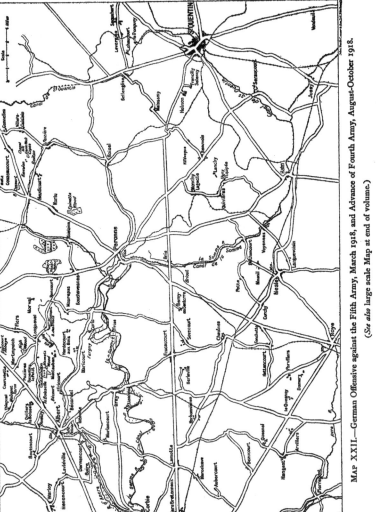

MAP XXII.—German Offensive against the Fifth Army, March 1918, and Advance of Fourth Army, August–October 1918.

(*See also* large scale Map at end of volume.)

the timely withdrawal of General Byng's forces from Monchy to prepared defences nearer Arras, but before the 24th dawned the enemy seemed to have a good chance of accomplishing his two principal objects, the severance of the French and British Armies and that of the Fifth and Third Armies.

Thus the task before the British on the 24th was not a simple one. The preservation of liaison with the French hinged upon the ability of our troops to stem the German advance between the Somme and the Oise; in our struggle to effect this we could count on French assistance. In addition, General Gough had to hold the line of the Somme between Ham and Peronne, and efforts had to be made to close the gate between the Fifth and Third Armies. As regards the first two parts of our task the results of the fighting on the 24th were fairly satisfactory, but the situation as regards the third became exceedingly precarious, owing to a successful Boche thrust into the territory of General Byng's army. By securing possession of Combles the Germans compelled the Third Army to surrender the whole of the old Somme battlefield, and enhanced their prospect of severing the connection between the forces of General Gough and General Byng.

Encouraged by this substantial measure of success, the Boches pressed their pursuit with sustained fury on the 25th March, and drove the southern portion of the Third Army back to the old Ancre defences, thus uncovering the left wing of General Gough's force, which was in consequence compelled to abandon the line of the Somme. Our liaison with the French continued to be precarious, for the hostile attempt near Roye to drive a wedge between the armies of the Allies had not yet been frustrated. Moreover, there were several ominous rents in the British line, the most disturbing being those between the V. and the VII. Corps, and between the IV. and the V. Corps. Fortunately, reinforcements were now arriving, and with their aid General Byng, on the 26th, succeeded in stabilising his line; but General Gough was so hard pressed that on the 27th he was obliged to continue his retreat to a line stretching approximately from Bouzencourt near the Somme to Arvillers.

Extensive and rapid as had been the advance of the enemy, his prospects became more tenuous as the hours sped on. Our infantry showed the fine quality of their mettle by refusing to be stampeded, and in spite of the most frantic efforts of the enemy, the unity of the British front was re-established by the 27th March. Thus the fate of the battle hung on the result of the German attempts to break through between the French and the British. The enemy had now enormous difficulties to surmount; his communications straggled across a devastated battlefield, and were rendered more unsatisfactory by downpours of rain, while his front of attack had shrunk from 50 to 20 miles, and his left flank was no longer shielded by the River Oise, which the resistance of the French had compelled him to quit west of Noyon. The Germans had secured possession of Montdidier, but they had no assurance of capturing Amiens and severing the liaison between the Allies, unless they could extend to the flanks and widen the front of their assault. With this object they organised a grand attack against Arras, but they sustained a crushing defeat, and this check, as things turned out, proved decisive as far as the Somme was concerned. The enemy reaped a few more gains, but he was unable to advance far from Montdidier and could not prevent the French from

II   2 N

linking up firmly with the British at the River Luce. In a final push to reach Amiens, the Germans ejected our troops from the angle formed by the Luce and the Avre, and from the western bank of the latter, but beyond this they made no headway.   Since the opening of the battle, thousands of prisoners, numerous guns, and a colossal amount of war material had fallen to the Germans, who had in addition captured incomparably more territory than had the Allies in any of their offensives on the Western front, but they had just failed to dissolve the Allied line, which was the great strategical objective of their drive.

The fact that during these strenuous days, with numerous gaps appearing in different parts of the line, our troops did not succumb to panic, forms the most eloquent proof of their discipline and courage.   The perspiring marches followed by long halts in the chilliness of the night, when the jarred flesh seemed to quiver with innumerable aches, the scanty moments available for slumber, and the knowledge that an eager foe was pressing on their heels combined to constitute a strain which only first-rate troops could have endured without stampeding. Even such disorganisation as occurred was of a disciplined character, for though formations here and there were disrupted, few were overwhelmed by the sense of blind unreasoning terror that prompts men to divest themselves of equipment and weapons and seek ruinous safety in ignoble flight.   Where leaders appeared, the men stayed their retreat and willingly answered all calls that were made upon them.   The pressure on our troops in the spring of 1918 was probably more relentless and sustained than that during the retreat from Mons; in the latter case a battalion was not constantly in contact with the foe, whereas during the retirement from the Somme units for days at a stretch were grappling desperately with their pursuers. The discipline and fighting qualities of our troops in the face of gigantic odds wore down the German attack and gave time for the arrival of reserves, with the aid of which a line was at last formed impervious to every hostile thrust.

In what follows, a separate account is given of the part played by each of the battalions of the Royal Scots in the great battle. In the southern portion of the battlefield we are at the outset concerned with three battalions, the 9th, 11th, and 12th; in the later stages the 17th Battalion arrived to assist in stemming the Boche advance.

The sector near St Quentin, occupied by the Sixty-first Division, was furiously attacked by the Germans on the 21st March. The 9th Royal Scots, who were at Beauvois on the 20th, were sent up to garrison the second or battle zone, and were not actively engaged in the fighting on the first day. Gallantly though the division resisted, the Germans by noon had penetrated the forward defensive zone and obtained a footing in the battle position at Maissemy. Terrific shell fire now ravaged the lines of the Royal Scots, and caused many casualties among "A," "B" and "C" Companies, but the enemy was firmly held at Maissemy on the 21st, and made no further gains at the expense of the Sixty-first Division. On the following day the hostile attack gathered vehemence, and a hurricane of shell fire swept the Royal Scots. The German progress south of St Quentin ultimately made it necessary for the Sixty-first Division to abandon its battle position, and shortly after noon the 9th Royal Scots were instructed to move back towards Villévécque, the retirement of the battalion being splendidly covered by "C" Company, whose accurate shooting served to keep the Boches at a respectful distance. Villévécque brought the men only a short respite, and in the late afternoon the retreat was continued to Beauvois, in front of which the Royal Scots occupied four lines, with "C" Company, which had lost two officers and thirty other ranks during its rear-guard action, in rear. The situation was extremely grave, not merely on account of the fact that the defences of the third zone were incomplete, but because during the retreat gaps had developed between the Sixty-first and the divisions on its flank. But the men did not tremble before the hazards that surrounded them, and their resistance defeated the most persistent efforts of the Boches to crumple up the division, on the left flank of which the 9th Royal Scots with rifle and Lewis-gun fire inflicted enormous losses on their field-grey adversaries.

It was at this juncture that General Gough decided that a general retreat to the line of the Somme was essential for the salvation of his army. This movement was commenced on the 23rd March, and the 9th Royal Scots skilfully extricated themselves from Beauvois and passed through Voyennes to Languevoisin and Nesle. In imposing array came the pursuing Germans; behind a screen of skirmishers marched their infantry battalions in artillery formation, and in rear of these, all roads and paths were packed with transport, including motors to which were attached observation balloons. Even in the stress of retreat the 9th Royal Scots could not refuse a tribute of admiration to the brilliant Staff work which had made such skilful use of the resources of Germany. The Royal Scots on reaching the Somme had to curb the impatience of a sapper officer who was anxious to demolish the bridge before the whole of the battalion had crossed to the western bank. At the end of the long day's march the men were grouped at Languevoisin and Nesle, near which they held bridge-heads across the canal. Those quartered at the latter town found a store full of eggs and champagne which provided officers and men with a luxurious and stimulating breakfast on the following morning.

The Somme Canal did not prove the safe line that we had hoped, for on the 23rd the Germans cleverly effected a crossing at Ham. It was vital to our safety that the enemy should be prevented from exploiting his advantage, and on the 24th the 9th Royal Scots were ordered to take part in a counter-attack on Béthencourt on the Somme. Shortly after noon they began their advance, supported by a light artillery barrage, but the hostile machine-gun fire was so intense that the attack ultimately came to a halt in front of Mesnil. Captain Paulin, the Adjutant, with the assistance of 2nd Lieut. Findlay, rapidly reorganised the line, which the battalion maintained until it was relieved. Officers and men did not fail to respond to the magnificent lead of Brig.-General Spooner who, mounted on horseback, was never far from the point of danger, and by his example infused fresh hope and courage in the most timid breast. The attack of the Royal Scots had retarded the advance of the enemy. On relief by the Argylls the battalion returned to Nesle, from which after a brief rest it was sent forward in the evening to fill a breach in the line between Curchy and Potte.

A fair measure of success had attended our efforts on the 24th, but on the 25th March the Fifth Army's power of resistance was all but broken, and another long retirement had to be made. In the early morning the unit on the right of the 9th Royal Scots withdrew from its positions and the latter were obliged to conform. The enemy followed up with vigour, and a critical rearguard action was waged till the 9th Royal Scots turned and faced their pursuers on a line about 200 yards

II   2 N 2

south of the railway near Curchy. Splendidly handled
by Lieut.-Colonel Green, the men fought with fine spirit
and smashed a succession of German thrusts. Many
did notable work, but none more so than C.S.M. D.
Walker, who rendered yeoman assistance to his C.O.
by the admirable manner in which he rallied his men
under heavy fire. The attack was becoming fiercer,
and the Royal Scots were dwindling in number when,
opportunely, the Twenty-seventh Division arrived and
advanced to counter-attack the enemy. In small
groups the survivors of the 9th Royal Scots marched
to Fonchette and were attached to the 72nd Brigade.
Later, the battalion proceeded through Hatten-
court to Le Quesnel where it rejoined the Sixty-first
Division.

The next two days brought comparative ease to
the 9th Royal Scots, who proceeded to Beaucourt on
the 26th. The Scottish Brigade of the division had
been so sadly reduced by the desperate fighting in
which it had been engaged that it was organised into
a composite battalion under Lieut.-Colonel Green ; two
of the companies were formed by the 9th Royal Scots
and one each by the 8th Argylls and 5th Gordons.
This composite force was despatched to a position west
of Beaucourt, where it held an outpost line astride the
main road between Amiens and Roye. A respite from
fighting came on the 27th, when the battalion was
sent to Hangest to hold a position to the south-west
of the village.

On this day Captain E. P. Combe, a former Adjutant
of the 2nd Royal Scots, with a party of 100 officers
and men, accomplished a glorious feat of arms near
Le Quesnoy. This gallant band, which was detailed
to cover the withdrawal of the Twentieth Division,
"successfully held the enemy at bay from early morning

until 6 P.M., when the eleven survivors withdrew under orders, having accomplished their task."[1]

Relieved by French troops on the night of the 27th/28th March the 9th Royal Scots had reason to believe that they were being withdrawn from the battle, but their hopes were disappointed, for after being conveyed by omnibus to Marcelcave, they were met with orders to deliver an attack on Lamotte. A brilliant stroke on the part of the Germans had carried them past the line of the Somme and allowed them to dash through to Lamotte near the main Amiens Road, about 9000 yards behind the fighting front of the Fifth Army. At 6.30 A.M. the Royal Scots moved to a position north of the railway and south-west of the village. "A" Company was directed to carry the village, and was only 200 yards away from it when it was pinned to the ground by raking machine-gun fire. But though the enemy retained his prize, his advance was delayed. The Royal Scots, after lying in front of Lamotte for over twelve hours, were instructed to re-assemble south of Marcelcave, and the retirement of the battalion was skilfully protected by the fire of a Lewis gun under the command of Corporal W. Telfer. The Germans were now within easy reach of Villers-Bretonneux, and there was a general feeling that if they secured that village, Amiens would have to be abandoned. The enemy made a very determined effort to take it, and there was savage fighting on the 29th March, but he was prevented from deploying from Aubercourt by a magnificent counter-assault delivered by Australians on the 30th. This successful stroke was materially assisted by the action of "C" Company of the Royal Scots, which under Captain Wakelin stopped the Germans from pressing along a valley lying between

[1] Sir Douglas Haig's Despatches, p. 206.

Villers - Bretonneux and a wood to the north of Aubercourt.

The 9th Royal Scots remained in the neighbourhood of Villers-Bretonneux till the 3rd April, but were not involved in any active operations. Throughout the retreat they owed much to their Medical Officer, Captain A. C. McMurtrie, who took innumerable risks to succour the wounded, especially at Béthencourt, where under heavy fire he dashed over open ground and brought back wounded men. The casualties of the battalion during its protracted ordeal were inevitably severe, and with the enemy pressing closely on its heels, it was not always possible to evacuate the injured. Between the 21st and the 31st March Major G. D. Cowan, Captain S. Mountford, 2nd Lieut. J. M'Millan, and forty-five other ranks were killed, fifteen officers, including the Adjutant, Captain Paulin, and two hundred and eighty-seven other ranks wounded, and one hundred and thirty-eight other ranks missing. Relieved on the 3rd April the 9th Royal Scots remained in the back areas of the Somme till the 10th April.

The Ninth Division, holding a sector near Gouzeaucourt, lay on the south side of the Flesquières salient and was the left formation of General Gough's army. It was not in the scheme of the Boches to deliver a frontal assault on the salient, and the only portion of the line of the Ninth Division that was seriously engaged on the 21st March was the right. This flank was dominated by an eminence, Chapel Hill, which comprised part of the territory for which the Twenty-first Division was responsible. The enemy twice carried this height but was twice driven off by the South African Brigade, and for a time our position was tolerably secure.

The 27th Brigade was in divisional reserve when the battle opened, the 11th Royal Scots[1] being at Heudicourt and the 12th at Dessart Wood.   Torrents of shells, many of them filled with gas, descended, and for more than two hours the men of the 11th and the 12th had to wear their box respirators.   The thrusts of the Boches against Chapel Hill indicated that the south was the quarter from which trouble was to be expected.   The enemy was in fact making disquieting progress in the area of the Twenty-first Division, and since Brig.-General Croft was responsible for the protection of the flanks of the Ninth, he ordered the 11th Royal Scots to despatch scouts and strong patrols to Railton, and to reconnoitre the country in the direction of Peizière.   These parties were given instructions to gain touch with the troops of the Twenty-first Division, and as far as possible to ascertain the dispositions of the Germans.   Captain Kennedy, the Scout Officer of the 11th, succeeded in reaching Peizière, and the information which he sent back to Brig.-General Croft showed that the possibility of the right flank of the division being turned was far from remote. Behind the scouts, a patrol under Lieut. Millar surprised and captured a group of Germans near Genin Well Copse, and a second patrol led by Sergeant Robertson, showing great daring, picked up a surprisingly large "bag" of prisoners, consisting of one officer and thirty-three men.   These vigorous reconnaissances temporarily established the flank of the division, which was still in possession of its forward positions when darkness fell.

During the night extra territory was taken over by the Ninth from the Twenty-first Division, and in order

---

Commanded during this action by Major A. C. Campbell, Lieut.-Colonel Sir John Campbell being on leave.

that the additional ground might be adequately guarded the 11th Battalion was lent to the South African Brigade, two of its companies being strung out to form a protective flank from Chapel Hill to Railton.   Troubles multiplied on the 22nd, when, veiled by the morning mist, the Boches hurled themselves against the South Africans. The latter were still clinging grimly to their positions, when orders arrived for the division to fall back to a line in front of Nurlu ; the first phase of this retreat, to a line near Heudicourt, was to be carried out during the afternoon, and the final stage in the evening.   The task of Brig.-General Croft was to post his men so as to relieve the strain on the two front brigades, which had to perform a trying and complicated manœuvre. The 12th Royal Scots accordingly were stationed to the north of Nurlu, while the 6th K.O.S.B. were posted between the village and Epinette Wood.

The enemy probably anticipated a withdrawal on our part, and he did his utmost to take full advantage of it.   Nevertheless, the first phase of the retreat was accomplished with comparatively little difficulty ; it was the final stage that caused embarrassment.   For all the troops on the right flank, locked in close conflict with the foe, the retirement was an exceedingly difficult operation and some of them could not be extricated. "B" Company of the 11th Royal Scots, which at Revelon Farm was engaged all day in waging unceasing battle against frantic odds, failed to win clear.   The men fought with the tenacity that is characteristic of the true Lowlander, and when last seen the survivors under Lieut. Cowans were fighting heroically against a ring of foes.   The sacrifice of the few assured the safety of the many, and during the night the division, still practically intact, formed up on its new position in front of Nurlu.

It was a night such as in olden times men might have believed that the powers of darkness stalked abroad, and there were few who could wholly shake off a superstitious thrill, as in ghost-like fashion the troops groped their way past smoking dumps and burning villages. The inky blackness of the night was ripped by flashes of brilliant flame as innumerable rockets and flares soared skywards, the leaping lights against the dark curtain of the night forming a baroque spectacle as fantastic as the visions of a lunatic. By the flickering glow of burning houses the Royal Scots caught glimpses of shadowy groups of men on business similar to their own. None knew for certain where the Germans were, and all felt a vast sensation of relief when at last they reached their allotted positions. When the adjustments were completed, the 27th Brigade held the right front of the division.

It was at this stage that the liaison between the Fifth and the Third Armies became wobbly. The right division of the latter had not retired in conformity with the movements of the Ninth on the 22nd March, and an attack in the evening by the Germans forced the right Corps of General Byng's command away from its boundary, so that a co-ordinated retirement by the two armies was rendered almost impossible. Thus the Ninth Division found its left as well as its right flank exposed.

A general retreat to the Somme having been decided on, Brig.-General Croft was informed at an early hour on the 23rd March that his brigade was to retire to a line near Moislains-Vaux; but before these instructions could be issued to the troops all the battalions were striving desperately to beat back the eager Germans, who had discovered that the right flank of the 27th Brigade was in the air. The retirement therefore had to be carried out in the face of an attack, but it was conducted with a marvellous skill and assurance that reflected the utmost credit on the officers and men.   In a protracted rear-guard action the 11th and the 12th Royal Scots kept the enemy at bay, and at 11 A.M. arrived at a line selected for defence near Moislains and Vaux Wood.   But this, to the surprise of the men, who had no knowledge of the general situation, was only a stage in the retreat; for the right flank of the division was still in peril, and an alarming gap had developed between the 27th Brigade and the 26th Brigade on its left, so that the whole division appeared to be on the brink of destruction.

The situation in fact had become so grave that orders were issued for the Ninth Division to withdraw to a new position near Bouchavesnes, but through some mischance they never reached Brig.-General Croft. During the day the hostile pressure against the 27th Brigade increased in intensity, and it was only through the indomitable pluck of the men that the 11th and the 12th Royal Scots were not utterly overwhelmed.   In the evening Brig.-General Croft realised that his brigade had no friendly companions, and that the Germans were passing round on both flanks.   At one time indeed the 12th Royal Scots were almost surrounded, but fighting with great coolness and determination they cut their way through the foe.   The stubborn gallantry of officers and men saved the brigade from the destruction to which it had seemed to be doomed, and under the screen of darkness the 11th and the 12th Royal Scots broke clear from their pursuers.   This incident was typical of what occurred in many parts of the battlefield.   For all their skill in taking advantage of our weakness, the Boches lacked the necessary resolution and vehemence to round off their success, and time and again their victims slipped away from their clutches and continued to form fresh barriers to their progress.

Thus, though the odds seemed heavily against them, the units of the 27th Brigade broke away from the Germans, and with their organisation still intact reached St Pierre Vaast Wood, where they formed up in line with the remainder of the division. The enemy followed in pursuit, and there were several lively skirmishes during the night, but our line stood fast. Spent and weary after three days and nights of continuous strain, the men, on the 24th March, had to face the most trying day that they had experienced since the commencement of the battle. Searching for an opening, the Germans soon realised that the 27th Brigade was still isolated, and violently assailed it from the front and both flanks.

Brig.-General Croft had posted his reserve near the right flank, and fortunately it was on this side that the main weight of the German onset fell. Virtually surrounded, the 11th Royal Scots resisted with unflagging courage, and handled by Major Campbell with consummate skill, successfully extricated themselves after inflicting terrific punishment on the enemy. The 12th Royal Scots on the left were not so closely beset, and braced up by the coolness of Lieut.-Colonel Ritson and by the buoyant cheerfulness of their popular Adjutant, Captain S. McKinley, they repelled every hostile thrust with apparently effortless ease. Only well-trained troops could have been drawn off under a pressure so colossal without being broken, and it was the alliance of skill and courage that brought the men of the 27th Brigade to safety. Though they had to contest every yard of the way the 11th Royal Scots fell back in good order to Guillemont Ridge. Perils menaced them from the air as well as on the ground, for during their retreat they were constantly harassed by low-flying hostile aeroplanes, which dropped bombs on them and sprayed them with machine-gun fire; many of these machines sported British colours, and one of them fired vigorously at Brig.-General Croft, to his intense annoyance. After a short halt on the Guillemont Ridge the retirement was continued to a position between Maricourt and the Somme.

The withdrawal of the Fifth Army was conducted amid a blaze of burning huts and canteens. Captain W. Y. Darling of the 11th Royal Scots, attached to the staff of Brig.-General Croft, was entrusted with the duty of demolishing canteens, and he performed his office with zest. After issuing the troops with such goods as they demanded from the stores, he poured petrol over the remainder and set the building alight. In spite of the difficulties of the situation, and the impossibility of determining exactly where any unit would be at a given hour, the Quartermasters of the 11th and the 12th Royal Scots carried out their duties with conspicuous success and managed to provide the men with their daily rations, but the additional supplies which the troops secured from the canteens were gifts not to be despised. The men suffered from strain and want of sleep, but at any rate they were spared the pangs of hunger.

On the 24th March the South African Brigade was lost in a glorious fight to the death, but the situation as regards the Ninth Division was considerably eased by the arrival of new divisions, including the Thirty-fifth. Hence in the early morning of the 25th March the 11th and the 12th Royal Scots were relieved by battalions of the 106th Brigade, and were taken to Etinehem where they snatched a brief rest. In the evening word was sent to Brig.-General Croft that his brigade was to take up a line from the east of Méaulte to Albert. This involved an arduous night march along roads thick with traffic, and the Royal Scots progressed slowly through the press till they reached the Bray-Corbie Road, when the stream of traffic suddenly ceased. So deserted was the road from this point that in addition to the advanced guard a flank guard was put out, but no enemy was encountered, and the Royal Scots arrived at Méaulte in time to cover the withdrawal of the Seventeenth Division, which had come into the battle on the left of the Ninth.

The line was held by the 12th and the 11th Royal Scots. Brig.-General Croft's dispositions had just been completed, when scouts of the Royal Scots brought in tidings at 11 A.M. that the Boches were advancing from the direction of Fricourt. Soon afterwards the outposts of the Royal Scots were exchanging shots with hostile patrols, but the main forces of the enemy did not appear till 1 P.M., when a very violent assault was launched against the 12th Battalion. On this occasion the Germans displayed unwonted audacity and unlimbered a battery on a ridge to support their infantry, but the onslaught was repulsed with heavy loss to the enemy, and the battery was put out of action by the deadly accuracy of the battalion's Lewis-gun fire.

Baffled in their frontal approach, the Germans endeavoured to circumvent the 12th Royal Scots from the right flank, which had been uncovered by the withdrawal of the Thirty-fifth Division. Brig.-General Croft despatched a company of the 9th Seaforths to form a defensive flank, but the enfilade fire from German machine-guns posted on the Bray Road caused many losses among the 27th Brigade, and its position became wholly untenable when the division on the left also retired. Behind the brigade lay the Ancre, and the retirement across the river was carried out in perfect order, though the 12th Royal Scots suffered considerably as they passed through Méaulte. After reorganising on the west side of the Ancre, the brigade, unmolested, took up a position along the Amiens-Albert Railway, with the 26th Brigade on its right and the Twelfth Division on its left.

The 27th March was an uneasy day, for stories, born of panic, about a disastrous breach in our southern front were spread broadcast along the line, and kept officers and men in a state of nervous tension. The night had been restless with sporadic firing, and a hostile machine-gun on the flank of the 11th Royal Scots was a constant source of annoyance. This gun at last made itself such a pest that Major Campbell organised a small party which raided it and succeeded in destroying it; unfortunately the gallant Major, who led the charge, was hit by several bullets, and afterwards succumbed to the effects of his wounds. Several times on the front of the Royal Scots the Germans appeared to be making preparations to muster for attack, but so excellent was the liaison between the infantry and the gunners that every attempt of the enemy to concentrate was frustrated by our shell fire. At a wood, about 1000 yards east of Vivier Mill, the Royal Scots could see piles of dead Germans who had been caught by our gun fire when they were endeavouring to assemble. At no time during the day did the hostile infantry get an opportunity of attacking the front of the 27th Brigade, and at night the 11th and 12th Royal Scots were withdrawn from the battle. During the seven successive days and nights in which they had been engaged in the fight they had never been broken, and though their losses[1] had been heavy they had inflicted a much greater number on the enemy. Like many of the battalions relieved at this time, they were sent to hold a part of the line in the far north.

The Thirty-fifth Division, hurriedly brought down from Passchendaele, came into the battle line near the Ninth Division on the 24th March. Leaving one company to unload for the brigade, the 17th Royal Scots, continually on the move since midnight of the 23rd/24th, in the late afternoon of the 24th occupied a defensive position in the Somme Valley in the vicinity of a road running south from Maurepas. Shortly afterwards, along with the 105th Brigade, to which it had been attached, the battalion was withdrawn to a line between Curlu and Hardecourt-Aux-Bois, where it manned the firing-line near the cross-roads north of Curlu. Early in the forenoon of the 25th the Germans barraged the road lined by the battalion, and soon afterwards their infantry, advancing to the attack, fell violently on the left flank of the 17th Royal Scots, who were gradually pressed back. Fighting a stubborn rear-guard action, the battalion withdrew slowly towards Maricourt and lined a small path over 1000 yards to the south-east of that village. In this position it maintained itself till nightfall, when it was relieved and moved back to Bray, where, at 2 A.M. on the 26th, it took up a position along the Bray-Albert Road, some distance north of the former village.

The morning of the 26th March passed quietly,

---

[1] 11th Battalion—four officers (Major A. C. Campbell, Captain A. Kennedy, Lieut. A. O. Keen, 2nd Lieut. E. T. Caird) and eighteen other ranks killed; eight officers and one hundred and sixty-eight other ranks wounded; and six officers and two hundred and thirty-eight other ranks missing. 12th Battalion—sixteen other ranks killed; eight officers and eighty-eight other ranks wounded; and ten officers and two hundred and eighty-seven other ranks missing.

but at noon a report reached Lieut.-Colonel Heathcote that the Germans were advancing from the direction of Maricourt ; by 2 P.M. they were in Bray, and the swiftness of their advance imperilled the right flank of the 17th Royal Scots, who at 4 P.M. were ordered to retire across the Ancre. At 5.30 P.M. the battalion reached Morlancourt, where it steadily fought a rear-guard action with the Germans, while the remainder of the division passed through. By 7 P.M. Morlancourt was cleared. The 17th Royal Scots began to retreat, and favoured by the tardiness of the pursuit crossed the Ancre without molestation. Having efficiently accomplished its task, the battalion passed into divisional reserve and marched to Laviéville, which it reached about midnight.

On the 27th March the 17th Royal Scots were ordered to take over a portion of the line along the Amiens-Albert Railway near Dernancourt and relieve the 4th North Staffordshire Regiment, but before this was done rumours arose that the enemy had already cut the railway to the north of Dernancourt. In this uncertainty Lieut.-Colonel Heathcote was directed to lead his men to the village and if possible relieve the English battalion, but if not, then to use his men to strengthen the line. Fortunately the rumours proved to be unfounded, and on reaching Dernancourt Lieut.-Colonel Heathcote experienced not the least difficulty in relieving with two companies the North Staffordshire Regiment on the line along the railway. A third company was sent to a position near Buire, and the fourth, which since the 24th had been employed as the brigade unloading party, on this day rejoined the battalion. The 17th Royal Scots maintained their position throughout the 28th March, the day on which the Boche hopes of success were dissipated by the

failure of their attack at Arras. Our line in this part
of the front was beginning to solidify, and though
anxiety was not at an end for many days and nights,
the 17th Royal Scots had no more brushes with the
German infantry in the Second Battle of the Somme.

Relieved on the 29th March, the battalion returned
on the 6th April to the line near Aveluy to the north
of Albert, and remained in this sector till June. Its
casualties from the 24th till the 30th March were:
three officers (Captain A. Currie, Lieuts. F. A. Raynes
and M. S. Barclay) and thirty men killed; two officers[1]
and one hundred and fifty-five other ranks wounded, and
forty other ranks missing.

[1] Captain N. B. Graham, the Medical Officer, and 2nd Lieut. N. U. Bird.

CHAPTER XXXIII

March 1918

Position of Fifty-first Division. Action of 8th Battalion, 21st to 26th March. Death of Lieut.-Colonel Gemmill, 25th March. Position of Thirty-fourth Division. Action of 15th and 16th Battalions, 21st to 23rd March. Third and Fifteenth Divisions near Arras. Readjustment of line, 22nd/23rd March. Great German attack, 28th March. Action of 2nd and 13th Battalions. 5/6th Battalion at Ayette.

THE battalions of the Royal Scots with the Third Army were, from right to left, the 8th, 15th, 16th, 2nd, and 13th; the 5/6th arrived at the end of the month.

The Fifty-first Division held the sector in front of Louverval and Doignies at the northern angle of the Flesquières salient, and the safety of the garrison of the salient hinged upon the ability of the division to maintain its ground. Consequently it is not surprising that on the morning of the 21st March the Fifty-first Division was furiously assailed by the Germans, who, having partially smothered the defence by the volume of their artillery fire, burst through between the Fifty-first and its left-hand neighbour, the Sixth Division. Boursies and Louverval, north of the Bapaume-Cambrai Road, were lost, and the Highland Division, fighting valiantly, was driven back to the Beaumetz-Morchies line.

On the eve of the battle the 8th Royal Scots lay near Fremicourt, and early on the 21st they had clear

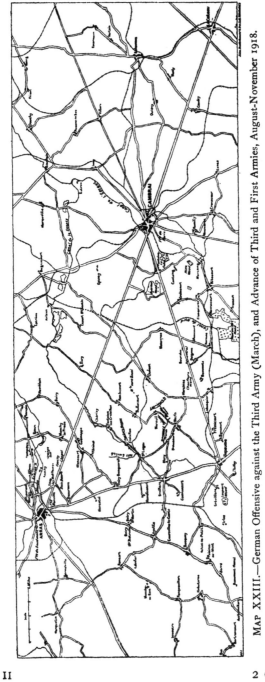

MAP XXIII.—German Offensive against the Third Army (March), and Advance of Third and First Armies, August-November 1918.

(*See also* large scale Map at end of volume.)

warning that the Germans had begun their offensive by the storms of artillery fire which swept our hinterland. All forward communications were shattered, and for some time no one possessed certain knowledge of what was taking place in front. Lieut.-Colonel Gemmill, shortly after the opening of the hostile bombardment, was ordered to send two companies to a position near Lebucquière, and "A" and "C" Companies accordingly mustered in a sunken road near that village. The road, however, was one of the enemy's artillery marks, and to avoid casualties Lieut.-Colonel Gemmill disposed his men in shell-holes slightly to the rear of it. The fighting continued to favour the Boches, and soon after midday Lieut.-Colonel Gemmill was instructed to deploy "A" and "C" Companies in support of the 153rd Brigade along a sunken road between Beaumetz and Morchies, and to deliver a counter-attack should the foe establish a footing in the Beaumetz-Morchies line. The remaining company of the battalion, "B," had been placed under the command of the 152nd Brigade, and had been sent at 6 A.M. to occupy a position in a sunken road east of Beaumetz, where it remained throughout the day, undisturbed except by occasional shelling.

Though it had been forced to yield some ground on the 21st, the division maintained a continuous front and was full of confidence when the 22nd dawned. Owing to the evacuation of the Flesquières salient, which was now in process, the right wing of the division was brought back to Hermies and thence its line stretched to Beaumetz. The early morning attacks of the Boches, though cloaked by mist, were easily dealt with, but the chief danger to the division came from the inroads which the enemy was making to the north of it. On this day the 8th Royal Scots proved that in their long spell of work with pick and shovel they had not forgotten how to use their rifles. At daybreak the position of the battalion was as follows: H.Q. and two platoons of "A" Company lined part of the sunken road between Beaumetz and Morchies, the other two platoons being in a trench about 300 yards behind the road, while "C" Company occupied a post which it had dug that morning near the north-west corner of Chaufours Wood. In the early hours "C" Company gave up its post to an English battalion, and while it was still without cover a terrific cannonade crashed down on it; but the pioneers were hardened to working under shell fire, and in an incredibly short space of time they had consolidated a line of shell-holes near their original post.

The crisis of the battle occurred in the afternoon. About 2 P.M. the men of "A" Company were violently shelled, and under cover of this bombardment the Boches crept close to the left of the trench occupied by the pioneers. The enemy had broken through north of Morchies and was endeavouring to turn the left flank of the Fifty-first Division. "A" Company at once extended its line to the left behind Morchies and stuck doggedly to this position till 6 P.M., repeatedly beating back by steady firing the swarming infantry of the Germans. The platoons commanded by Lieut. W. G. Young and 2nd Lieut. Blackwood did particularly good work, and even veterans of the old regular army would have found it difficult to better the fire control shown by the pioneers. After exacting a prodigious toll from the adversary, "A" Company timeously retired across the road just as the enemy entered it on the right, and took up a position in rear of Morchies on the left of "C" Company.

The latter had been heavily shelled during the afternoon, and had, moreover, sustained many losses from machine-gun fire. The persistence and weight of the enemy's attacks were now making themselves felt and our men began to give way, but Lieut.-Colonel Gemmill, who proved himself during these days of stress a born leader of men, rallied them and led them back through a scathing fire to a new position 200 yards in rear of Morchies. Fortified by the glorious example of their C.O., " A " and " C " Companies successfully held off every assault and only vacated their position at 9 P.M., when they were ordered to withdraw into reserve at Fremicourt, where they were rejoined by " B " Company. Like " C " Company, " B " had suffered much from hostile shelling, and included among the wounded was Captain H. E. R. Jones. In the evening, as the Germans were making alarming progress on the north side of the Cambrai Road, a platoon under 2nd Lieut. J. Robbie went forward and helped the 6th Seaforths to form a defensive flank to the north of Beaumetz, where it easily repulsed an attack by some German bombers and captured one prisoner.

In consequence of the German infiltration to the north, the line of the Fifty-first Division, pivoting on Hermies, had been swung round till it was facing nearly due north. At the same time our losses in the south had loosened the right flank of the division, and a retirement to the east of Bapaume had to be made on the 23rd. The enemy's assaults were resumed in the morning, and the 8th Royal Scots at Fremicourt, being heavily shelled, withdrew to a position west of the village facing the Cambrai Road. During the bombardment the Adjutant, Captain A. D. Jones, was wounded and his place was filled by 2nd Lieut. Calder. At 11.30 A.M. Lieut.-Colonel Gemmill received instructions that his men were to consolidate a position stretching east from Bancourt to the Cambrai Road;

this was done without any difficulty and the day ended with the enemy at a safe distance.

When morning dawned on the 24th the line taken over by the 8th Royal Scots had been converted by their skilled labour into a fairly strong position. "C" Company was on the right, "B" in the centre, and "A" on the left, the reserve consisting of a platoon of "B" Company under 2nd Lieut. Irvine. There was no action during the forenoon, but later in the day patrols brought in word that the troops in front were retreating, and that the Nineteenth Division would fall back through the line held by the 8th Royal Scots. When this had been accomplished, the pioneers found themselves in the forefront of the battle. At 2.30 P.M. a vicious bombardment burst on their trenches and on the sunken road behind them and casualties were numerous. About 4 P.M., just as the enemy's infantry attack was on the point of developing, Lieut.-Colonel Gemmill was ordered to take back his H.Q. to a dug-out on the Bancourt-Bapaume road. Soon afterwards kilted men on the right, remnants of the 153rd Brigade, were observed to be retiring, so the right platoon of "C" Company was swung round to form a defensive flank. The hostile pressure then became so menacing that the whole unit fell back a short distance, but on descrying the first indications of this retrograde movement, Lieut.-Colonel Gemmill dashed from his H.Q. and led his men back to their line. But the position of the battalion was very critical, since its right flank was completely in the air, and Lieut.-Colonel Gemmill was obliged to give the word to withdraw. The movement was carried out deliberately and gradually, platoons retiring in succession from the right, and was splendidly covered by the fire of the reserve platoon under 2nd Lieut. Irvine, which inflicted considerable casualties on the enemy. At nightfall the battalion was ordered to assemble at the cross-roads, Bapaume-Albert, Grévillers-Thilloy, from which point it marched to a position behind Loupart Wood to the west of Grévillers.

The whole British line was in flux, and the connections between formations were very fragile. Like many other divisions, the Fifty-first, on the night of the 24th/25th, appeared to have no friendly neighbours on either flank, but there was a fair assurance about the left flank, for the position of the Nineteenth Division was known; it was otherwise as regards the southern flank, which for several consecutive days was in peril of being turned.

The 8th Royal Scots, on the left wing of the division at Loupart Wood, were reinforced during the early morning of the 25th by 2nd Lieut. Robbie's platoon, which since the 22nd had been attached to the 6th Seaforths. About 11.30 A.M. the battalion was fiercely attacked from the direction of Grévillers by parties of Germans who, aided by a stretch of dead ground, were able to get up close to the right flank without being observed. On the other flank, where the lie of the ground gave the defenders a clear advantage, masses of Germans, about 3000 yards off, were seen advancing; these were allowed to approach within close range, when the Royal Scots suddenly opened a withering fire with rifles and Lewis guns, which scattered the hostile columns and temporarily checked the onslaught from the north.

It was the weak southern flank of the division that brought peril to the pioneers. Germans had already established themselves up against the right wing of the 8th, and when the units on this wing began to retire, the battalion was in the gravest danger of being surrounded. The crisis came to a head about 1.30 P.M., when, cut off from all friends on the right, a platoon of "C"

Lieut.-Colonel W. GEMMILL, D.S.O., 8th Battalion, The Royal Scots.

[*To face p.* 588.

Company under 2nd Lieut. Mackenzie was swung round into the wood to form a defensive flank. All attacks were repulsed till after 2 P.M., but during this critical fighting the gallant C.O., Lieut.-Colonel Gemmill, regardlessly exposing himself while encouraging his troops, was killed by a shell. The loss of such a leader at so critical a moment was a cruel blow, but his majestic example had accomplished its purpose, and the Royal Scots, inflamed with a desire to avenge the death of their Colonel, wrought enormous havoc in the opposing ranks. Not till 2.30 P.M. did the pioneers, now led by Captain Fleming, give ground before the surging tide of the Boche onset, and the battalion, though Germans were by this time established in its rear, tore itself free from the encircling foe. " C " Company, followed by " B " and " A " in succession, fell back slowly and in good order, taking no small toll of the Boches as they retreated. One platoon of " A " Company under Lieut. Meek held on long enough to cover the rest of the battalion by its fire, and then successfully extricated itself. Once out of the clutches of the enemy, the majority of the battalion mustered and reorganised on a ridge to the south-east of Achiet le Petit, but a party of fifty, comprising Lieut. Meek's platoon and some stragglers under 2nd Lieuts. White and Mackay, was forced back in the direction of Irles, where, though entirely un-supported, it took up a commanding position and held its ground for some hours, inflicting many losses on its assailants, who were advancing in large numbers against Irles.

The bulk of the battalion, amounting in all to twelve officers and one hundred and twenty men, dug in on the forward slope of a ridge in front of Achiet le Petit, where further casualties were sustained from the machine-gun fire which the enemy from an opposite

ridge was able to direct on the position. Fortunately the Sixty - second Division had now arrived
to strengthen the line, and the parties under Captain
Fleming and Lieut. Meek were relieved and re-formed on
the sheltered side of the ridge. The battalion's part
in the Second Battle of the Somme was ended. At
midnight the survivors of the 8th Royal Scots concentrated at Hébuterne and on the 26th March proceeded
to Fonquevillers. After reorganising they continued
their western march to Souastre, near which place
they dug in because of an alarm that the Germans
had broken through our lines and were within a short
distance of the village. Fortunately the rumour had no
foundation in fact, and the battalion, after spending the
night at Pas, marched on the 27th to Frévent, where it
entrained for Lillers. While the unit was waiting at
Frévent for the train, His Majesty the King passed
through, and his few words of cordial praise inspired the
men with fresh courage by making them feel that their
self-sacrificing efforts had been gratefully appreciated.

The casualty list of the pioneers ran to a dismal
length : besides Lieut.-Colonel Gemmill, Lieut. E.
Jeffrey and thirty-three other ranks were killed; four
officers [1] and one hundred and thirty-three other ranks
wounded, and forty-five other ranks missing.

Few divisions in the Third Army had a more
shaking experience than the Thirty-fourth on the 21st
March. The divisional front ran across the valley of
the Sensée river opposite the village of Fontaine les
Croisilles. A German prisoner, captured on the night
of the 9th/10th, had indicated that the main attack
would be through Bullecourt, garrisoned by the Fifty-
ninth Division on the right of the Thirty-fourth, and

---

[1] Captain and Adjutant A. D. Jones, Captain H. E. R. Jones, 2nd Lieut.
Lawrie, and Captain Morgan, the Medical Officer.

his information proved to be substantially correct. When the battle opened, the 101st Brigade was on the left of the front, the 15th Royal Scots being on the right and the 16th in reserve. At 5 A.M. a frenzied barrage burst on the whole divisional sector, and battery areas were drenched with gas, the 16th Royal Scots being compelled to wear their respirators for over four hours. Meanwhile the German infantry, unleashed against the Fifty-ninth Division, broke through the forward defences and attempted to roll up the Thirty-fourth Division from the south.

The progress of the Germans was appallingly rapid, and shortly after noon the 15th Royal Scots were amazed to find Boches on their right flank, while parties of them in artillery formation were seen advancing along the valley. Lieut.-Colonel Guard, however, had anticipated this manœuvre, and his right flank, thrown back to meet an attack from the south, temporarily checked the thrust. A little after 3 P.M. Major Warr,[1] commanding the 16th Royal Scots, who had suffered dreadful losses from the barrage, noticed with uneasiness that large forces of the enemy, at least four hundred strong, were closing in on Croisilles. There could be no reasonable doubt that the right brigade of the division had been overwhelmed, and that the 101st was in imminent danger of being similarly swallowed up, for the Germans, having pierced the forward defences, were now biting into the battle zone.

The crisis demanded immediate action, and Major Warr at once despatched Lieut. R. A. Inglis with two platoons to hold a defensive position in front of Croisilles. Lieut. Inglis was killed after leading his men to their places, but the remnants of his command pluckily held on till nightfall and beat off a number of attacks.

[1] Lieut.-Colonel Stephenson was at home on leave.

With the personnel of his H.Q. Major Warr manned
a trench on the western outskirts of the village, while
three platoons from each of his centre and left companies
were sent to hold a trench in the Croisilles Switch line
just behind his H.Q. By these timely measures he
buttressed the weak flank of the other two units of the
brigade. After 7 P.M., observing that the two forward
platoons were now dangerously exposed, he withdrew
them to form a protective screen to the south of his
battalion H.Q.

All this time the 15th Royal Scots were engaged in
a murderous bombing conflict with the Germans, who
were endeavouring to force a passage northwards
along the trenches from which they had ejected the
102nd Brigade. The primary duty of Lieut.-Colonel
Guard was at all costs to maintain his right flank,
which was gradually being strung out as the Boche
attack widened, and in order to find the men to effect
this object he had to surrender his front and fall back
to his support trench. But even with this adjustment
his depleted forces were barely adequate to hold their
extended positions, and when night came he withdrew
his front line to the Sensée Reserve Trench, with his
right flank stretching along Factory Avenue towards
Croisilles, where it was linked up with survivors of
the 102nd Brigade. Major-General Nicholson had by
this time thrown his reserve brigade, the 103rd, into
the battle, and it arrived in front of St Leger just in
time to prevent the Boches from smashing an entrance
into the third defensive zone.

The hostile infiltration to St Leger was one of the
worst shocks experienced on the 21st March, and
entirely upset the complacence of the Third Army.
But the situation might easily have been worse. Every
yard of the ground had been stoutly contested by the

Thirty-fourth Division, and its obstinate defence gained time for the Fortieth Division to come up and strengthen the line.

Night brought no breathing-space for any of the troops, since under the cloak of darkness they had to move to new positions better adapted for defence. The 15th Royal Scots were drawn back to a position just north of Croisilles; on their left were the 11th Suffolks, and on their right the remnants of the 102nd Brigade; the 16th Royal Scots occupied positions in support. The day of fighting, followed by a night of marching, imposed a terrible strain on the men; hollow-eyed and gaunt, all showed traces of the ordeal, but their discipline stood the test, and in grim silence they did all that was required of them. It is not surprising that amid the general confusion some mishaps occurred. A platoon of the 16th Royal Scots never received notice to retire, and it was only at daybreak that 2nd Lieut. Cowan realised that his small party was isolated; then, leading his men from their position, he took them along the Sensée until he secured touch with the 11th Suffolks and came into the firing-line on their right flank.

Shrouded by a sticky, blinding mist, the Germans, on the 22nd, launched a ferocious attack which was within an ace of proving fatal to the Thirty-fourth Division. The hostile blow was skilfully directed at the junction of the 101st and 102nd Brigades, and about 9 A.M. the 15th Royal Scots were assailed simultaneously from the front and the right flank. Hastening through the gap between the two brigades, Germans began to fire on the battalion from behind, and Lieut.-Colonel Guard was compelled to withdraw his men to a trench, Hill Switch, to the north and west of Croisilles. In all probability this retirement was only rendered possible through the heroic self-sacrifice of Captain Brown, who single-handed held a block to allow the safe retreat of his men. In Hill Switch the 16th Royal Scots were already in position. With scarcely a pause the Germans continued the attack with vigour, and, directed by air-scouts, their gunners savagely barraged the switch, which was a mere scrape in the ground incapable of affording any shelter against concentrated shell fire.

The Royal Scots were near the end of their tether, and when the Boches swarmed down upon them from Croisilles, they began to betray signs of unsteadiness. The breaking-point came when shells from our own guns also rained into the trench ; the men, temporarily demoralised, fled rearwards in batches, and only by dint of numerous appeals and threats were Lieut.-Colonel Guard and Major Warr able to arrest the rout at a trench in the third system of defence, where the shattered battalions were reorganised. Happily, the rent created in the line by this withdrawal did not bring about the collapse of the division, and the other units after a valiant resistance also reached a position in the third system in line with the Royal Scots, where the Germans were kept at bay till nightfall.

The 15th and the 16th Royal Scots never welcomed a relief with greater thankfulness than that on the night of the 22nd/23rd March, when the arrival of units of the Thirty-first Division allowed them to be withdrawn from the battle. By easy stages the war-worn division was taken to St Pol, whence at the end of the month it was sent to take over a familiar sector on the Lys front near Armentières. The casualties sustained by the battalions were : 15th—three officers (2nd Lieuts. J. W. Paxton, W. S. J. Noble, and J. Thomson) and eleven other ranks killed, four officers and eighty-eight other ranks wounded, eight officers and two hundred and eighty-two other ranks missing; 16th—four officers (Lieut. J. W. Stewart, 2nd Lieuts. G. F. Howie, R. A. Inglis, and R. S. Barclay) and eleven other ranks killed, three officers and one hundred and thirty-seven other ranks wounded, and two officers[1] and sixty-eight other ranks missing.

The Third and Fifteenth Divisions were not so closely affected by the German offensive in its first stages as were the other divisions with which we are concerned. The latter, which was mainly responsible for the defence of Arras, was in fact not seriously attacked till the 28th March, and the former, being on the wing of the Boche north attack, was only partially involved in the early fighting.

Holding the Third Divisional front east of Guémappe and Héninel were the 9th Brigade on the right, in touch with the Thirty-fourth Division, and the 8th Brigade, of which the right front battalion was the 2nd Royal Scots. The heavy enfilade attack against the Thirty-fourth Division to a certain extent affected the 9th Brigade, which was obliged to make a slight withdrawal. Hence the 2nd Royal Scots had to construct a block in their front line and post a section to watch the southern flank, but there was no attempt by the Germans to rush the defences. Just before midday the Boches began to probe our line, and a few of them, who were detected crawling towards one of our posts, were dispersed by rifle and Lewis-gun fire. The hostile barrage on the trenches held by the 8th Brigade had been unusually light, but the Royal Scots were inconvenienced by the gas fumes that drifted along their lines from the south. About noon evidence

[1] The wounded officers of the 16th were Captain J. F. Mackintosh, Lieut. W. S. Gavin, and 2nd Lieut. T. C. Laidlaw; the missing were Captain C. S. Lambert and Lieut. P. M. MacAndrew.

II   2 P

accumulated that the enemy was preparing for a serious attack; field-guns had opened on our front trenches, while numerous aeroplanes scudded low across our lines, peppering the troops with machine-gun fire. At 3.30 P.M. the long-expected infantry attack was launched, but the hordes of Germans who threw themselves against the trenches held by the left company were shaken and scattered by the "mad-minute"[1] practice of the Royal Scots. Meantime the men countered the Boche aircraft with Lewis-gun and rifle fire, and registered a hit on one aeroplane which crashed earthwards in the direction of Chérisy. Through the faint light cast by the westering sun the Royal Scots observed Germans creeping from shell-hole to shell-hole, while the extraordinary amount of movement in the neighbourhood of Chérisy clearly indicated that the Germans had more men opposite our front than were essential for manning their trenches. Having held on to all their positions, the Royal Scots were in good heart when the day ended, and took precautions against a surprise attack on the morrow by sending out patrols to prevent the Boche skirmishers from establishing themselves too near our wire.

Compared with what was happening to the south of them, quietness prevailed on the front of the Third and Fifteenth Divisions on the 22nd. At this time the Germans were trying to force an opening between the Fifth and the Third Armies, and the whole of the assailed front was so unstable that it became imperative for us to improve our defences round Arras; for our line girdling the city, as a result of hostile progress in the south, now bulged eastwards in an awkward salient, and a successful onslaught by the enemy at this juncture,

---

[1] The nickname for the rapid fire practice in the British Army Musketry Course, in which a man was given one minute to fire fifteen rounds.

when the westward movement of the Fifth Army was in full swing, might well have involved us in a terrible military disaster.   Accordingly it was determined to draw back the defenders of Arras to a more favourable position, and the necessary adjustments were made on the night of the 22nd/23rd March.   All the outposts and forward positions were vacated, and the 2nd Royal Scots withdrew to trenches near Wancourt ; similarly the units of the Fifteenth Division retired from Monchy to a system of trenches east of Orange Hill in front of Feuchy Chapel.   Two of the 13th's companies, "A" and "D," held a portion of this line while the movement was being effected, and the remainder of the battalion occupied a position in front of Tilloy.   About 11 A.M. on the 23rd Lieut.-Colonel Hannay was ordered to form his battalion along a position overlooking the Wancourt valley, but this step was merely in the nature of a precaution, since the whole of the operations had been admirably conducted, the Fifteenth being in touch with the Third Division on its right.

This opportune and skilful withdrawal upset the plans of General Buelow, who had made elaborate preparations for a colossal attack on Arras, and possibly prevented our Fifth and Third Armies from being irretrievably broken.   The Boches spent the 23rd in groping forward to gain touch with our troops, and during the afternoon small clusters of them were seen on a ridge above Wancourt and Héninel.   The time gained was profitably used by our men in preparing to meet the assault which they knew could not be far distant.   After the 23rd the enemy's shell fire increased in intensity, and from the reports of the observers of the 2nd and 13th Royal Scots as to the movements and activity of the foe, it was clear that the arrangements of Von Buelow were nearing completion.   A hostile reconnaissance in force was made against the 8th Brigade on the 24th, when the German infantry, without gaining ground, sustained heavy losses from the fire of the 2nd Royal Scots. Incessant vigilance was maintained, and our troops lived in continual suspense till the great blow was at last dealt on the 28th March.

On the date of the attack the 2nd Royal Scots were in reserve near Mercatel. There had been considerable liveliness on the previous day, and a report reached the battalion that the two front battalions of the 8th Brigade were being forced back. The battle attained its height on the 28th, and at 2 P.M. parties of the 2nd Royal Scots Fusiliers, fighting lustily, retired through the Royal Scots and reorganised behind them in a sunken road. The Royal Scots now held the front of the brigade, but so grievously had the enemy been punished in making his advance that he did not venture to come within 1000 yards of the 8th Brigade front, and made no real attempt to drive in the Royal Scots. The latter indeed were surprised that the Boche effort was so feeble, and after their relief on the 29th/30th by the Second Canadian Division, they recorded in the war diary that "during the whole of the time the battalion kept absolutely intact and in touch with units on the flanks, and at no time did the battalion consider the situation out of hand." Its casualties for the period were three officers (Captain T. Newlands, Lieut. R. G. N. Gibson, and 2nd Lieut. R. Anderson) and nineteen other ranks killed; two officers[1] and seventy-eight other ranks wounded. After leaving the line the battalion arrived at Lozinghem on the 1st April and came under the orders of the First Army.

The thrust on which the enemy staked his chances of success was directed mainly against the Fifteenth

[1] Captain V. Shearman and 2nd Lieut. R. H. Westley.

Division. After midnight on the 27th/28th the 13th
Royal Scots moved up from the support to the front
positions east of Orange Hill astride the main Arras-
Cambrai Road; the front companies were "A" and "D,"
supported by "B" and "C." The battalion was fated
to have the proud honour of taking a principal rôle
in the gigantic battle that was to dash the hopes of
Germany. Its patrols speedily discovered that the
stage had been set for the performance, for within easy
reach of our trenches a line of shell-holes had been
consolidated and manned by Boche infantry.

The prelude of the action was the customary
bombardment, which opened at 3 A.M., and for over
three hours the guns, German and British, roared like
the wrath of God. Against the accurate gunnery of
the enemy the wide trenches of the Royal Scots were
but death-traps, and the shells, plunging in, annihilated
batches of men in a moment. Apparently unconcerned
by the pitiless deluge, Lieut. Forbes of "A" Company
picked his way from point to point, exhorting his men
to stand firm and cheering them with the assurance
that their turn would come when the hostile infantry
began to advance, until he was laid low by a shell.
His wonderful example was imitated with admirable
sang froid by his successor, 2nd Lieut. Mathieson.
But death continued to gather a rich harvest, and one
platoon under 2nd Lieut. Higgins, stationed near the
Cambrai Road, was wiped out; before dawn broke the
great majority of both "A" and "B" Companies, posted
near the fatal road, had been either killed or wounded.

The awful tornado of shells seemed to those within
its scope to last for æons, and nearly all who did not
lose their lives lost their senses. At 7 A.M. the German
infantry, confident that all immediate resistance must
have been shattered by the barrage, pushed down the

Cambrai Road, but on this occasion they were not sheltered by a screen of mist, and many fell under the artillery and machine-gun fire that burst upon them. Moreover, several of the scanty survivors of "A" and "B" Companies, recovering marvellously from the stupor caused by the cannonade, fought with the desperation of fanatics, and though they were surrounded and overwhelmed by sheer force of numbers, their stand availed to give a slight respite to "D" and "C" Companies on the left. These, commanded by Captain Kelly and Captain Considine respectively, had not suffered so lamentably from the devastating effects of the barrage, and contesting every inch of the ground, fell back methodically step by step to a line of trenches behind Orange Hill. This retirement was pluckily covered by 2nd Lieut. Brown of "C" Company, who, having found a Vickers machine-gun in a narrow trench, turned it against the enemy, and continued to fire it until he had exhausted all his ammunition.

Meantime Lieut.-Colonel Hannay, with his H.Q. west of Feuchy Chapel cross-roads, could only conjecture what was happening in front, for the Boche barrage demolished all communication between him and his companies and every effort to restore it proved unavailing; although numerous runners were sent forward to gather information, not one returned. But the fate of the companies astride the Cambrai Road could not be doubted when, before 8 A.M., knots of Germans were seen topping the ridge on the north side of the road. Lieut.-Colonel Hannay promptly turned out every available man to form a line in front of his H.Q., from which rapid fire was opened on the approaching enemy. At this time there appeared reason to fear that a debacle had occurred, for men from various units of the division

were now moving westwards, but these were stopped and
commandeered to reinforce Lieut.-Colonel Hannay's line.
These measures decisively checked the German advance
in this quarter, and the foremost Boche troops were
driven to seek cover in the quarries near the cross-roads.

The resistance of the H.Q. staff helped to ease the
strain on the companies which had rallied to the rear
of Orange Hill. Their right flank, however, was
turned by the Germans who advanced up the trench
from the road, and 2nd Lieut. West and a few bombers
had to fight obstinately to give their comrades time
to reorganise. Having re-formed, "D" and "C" Companies withdrew to the banks of the road leading
north from Feuchy Chapel, and here with the opportune
assistance of two machine-guns, which fired over their
heads, the Royal Scots held the Germans at bay for
some hours. There was still a danger of the position
being turned from the right, but happily the fire of
Lieut.-Colonel Hannay's force prevented the enemy
from leaving the quarries.

After midday the enemy lost heart. His casualties
had been enormous, and he had been surprised by the
vigorous resistance which our infantry, in spite of the
pounding to which they had been subjected, were
able to offer. No more than the forward and least
vital parts of our defences had been lost, and about
1.30 P.M. the scattered platoons and companies of the
division, which had stemmed the enemy's furious
attack, after re-forming and reorganising, fell back to
a strong position east of Tilloy Wood.

The survivors of the 13th Royal Scots retired in
two parties, one on either side of the Cambrai Road.
With the southern group was Sergeant Watson who,
having spotted a platoon of Germans entering a
Y.M.C.A. tent in the Bois des Bœufs, trained a

machine-gun on it, and, when the last foeman had vanished beneath the canvas, raked it with bullets from top to bottom. A few hours later when a reserve battalion delivered a counter - charge it discovered eighteen dead Boches in the tent.

This counter-attack carried our line beyond the Bois des Bœufs, and by nightfall the German onset had been decisively repulsed. From Tilloy Wood the remnants of the 13th Royal Scots were withdrawn at midnight to a tunnel behind Tilloy, from which after a brief rest they marched up to Telegraph Hill ready to repel any further assaults. But the enemy made no move. There remained of the Royal Scots scarcely sufficient men to form a strong company; two officers, Lieut. D. Forbes and 2nd Lieut. K. Maclean, were killed, eight (Lieut. J. R. Mitchell, 2nd Lieuts. A. A. Farquharson, H. S. Higgins, J. McGregor, L. W. Guthrie, J. Hobbs, S. C. Cumming, and A. Mathieson) were missing[1]; six other ranks were killed, one hundred and forty wounded, and two hundred and thirty missing.

By the time the Thirty-second Division arrived in Third Army territory the storm had been weathered, but much remained to be done before the defence was ship-shape. Minor operations were necessary to eject the foe from commanding positions, and in one of these the Thirty-second Division took part. The 5/6th Royal Scots entered the line on the 2nd April near Ayette, a village lying north-west of Courcelles le Comte and held by the enemy. On the night of the 2nd/3rd the battalion co-operated with the 15th Highland Light Infantry in an operation which had as its object the capture of the village. The enterprise was successful. Ayette fell to an attack in which the Royal Scots were represented by two platoons of "D" Company

[1] It was later ascertained that Lieut. H. S. Higgins had been killed.

on the right wing, and two hundred prisoners, including a battery commander and three officers, and numerous machine-guns were secured. The captured positions were then taken over by two and a half companies of the Royal Scots, who had a troublesome time from Boche retaliation on the 3rd.

The Germans established themselves in a sunken road near our lines, and sadly harassed the Ayette garrison with machine-gun and rifle fire. One hostile machine-gun was accounted for by a brave exploit of Privates Cunningham and Young who, working round the enemy's flank, seized the gun and two prisoners. Lieut. W. O. Steuart handled his platoon with great skill, and his men, by well-controlled Lewis-gun fire, ultimately forced the Boches to quit the sunken road. The night passed without any counter-attack, and on the 4th April it became clear that the enemy had for the time given up any idea of disputing the possession of Ayette. There was one unusual incident. Just before daybreak Sergeant Smith of "C" Company heard a shot that seemed to be fired from our lines, and on looking over the parapet saw a German creeping from our wire. The Boche slunk into a shell-hole, but Sergeant Smith dashed after him and took him prisoner. The casualties of the battalion in this successful enterprise were not unduly heavy; one officer, 2nd Lieut. Nairne, was killed, two were wounded, and the losses in other ranks in killed and wounded totalled forty.

By the beginning of April the stir on the battlefront had died down considerably, but it was generally realised that the breathing-space would be short, and our shattered divisions, withdrawn from the line, were hastily preparing for what they called "the third round of the Somme"; but the next attack of the enemy was directed against another sector.

CHAPTER XXXIV

THE GERMAN OFFENSIVE ON THE LYS

April 1918

German Break-through at Lys, 9th April. Attack on Givenchy repulsed. German advance on Merville and Béthune. Action of the 8th, 2nd, and 9th Battalions. German advance on Bailleul and Hazebrouck. Action of 15th and 16th Battalions. Armentières abandoned, 10th April. Loss of Bailleul, 15th April. 11th and 12th Battalions near Hollebeke; German Attack on Kemmel, 25th April. Action of 11th and 12th Battalions. Hostile advance checked.

THE situation at the beginning of April 1918 was not entirely satisfactory to either of the contesting forces. The British had prevented Ludendorff from achieving his strategical objective, but they had been pressed back so far that they had no margin for further retreat, if the important city of Amiens were to be preserved; the Germans in spite of their prodigious captures had failed to sever the armies of the Allies, and for the time their attack had spent itself. Their forces lay within striking distance of Amiens, but their communications extended across a hinterland so torn and devastated that the task of making preparations for a resumption of the offensive on an adequate scale presented stupendous difficulties. From a military point of view the new German line was not adapted for an economic defence, and on the south it was quite unsound owing to a long weak flank, against which the French were favourably situated to launch a counter-attack as soon as the enemy lost the initiative.

Military considerations, therefore, seemed to indicate

604

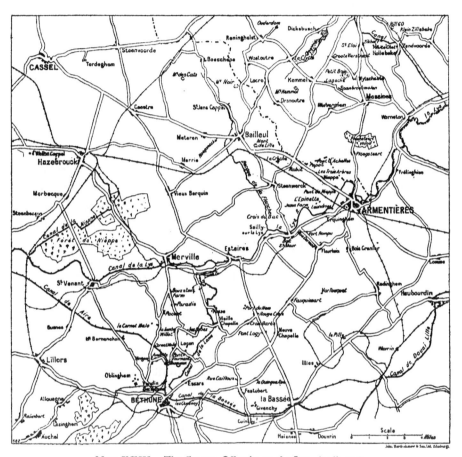

MAP XXIV.—The German Offensive at the Lys, April 1918.

(*See also* large scale Map at end of volume.)

that the Germans would resume active hostilities on the Amiens front, and no doubt it was the intention of Ludendorff that they should do so.   Meantime, feeling that he had disturbed the balance of the British, he resolved to harass them by a diversion in a sector where he knew that they were weak.

Previous to the 21st March the British line was more thickly garrisoned in the north than in the south, but when the Second Battle of the Somme opened, Sir Douglas Haig was obliged to thin his northern front by sending reinforcements to the south.   The Salient and the sector between La Bassée and Arras were of such vital importance that they could not safely be weakened, and most of the reinforcements were drawn from the line between these two limits.   The troops sent to assist the Fifth and the Third Armies were replaced by divisions depleted by the fighting at the Somme ; these, hastily filled up by mere boys, were given no adequate time to assimilate their drafts before they were despatched to hold the line.   Thus the Thirty-fourth Division was sent into Armentières sector, and the Ninth to the neighbourhood of Hollebeke ; in the hinterland of the front from La Bassée to the Salient were the Third, Fifty-first, and Sixty-first Divisions.

All this was known to Ludendorff, and furnished a good reason for an offensive on the Lys.   And though since he employed only nine fresh divisions in the attack, he apparently contemplated nothing more than a diversion for the purpose of weakening British morale, there were substantial prizes to reward victory.   First of all there was the alluring prospect of turning our defences on the Vimy Ridge and the high ground east of Arras by the capture of Givenchy, and if this object were attained the whole British front would become fluid, and the offensive against Amiens could be resumed with every promise of success.   Failing this, there remained the possibility of seizing important centres like Béthune, Merville, and Hazebrouck, thus weakening the lateral communications of the Allies; or, the least of the prizes, the Germans might make a bid for the ridge of hills stretching east from the Mont des Cats, the capture of which would put them in a favourable position for expelling us from Ypres, and even perhaps for gaining Dunkirk and Calais.

Sir Douglas Haig was aware that the Germans were planning an operation against our positions north of La Bassée, and, being particularly anxious about the security of the front near Neuve Chapelle, which was manned by Portuguese troops who had undergone a long spell of trench duty, he issued instructions for this sector to be taken over by British troops.   But before this could be carried into effect, the German blow fell.

A hostile bombardment along our front from Lens to Armentières began on the night of the 7th/8th April and reached its greatest volume on the morning of the 9th, when German storm-troops issued from their lines and scattered the Portuguese in rout from all their positions. Thus an extensive gap was immediately created between the Fifty-fifth and Fortieth Divisions on the flanks of the Portuguese, and the enemy naturally endeavoured to exploit this opening to the best advantage.   A very determined effort was made to drive the Fifty-fifth Division from Givenchy and thus turn the all-important Vimy Ridge from the north, but the glorious resistance of this division wore down every assault, and the enemy was forced to concentrate his efforts on the lesser prizes. The German attack then developed westwards and north-westwards.   In the former direction they pushed on towards Béthune, but they were ultimately brought to a standstill by the resistance of the Fifty-first, Third, Sixty-first, and other Divisions; simultaneously they rapidly progressed to the north-west, rolling up the flank of the Fortieth Division, and when by the 13th April their designs on Béthune were frustrated, they threw all their weight into this attack. Bailleul and other noteworthy places fell into their hands, but by the 16th April Hazebrouck was reasonably safe. The turning movement of the enemy had regained for him the possession of the Messines Ridge, and after the 16th April he concentrated on the line of hills commanding Ypres from the south. But as the front of attack contracted, the task of defence became simplified, and though the Germans carried Mont Kemmel they were prevented from making dangerous progress beyond it, and the Lys offensive came to an end without Ludendorff having secured any of the prizes that dangled so tantalisingly before him.

This chapter is devoted to showing the part played by battalions of the Royal Scots in stemming the German advance, firstly on Merville and Béthune, secondly on Hazebrouck, and finally on the Salient and the Channel ports.

1. The Fifty-first Division, which was reorganising to the north-west of Béthune, was immediately available to be thrown into the breach created by the flight of the Portuguese, and by nightfall on the 9th April the division was linked up west of the Lawe Canal with the Fifty-fifth on the south and the Fiftieth on the north. The 8th Royal Scots, now commanded by Major Humphreys of the Black Watch, were at Bas Rieux near Lillers when the news of the German break-through was received, and during the afternoon of the 9th April they marched to Mont Bernenchon, where they halted for the rest of the day.

The fighting experienced by the division on the 10th was very severe, but the Highlanders kept their line intact. The 8th Royal Scots, who remained in reserve, were ordered to move forward to Pacaut, and coming within the zone of the hostile artillery fire sustained several casualties. After dark " B " Company under Captain Richardson advanced by platoons to a position in front of Paradis, where it dug and occupied a trench in close support of the 7th Gordons, who lay west of the Lawe near Foss.

The battle continued with unabated fury on the 11th April, and fighting dourly, the Fifty-first Division was thrust back from the line of the Lawe. " B," the advanced company of the 8th Royal Scots, was early involved in the conflict, and being forced to retreat, was mixed up with the units of the 153rd Brigade. A continuous rear-guard action followed until the railway line near Merville was reached, and here " B " Company, acting in co-operation with the 7th Black Watch, succeeded in stopping the enemy. " C " Company also had a trying ordeal. Before dawn it advanced from Pacaut and dug itself in about 500 yards east of Paradis Church, where a gallant stand, which broke a dangerous German attack at 8 A.M., cost the company many losses: Major Humphreys, Captain Fleming, Lieuts. Dodds and Burnet were all wounded, and for a considerable period a Warrant-Officer, C.S.M. Dickson, was in command. Lieut. the Hon. R. B. Watson came up from Pacaut to take charge of the company, but he was hit by a bullet soon after his arrival.

The third company, "A," moved west from Pacaut at 7 A.M. and dug a trench about 1000 yards to the south-west of "C" Company. The tide of battle reached it at midday, when groups of Germans established themselves in houses close to its position. Artillery fire was immediately directed on the Boches, and when they scurried across the open from the houses, the Royal Scots brought many of them to the ground by rifle and Lewis-gun fire. Meantime Lieut. A. B. Falconer had succeeded in reaching "C" Company, which about noon beat off a very violent assault. But the flanks of the company were by no means assured, and Major Todd, who was now in command of the battalion, ordered it to withdraw slightly so as to maintain liaison with the units on its wings. A few men of "B" Company, under Lieut. Munro, came up in the afternoon and occupied a position in support of the troops on the left of "C" Company.

Though the Fifty-first Division had been forced away from the Lawe and many of its units were disorganised, it succeeded in presenting a continuous front to the enemy, and the situation was becoming less critical owing to the arrival of reinforcements. Thus the Third Division was already in position to support the Fifty-fifth and the right of the Fifty-first Division, while the units of the Sixty-first Division were moving up to prevent any break-through between the Fifty-first and Fiftieth.

The 2nd Royal Scots had been at Fouquereuil since the 4th April, and remained there until the morning of the 11th, when Lieut.-Colonel Gillatt was ordered to assemble his battalion on the road between Oblinghem and Hinges. From this point the battalion advanced and deployed along a line extending from the west of Locon south to the Lawe Canal. Stirred by a rumour that Germans were already in Locon, the Royal Scots lost no time in cutting trenches and felt that they were lucky in being able to finish the work without sustaining an attack.

The 9th Royal Scots were rushed up from the Somme area by train on the 10th, arriving at Steenbecque about 1.30 P.M. on the 11th. After detraining, the men, at 7 P.M., were sent to occupy a position along a road to the south of Merville.

From the general situation on the night of the 11th/12th April it seemed that the worst of the storm as regards the southern part of the battle had been weathered, but our confidence was rudely shaken by the events of the 12th.

The front of the Fifty-first Division extended approximately from La Tombe Willot to Bouzateux Farm, and the bulk of the 8th Royal Scots manned the centre of this position. The night passed in deceptive peace, for before dawn the Germans launched a tremendous attack which took us unawares. The enemy broke through on the left of the pioneers, who for the rest of the day were involved in desperate and confused fighting, in the course of which companies and platoons were often isolated. Lieut. Munro and his party were cut off and overwhelmed. The Germans worked round to the rear of the Royal Scots, surprising the battalion H.Q. and capturing Major Todd and his Adjutant, Captain Jones. "A" and "C" Companies were surrounded, but, fighting with grim desperation, the majority of them broke through the enemy. Three platoons of "A" Company crossed the La Bassée Canal near Bernenchon, while the other platoon, forced away from its neighbours, retired south with a mixed body of men belonging to the 152nd Brigade. "C" Company, on extricating itself, joined a party of sappers, and with their assistance formed a line through Pacaut Wood, where it kept the Germans at bay till dusk. The troops on its right retired, and the Royal Scots and sappers flung out a defensive flank, and only withdrew across the La Bassée Canal when darkness hid their movements from the enemy. The survivors of the company were then instructed to

II   2 Q proceed to Busnes, where the whole battalion was to assemble.

The enemy's drive, carrying him almost up to the line of the La Bassée Canal, jeopardised the positions of the units on the flanks of the Fifty-first Division. Thus the 2nd Royal Scots came into action on the 12th. Before daybreak the battalion advanced and relieved the 7th Argylls of the Fifty-first Division on the east side of Locon, and when all adjustments were completed, it had the Fifty-fifth Division on its right and the 1st Royal Scots Fusiliers on its left. The line consisted of a few holes, hastily excavated in open fields and unprotected by any obstacles, while the country in front was thick with enclosures, rendering it possible for the enemy to come within close range of the battalion without being detected. On the right stretched out a large area of dead ground which would assist the Germans when they elected to attack. Boche aeroplanes, cruising over our lines from an early hour, quickly took stock of the defects of our position, which about 10 A.M. was savagely barraged.

The forenoon sped past without any infantry action, but immediately after noon the Royal Scots Fusiliers on the left were seen to be withdrawing. An officer, despatched by Lieut.-Colonel Gillatt to reconnoitre the main Locon Road, returned with the alarming information that the Germans had worked round the left flank of the Royal Scots and were actually in rear of the front companies, which were closely engaged with the enemy. 2nd Lieut. Gordon and a group of men from battalion H.Q. then reconnoitred the Locon Road as far as the church, from which point they explored towards the canal in order to ensure that liaison with the Fifty-fifth Division was not severed. Meanwhile the front companies of the Royal Scots had become split into small groups, but by dint of hard fighting they temporarily checked the hostile advance. Some ground was yielded, and after midday the line held by the Royal Scots ran from Pont Tournant on the Lawe Canal to the church at Locon, whence it bent sharply back in a westerly direction.

From about 1.30 to nearly 4 P.M. there was a lull; after that, the left company became aware that the foe was preparing for a fresh drive, but every attempt of the German infantry to concentrate was frustrated by the admirable shooting of our field guns. Just, however, when the men were congratulating themselves that all trouble was over for the day, they noticed with dismay that the Royal Scots Fusiliers were moving still farther back. Lieut.-Colonel Gillatt at once swung round the left wing of his battalion and, mustering every man he could find from his H.Q., only six in all, sent them to hold Avelette. Fortunately the right flank of the Royal Scots was rendered entirely secure by the opportune arrival of two companies of the 7th King's Shropshire Light Infantry who took over the line near the canal. By this time the advance of the enemy, who had suffered heavy losses, was definitely checked on the left, and at night the Royal Scots, being relieved in the front by the King's Shropshire Light Infantry, took up a position in support some distance south of Les Chocquaux.

On the 12th April the 9th Royal Scots were not affected to the same extent as the 2nd by the Boche success. The units of the Sixty-first Division arrived in the Merville sector in time to hold up the enemy, though for some days the situation continued to be critical and Merville itself was lost. In conformity with the movement of the Fifty-first Division, the Sixty-first had to fall back slightly, but otherwise no ground was yielded. The 9th Royal Scots found little difficulty in keeping the Germans at a distance, and at 11 P.M. the battalion was relieved and marched back to St Venant, where for the second time since the 21st March the Argylls, Gordons, and Royal Scots were formed into a composite battalion under Major Moir of the Argylls.

Cleverly and persistently though the Germans had conducted their operations on the 12th April, they found to their chagrin that despite all their efforts our line at the end of the day had solidified in front of them, and, aware that we were being reinforced in this locality, they began to concentrate on Bailleul in the hope of cleaving a passage to Hazebrouck. Hence after the 12th April the pressure on the Third, Fifty-first, and Sixty-first Divisions sensibly diminished. Neither the 2nd nor the 8th Royal Scots were disturbed on the 13th; the former remained in the positions which they occupied at the close of the previous day, while the latter were organised at Busnes under Major Mitchell as the Royal Scots Company of the 153rd Brigade composite battalion. The 9th Royal Scots, who were nearer the centre of the crisis, manned trenches on the outskirts of St Venant during the morning and afternoon, but there were no infantry encounters. Before the day closed they were reorganised once more as a separate unit, and during the night they moved up to trenches in front of the village.

When the 14th April passed without any serious attack by the Germans, it became clear that the enemy had abandoned his designs on Béthune. The 2nd Royal Scots were relieved on the night of the 14th/15th and proceeded to quarters in Vendin les Béthune. The 8th Royal Scots remained in readiness to act with the 153rd Brigade till the 15th April, when they began to function again as a pioneer battalion, and under the command of Lieut.-Colonel W. Thorburn of the 9th Royal Scots, assisted the Sixty-first Division in constructing defences round St Venant. The 9th Royal Scots also found that the worst of their troubles were over. It grieved them to part with so tried and esteemed a leader as Lieut.-Colonel Green, who was promoted to command the 153rd Brigade, but they had the satisfaction of securing as their new C.O. a sterling commander in Lieut.-Colonel J. B. Muir, D.S.O. The St Venant sector continued to be the home of the battalion till near the end of May.

All three battalions suffered heavy losses during the fighting: 2nd Battalion, one officer (Lieut. R. Whyte) and fourteen other ranks killed; seven officers [1] wounded and missing; one officer and one hundred and seven other ranks wounded, and two hundred and forty-seven other ranks missing: 8th Battalion, four officers (Lieut. G. Brunton, F. A. Burnet, J. B. Dods, G. Reid) and thirty-one other ranks killed; seven officers [2] and ninety-two other ranks wounded; and five officers [2] and fifty-one other ranks missing: 9th Battalion, one officer and seventeen other ranks killed; seven officers and one hundred and thirty-five other ranks wounded; and one hundred and forty-four other ranks missing.

2. The German thrust against Bailleul and Hazebrouck began on the 9th April, and for six consecutive days the 15th and the 16th Royal Scots were in the thick of the fight.

These battalions were in wonderfully high spirits

[1] Wounded, 2nd Lieut. W. E. Dow; wounded and missing, Captains D. Kininmonth and J. Henderson, Lieut. H. Robertson, 2nd Lieuts. A. E. W. Maclachlan, R. Murchison, J. Todd, and R. C. Wilkie.

[2] Lieut.-Colonel H. J. Humphreys, Captains W. A. Fleming and J. Richardson, Lieuts. Hon. R. B. Watson, A. F. B. Anderson, 2nd Lieuts. A. H. Callender, J. H. Robbie, wounded; Major J. A. Todd, Captains A. D. Jones, J. M. Ross (M.O.), Lieut. A. Munro and 2nd Lieut. A. M. White missing.

when they took over trenches in the Armentières sector on the 30th March. They were in a district that was familiar to them and was intimately associated with their first experiences in France. But Armentières was no longer the happy town of 1916. The hospitable civilians had disappeared, and the estaminets, where many joyous hours had been spent in social relaxation, were neglected and forsaken, for in 1917 the town had been blighted by a cruel bombardment which reduced it to a mass of ruins. But it was difficult for the rank and file to believe that anything really devastating could happen at Armentières, and they entered the sector in the expectation that they would not be molested by the enemy.

Ordinary trench duty was resumed with zest, and on the 2nd April C.S.M. Mellor, with twenty men of the 15th Royal Scots, dispersed a large Boche patrol after a lively exchange of shots; how many Germans were wounded it was impossible to ascertain, but four corpses were picked up and one prisoner was captured. But however satisfied our men might be, Major-General Nicholson was aware that Armentières was not an easy place to defend. The front line and the larger part of the town lay on the east side of the canalised Lys, straddled by only seven bridges, and a successful attack by the enemy might result in the troops between the front line and the river being cut off. The town itself would be little better than a trap during an attack, since after a gas bombardment the poisonous fumes lingered in the houses and cellars for weeks. These fears were tragically borne out on the night of the 7th/8th April, when a heavy bombardment deluged Armentières with gas, which put out of action two companies of the 25th Northumberland Fusiliers. "A" and "C" Companies of the 15th Royal Scots were then attached to this English battalion, the former being posted along the railway embankment near the station, the latter occupying a trench running to the east of the town. The remainder of the battalion, the command of which was taken over by Major Osborne on the 5th, was billeted in the Laundries to the west of Erquinghem. In this village was also the 16th Battalion, which spent the greater part of the night of the 8th/9th working near Bois Grenier and did not return to its billets till 2 A.M. in the morning. On the eve of the German attack the line was held by the 102nd and 103rd Brigades, the 101st being in reserve.

A ferocious bombardment during the early hours of the 9th April was a clear token of the enemy's intentions ; it was so heavy and sustained that Lieut.-Colonel Stephenson was impelled to turn the 16th Royal Scots from the village of Erquinghem into neighbouring fields where the shell fire was less concentrated. No direct assault on Armentières followed the bombardment, but the Thirty-fourth Division was soon caught in the toils owing to the collapse of the Portuguese near Neuve Chapelle. Breaking through in this vicinity, the Germans spread out in fan shape to the south and north, and their northern drive rolled up the flank of the Fortieth Division, the southern neighbour of the Thirty-fourth, and forced it back to a position facing south between Bois Grenier and Sailly sur la Lys. Even this line could not be wholly maintained, and before nightfall the right flank of the Fortieth Division had to be drawn back to the western bank of the Lys at Bac St Maur.

The 101st Brigade was the only reserve available to assist at the moment the hard-pressed Fortieth Division, and at 11.25 A.M. Lieut.-Colonel Stephenson was instructed to send his battalion to line a sunken

road running north-east and south-west on the south
side of the Lys, approximately 1000 yards south-east
of Bac St Maur. A report from Major Warr, who
had been sent ahead to reconnoitre the position, to the
effect that German troops were already in Bac St Maur,
caused Lieut.-Colonel Stephenson to deploy his battalion
near Fort Rompu to form a defensive flank facing west;
here the 16th Royal Scots were in a position to protect
the weak flank of the Thirty-fourth Division. Already
the exigencies of the battle had created a certain amount
of disorganisation; two companies of the 16th Royal
Scots had been attached to the 119th Brigade and
posted north of the Lys, but Lieut.-Colonel Stephenson
was compensated by having " B " and " D " Companies
of the 15th Royal Scots placed under his command.
At this time his force was in touch with troops of the
Fortieth Division on the right and with the 11th
Suffolks on the left. The immediate object of the
Germans was to break through the Royal Scots and
thus cut off the Thirty-fourth Division, but though on
several occasions hostile parties penetrated our defences
they were met and driven back by vigorous counter-
attacks. The enemy, however, kept hammering at our
defences, and ultimately, in the afternoon, forced back
the Royal Scots to the Armentières-Warneton Railway.

When the units of the Fortieth Division that remained
south of the Lys were all driven in, the 12th Suffolks
came into position on the right of Lieut.-Colonel
Stephenson's command, which received a welcome
reinforcement in the shape of four Vickers-guns from
the Machine-Gun Corps. Fighting continued far into
the night and patrols of the Royal Scots had several
affrays with the enemy. Late in the evening Lieut.-
Colonel Stephenson was amazed to find that his troops
were being fired at from Jesus Farm, north of the

Lys and well in rear of the position held by the
Royal Scots.

This was an unmistakable warning that all our
troops south of the Lys were in imminent danger of
being cut off; the Germans in fact were within an ace
of demolishing the whole of the Thirty-fourth Division.
The Boches, pressing on from Bac St Maur, had reached
Croix du Bac, where for a brief space they were stayed
by the desperate resistance of the remnants of the
Fortieth Division and the two companies of the 16th
Royal Scots attached to the 119th Brigade.   Reinforcements reached the assailants more quickly than the
defenders, and having overcome all opposition, the
Germans began to swarm along the north bank of
the Lys.   If their progress had not been abruptly
checked, all our forces south of the river would have
been lost; but when matters were at their blackest, the
74th Brigade dramatically arrived, and by a dashing
counter-attack halted the enemy on the outskirts of
Croix du Bac.   This success temporarily eased the
position of our troops on the south bank, where the
Germans carried on their attacks till late in the evening.
The most menacing onslaught occurred at 9 P.M., but
the rifle fire of the Royal Scots sufficed to prevent the
hostile infantry from breaking through.   From this
time till daybreak comparative quiet prevailed on this
side of the river, but on the north bank grim fighting
continued throughout the night.

During the day there had been no frontal attack on
the Thirty-fourth Division, so that only the reserve
brigade had been in action.   For the present the enemy
was firmly held on the south of the Lys, where during
the night Lieut.-Colonel Stephenson was reinforced by
two Vickers guns and one hundred and fifty infantry
from various units, but the fate of the division hung

upon what took place on the north bank. A night attack delivered at 2 A.M., in which the two companies of the 16th Royal Scots assisted the 74th Brigade, just failed to drive the Boches from Croix du Bac, and consequently our adversaries were in a favourable position to resume the offensive on the following day.

The 10th April was a day of desperate and critical fighting. North and south of the Lys the Germans attacked with tremendous vehemence, and at 8 A.M., sweeping all before them, advanced from Croix du Bac to Steenwerck, where only the appearance of fresh troops of the 88th Brigade saved the Thirty-fourth Division from absolute disaster; for the enemy on the south side had also staved in our lines. The position of Lieut.-Colonel Stephenson's force was a curious one; to meet a Boche thrust from the west, part of the line ran due north from the railway facing Fort Rompu, while the other part stretched almost due east from the same point facing Fleurbaix. Just at the angle of this line the enemy, advancing simultaneously from Fort Rompu and Fleurbaix, delivered a furious assault and regardless of losses flung himself against the line and broke through. The Royal Scots in the Rue Dormoir were surrounded, and after a brief and gallant fight against impossible odds Major Warr and a few survivors were captured. With the resource of the born soldier Lieut.-Colonel Stephenson kept the rest of his force intact, and at length stemmed the onrush of the foe.

But on the other side of the Lys there was chaos. British troops were streaming back in disorder, and all attempts of Captain Bayliss, the Adjutant of the 16th Royal Scots, to rally them were in vain. The Boche pursuers established themselves in a position from which they opened a galling fire on the backs of

Lieut.-Colonel Stephenson's men, and when in the afternoon parties of Germans began to press into Erquinghem from the west, it seemed that our men south of the Lys were doomed. Fortunately a battalion of the Duke of Wellington's Regiment arrived in the nick of time and drove the enemy from the village.

This opportune stroke gave us time to withdraw all our troops from the south bank of the river, and orders to this effect were received by Lieut.-Colonel Stephenson about 3 P.M., his retirement being little hindered by the Germans who significantly evinced no inclination to come to close quarters. Some casualties were caused by the enemy's shell and machine-gun fire, but, using a pontoon bridge near the church in Erquinghem, all Lieut.-Colonel Stephenson's troops were on the north side by 6.30 P.M. Without delay the remnants of the 16th Royal Scots occupied trenches near Jesus Farm. Only Germans appeared to be on the right flank, but these were apparently too disorganised to make an attack. Lieut.-Colonel Stephenson's force numbered about five hundred all told; in addition to the men of his own battalion there were about fifty of the 15th Royal Scots, sixty of the 12th Suffolks, and a few Australian Tunnellers. Patrols were sent out to reconnoitre the ground to the west, and one of these surprised and captured a hostile trench-gun wagon and team which were travelling from Croix du Bac to L'Epinette.

The withdrawal of the 102nd and 103rd Brigades was by no means an easy matter, but after some sharp fighting the majority of the troops were brought over to the safe side of the Lys. "A" and "C" Companies of the 15th Royal Scots, attached temporarily to the 25th Northumberland Fusiliers, had on the whole a less exciting time than their comrades with Lieut.-Colonel

622 GERMAN OFFENSIVE ON THE LYS [APR. 11

Stephenson, but the former company was only able to make good its escape across a bridge near the Laundries after hard fighting.

When night fell on the 10th April, the position of the Thirty-fourth Division was still very precarious. The design of the enemy to roll up its right flank was now supported by a similar movement on the other wing, for the Germans, by their capture of Messines Ridge and their penetration of Ploegsteert Wood on the 10th, threw the Twenty-fifth and Nineteenth Divisions into flux. Thus the Germans still had rosy chances of cutting off the whole division. After Armentières was abandoned, the line ran from Jesus Farm parallel with the Lys to a point north of the Armentières-Bailleul Road and was held from right to left by the 101st, 103rd, and 102nd Brigades. There was a certain amount of disorganisation, which affected particularly the 15th Royal Scots ; the remnants of "B" and "D" Companies were with Lieut.-Colonel Stephenson, "C" Company was with the 102nd Brigade, "A" Company, which under Captain Bryson was isolated during the crossing of the Lys, found itself under the command of the 103rd Brigade.

The most sensitive spot of the division was the right flank, for by midnight the 74th Brigade had been driven beyond Steenwerck, and it came as no surprise to Lieut.-Colonel Stephenson when he received orders to fall back to a defensive position on the south of Nieppe. This movement was performed with no little fatigue to the men, owing to the darkness and to the fact that the roads were congested with terror-stricken civilians who were seeking safety in flight to the north and west. Nieppe was reached by 3.20 A.M., Lieut.-Colonel Stephenson's force being distributed along the Bailleul-Armentières Railway, with the 16th Royal Scots in the post of honour on the right in line with " B " and " D " Companies of the 15th Royal Scots and the 11th Suffolks.

The 102nd and 103rd Brigades, particularly the former, were savagely beset by the enemy on the 11th April. The 102nd Brigade after lively skirmishing was compelled to retire, and about noon the Boches secured a lodgment in Pont de Nieppe. Fissures were appearing in the brigade line, and the 25th Northumberland Fusiliers and "C" Company of the 15th Royal Scots were for a time cut off, but by sheer pertinacity they extricated themselves and a magnificent stand by "C" Company at Touquet Parmentier took heavy toll of the Germans and materially lessened the strain on the brigade. The 103rd Brigade assisted the 102nd with telling counter-attacks, and in front of Papot Captain Bryson, with "A" Company of the 15th Royal Scots, cleverly checked the Germans and delayed their pursuit. Both brigades fell back on the Nieppe system, where for a spell the Boches were securely held, but some of them, having broken through the Twenty-fifth Division, suddenly appeared in the rear of the 101st Brigade near Papot. Brig.-General Chaplin of the 103rd Brigade, hurriedly collecting a mixed force including a number of Royal Scots, launched an immediate and successful counter-assault, temporarily sweeping the Germans from the rear of the division. Meanwhile Lieut.-Colonel Stephenson's troops had experienced an unusually tranquil time, and the 11th April closed with the weakened division still presenting an unbroken front to the foe.

Unfortunately the Nieppe system was too advanced to be safe, and orders were issued for the division to fall back during the evening to the neighbourhood of Pont d'Achelles. "A" Company of the 15th Royal Scots began its retirement while its commander, Captain

Bryson, was making a report to Major Osborne at battalion H.Q. Captain Bryson, completely ignorant that a retreat had been ordered, strolled back with his runner to the place where he had left his company; great was his astonishment when he walked into a party of Boches who disarmed him and placed him and his runner in a stable near their front line. The sentry was unusually casual for a Teuton, and when he left his post to chat with some comrades, Captain Bryson and his runner seized the opportunity to slip away; the latter unfortunately was shot, but the former succeeded in reaching his company.

The night of the 11th/12th April was one of sore travail for the men, not merely because of the fatigue of marching after two sleepless nights, but also because the Germans, anticipating some such movement, viciously barraged the railway, which was the track followed by the men during the retreat. The 16th Royal Scots sustained many casualties before they reached Trois Arbres, where the battalion formed up and marched in column of fours to a rendezvous north-west of Steenwerck Station. "C" Company of the 15th retired with the 25th Northumberland Fusiliers, but the survivors of the other companies were grouped together and ultimately occupied a position in the neighbourhood of La Crêche.

By this retreat the worn-out Thirty-fourth Division was established behind the 74th and 88th Brigades, but the menacing turn that events took on the 12th April further involved its units in anxious fighting. The Germans made such progress south of Bailleul that the 16th Royal Scots were sent at 9 A.M. to line the stream known as the Becque de la Flanche, which meandered past the east side of the town. Patrols sent out by Lieut.-Colonel Stephenson were hotly engaged by the enemy as soon as they left the Becque, and it was evident that the Germans were in considerable force near the stream. Several attacks on the 16th Royal Scots were repulsed without difficulty, but these were little more than demonstrations, under cover of which the Boches completed their preparations for a grand attack which was launched about 5 P.M. At that hour a deadly barrage dropped on the trenches of the Royal Scots, who were at the same time pestered by low-flying aircraft, which swept the Becque with gusts of machine-gun fire. The bombardment was succeeded by a lively infantry attack, which by weight of numbers drove the Royal Scots from their front. But the enemy's success was only transitory, for he was brought to a standstill a few hundred yards north of the Becque, and under the cloak of darkness the Royal Scots again pushed forward and reoccupied the line of the stream.

Dangerous hostile assaults were also launched against the left of the 88th Brigade, and the remnants of the 15th Royal Scots assisted in repulsing three of these near La Crêche. Once more, however, the enemy's persistence set this part of our line in motion, and at night the 15th Royal Scots were ordered to proceed to the vicinity of Bailleul. It was well-nigh impossible for regimental officers to tell the whereabouts of friend or foe; thus to "A" Company of the 15th the fall of the Very lights seemed to indicate that Boches were all around it, but covered by a high embankment it safely reached its destination between Bailleul Railway Station and the Mont de Lille. Nerves were beginning to be affected by the long strain of defensive fighting, and when some of the 15th Royal Scots were nearing Bailleul they were fired on by other British troops, fortunately without sustaining any harm.

On the night of the 12th/13th April we still entertained hopes of preserving Bailleul. The enemy during the morning of the 13th contented himself with a desultory shelling of our positions, and the respite was used by the Royal Scots to reorganise the different groups of men. At 3.30 P.M., after half an hour's intensive cannonade, the Germans swooped down on the Becque de la Flanche, and heedless of the losses caused by our fire forced the 16th Royal Scots to retire from the stream. The battalion was too weak to counter-attack and fell back to a line on the south-east side of Bailleul. At this time Lieut.-Colonel Stephenson had only two officers, 2nd Lieut. Storer and the Medical Officer, Captain R. Lyn Jones, but throughout the whole battle he received invaluable help from the R.S.M., A. B. Ness. The 15th Royal Scots withdrew through Bailleul and took up a position on a ridge behind the town, from which "D" Company was sent to the support of the 74th Brigade at the Mont de Lille.

Our defensive cordon was drawn close round Bailleul on the night of the 13th/14th April, and during the readjustments that were effected under cover of darkness the 15th and the 16th Royal Scots were sent up to the station at Bailleul and aligned along the railway. From midday on the 14th the new position became the target of German gunners but our casualties were few. About this time Lieut.-Colonel Stephenson was summoned to take over the command of the 101st Brigade, whose well-tried and esteemed leader, Brig.-General Gore, had been killed by a shell. The fragments of the 15th and the 16th Royal Scots were then formed into a composite battalion under the command of Major Osborne. Intermittent assaults were delivered by the enemy in the course of the day, the most dangerous being on the flanks of the 101st Brigade, but every effort was frustrated, and there still seemed a possibility that Bailleul would be saved.

War-weary and utterly spent, the men were relieved
on the night of the 14th/15th April by units of the
Fifty-ninth Division and concentrated near St Jans
Cappel. Silently they marched along, braced up by
visions not merely of rest but of new clothes and baths.
The first they had in a measure, but none of the Royal
Scots had a chance of indulging in the other luxuries,
for on the 15th April a sharp attack by the Germans
turned the flanks of the Fifty-ninth Division and carried
them past Bailleul. The Thirty-fourth Division thus
found itself again in the thick of the battle, and was
distributed in a position to cover St Jans Cappel.
Since this line gave the defence a wide field of fire,
the enemy prudently probed other parts of our position,
but a stout resistance checked all his attempts to make
progress.

The tide was now turning against the foe. The
arrival of new divisions solidified our defences, and
our guns functioned with such effect that on numerous
occasions the enemy was prevented from mustering for
an attack. In the face of our hardening resistance the
Boche infantry were growing tired and disheartened,
and they attempted no onset against the Royal Scots
till the afternoon of the 16th, when so deadly was
our rifle and machine-gun fire that at no time did
they come within assaulting distance. Before the
16th closed our men were cheered by the sharp reports
that betokened the comforting presence of the famous
French 75's, and it became known that our blue-
tunicked Allies were arriving in considerable numbers.
No infantry action of any importance disturbed the 17th,
at the end of which day the Royal Scots were relieved
in the front line and occupied a position in support
near Mont Noir. As far as the Thirty-fourth Division
was concerned no further change in the situation took

II   2 R

place, and on the night of the 21st/22nd April it was relieved by the One Hundred and Thirty-third French Division and assembled near Boeschepe, where the remnants of the 15th and the 16th Royal Scots[1] were billeted.

The Battle of the Lys proved to be the last, but certainly not the least glorious chapter in the war record of the 15th and the 16th Royal Scots.   For twelve days and nights they had never been free from the pressure of the enemy, but throughout the manifold torments and anxieties of this chaotic period they had never surrendered to despair, and had at all times met the foe with unflinching resolution.   Their fine capacity for giving their best when matters were at their worst more than offset the skill and determination of their opponents, and they were eminently worthy of the praise which Sir Douglas Haig gave to the Thirty-fourth Division for its "high standard of efficiency, discipline, and courage on the part of both officers and men."[2]

3. Bailleul was a petty prize compared with Hazebrouck, but the Germans, realising that their attack in this neighbourhood had reached its high-water mark, began from the 16th April to concentrate on driving us from the ridge of hills commanding Ypres from the south.   A victory here would secure not merely Ypres but Dunkirk and Calais, and the effect of these captures on public opinion in Britain might dispose the despondent Allies to open negotiations for peace.

[1] The war diary of the 15th Battalion does not include the casualty list. The casualties of the 16th Royal Scots were: Officers, Captain N. W. Rawson, Lieut. F. C. Urquhart, 2nd Lieuts. A. S. McKay, W. C. Mollag, and G. Turnbull, killed. Captain P. Bayliss, Lieut. T. M. Miller and 2nd Lieut. A. McKenzie, wounded. Major A. E. Warr, 2nd Lieuts. W. Lawrie, A. Robinson, and H. Tonathy, missing. The losses in other ranks, in killed, wounded, and missing, amounted to five hundred and fifty-four out of a total of seven hundred and eighty-five.

[2] *The Thirty-fourth Division*, by Lieut.-Colonel J. Shakespeare, p. 245.

The Ninth Division on the northern wing of the Lys position was not without anxiety during the first days of the struggle. Conscious that it was responsible for the protection of the hinge of the famous Salient, it was aware that the Germans, screened from observation by Zandvoorde Ridge, were favourably situated to launch an attack on Klein Zillebeke Spur and Hill 60, from which vantage points they could threaten the communications of the Salient. Consequently unremitting vigilance was demanded of the battalions from the time when they entered the line near Hollebeke on the night of the 3rd/4th April.

The 9th April was uneventful on the divisional front, but the night of the 9th/10th involved the 11th and the 12th Royal Scots in an exhausting and disturbing march. This was owing to the fact that the Ninth had to take over the northern portion of the front of the Nineteenth Division, and since no time was available for exploring the new area, which consisted mainly of a dismal waste of shell-holes without any distinguishing landmark, commanding officers and adjutants were kept in a state of tension till they were satisfied that their units had not gone astray; it was a proof of good leadership and discipline that in spite of a purgatorial gas bombardment the battalions maintained their cohesion, and reached their proper positions shortly after daybreak on the 10th.

On this day the battle extended northwards, and the enemy in the afternoon attacked the right wing of the Ninth Division south of the Ypres-Comines Canal. The garrison at this point consisted of the 11th Royal Scots who, utterly exhausted by their experiences of the night, had found no opportunity of reconnoitring the ground in the vicinity of their posts. The enemy's rush surprised the outposts, all of which were overwhelmed before they had time to offer resistance, with the exception of a platoon commanded by Lieut. MacGregor. After a brief, stiff fight this platoon was overcome, and the Germans bore down on the next position where, luckily, the garrison was alert and halted the Boches by a shrivelling fire. At the same time the enemy crushed in the front of the Nineteenth Division, and then sought to turn the right flank of the 11th Royal Scots by an advance against the White Château; but Brig.-General Croft was ready for this stroke, and two companies of the 12th Royal Scots arrived at the château in time to repel the foe. Beyond that point the right flank was still bare, and two other units were sent up by the division to safeguard this wing. This, the sensitive point of the division, naturally became the hostile objective, and before daybreak on the 11th April the Germans endeavoured to break through on the right of the 12th Royal Scots near White Château, but their concentration was observed, and the attack was broken up by relentless artillery, machine-gun and rifle fire, the enemy bolting for shelter in terror-stricken panic. This rebuff kept the Germans quiet for several days, but the position of the Ninth Division was menaced by the enemy's capture of Messines Ridge on the 11th April.

From the 12th till the 15th April the front line and hinterland of the division were frequently and systematically shelled, many casualties being sustained; but our men felt that they were masters of the situation, and there was no doubt that our patrols were much more enterprising than those of the enemy. On the night of the 14th/15th April, Lieut. Tyler with a few men of the 11th Royal Scots invaded a Boche post near the canal and seized a prisoner. Stung to retaliation, the Germans, on the afternoon of the 15th, tried to rush a post held by the 11th, but they were easily repulsed.

Our line in the Salient and immediately to the south of it was becoming increasingly vulnerable owing to the enemy's progress at the Lys; it now formed a very pronounced bulge. Prudence demanded that our line should be flattened out and shortened, and on the decision being taken that it should be drawn closer to Ypres, the left flank of the Ninth Division was swung back. The White Château and Klein Zillebeke were given up, but Hill 60 was retained. The new line to which the 27th Brigade had to retire consisted principally of a fringe of posts facing south-east, so skilfully camouflaged that Brig.-General Croft and his Brigade-Major, Captain Duke, only located them through the latter falling head first into one. During the night of the 15th/16th when these adjustments were carried out, our patrols were so daring that the Germans never suspected that a retreat was in progress, and the 27th Brigade drew back without any interference.

Since the 9th April the Germans had won a series of victories more remarkable for brilliance than for profit; without having gained any important strategical objective they had considerably lengthened their line. They sought to improve their situation by widening their front of attack, but their efforts against the Belgian front north of Ypres and the British positions at Givenchy and Hinges on the 17th and 18th April respectively were unsuccessful. Then on the 25th they concentrated on the Kemmel sector.

In this quarter the line of the Ninth Division ran from Lagache Farm to Eikhop Farm, the right front from Lagache to Black Cot being held by the 12th Royal Scots; the 6th K.O.S.B. were in support and the 11th Royal Scots in reserve at Ouderdom. The

II   2 R 2

right flank was still the weak spot, being open to attack from Messines Ridge, and an operation for the recapture of Wytschaete was planned for the 26th April, but it was forestalled by the German offensive on the 25th.   On the eve of that event French troops were the neighbours of the 12th Royal Scots and held a low ridge running east from Mont Kemmel to Spanbroekmolen, which overlooked the trenches of the Royal Scots.

A vehement bombardment with gas and H.E. opened on the whole area of the Ninth Division at 2.30 A.M. and was followed at 5 A.M. by a general advance of the German infantry, who had been enabled to complete their concentration without disturbance owing to a thick enveloping mist, which prevented our men from seeing more than a few yards in front of them.   The barrage fell with such crushing force on the support trenches that two platoons of the 12th Royal Scots were virtually annihilated.   Happily the front trenches had not been so brutally ravaged, and though the Germans, suddenly emerging out of the fog, in their first rush broke through between "C" Company on the right and "B" in the centre, the 12th Royal Scots quickly recovered from their surprise, and fiercely counter-attacking, drove them back.   Subsequent assaults against the front of the battalion were repulsed with enormous losses to the Boches, and the 12th Royal Scots sent a cheerful report to Brig.-General Croft that all was well.   Lieut. Shaw, the commander of "B" Company, was severely wounded, but when he was carried away on a stretcher at 7.30 A.M. he consoled himself with the thought that the enemy had been soundly beaten.

The security of the 12th Royal Scots, however, wholly depended upon the ability of the French to keep the all-important ridge dominating their right flank, and when our blue-clad Allies were driven from this position

the Boches were advantageously placed to roll up the
Royal Scots from the right.	Pouring down towards
Kemmel and turning north they cut off the whole of
the 12th Royal Scots and part of the 6th K.O.S.B. in
support.	Hordes of field-grey figures swept down from
all sides on the devoted battalion, which fought till it
was practically wiped out.	A few groups favoured by
fortune cleft their way through the German ring and
made a perilous escape to the Cheapside Line, but the
great majority of the 12th Royal Scots fell at their posts.

Their heroic stand was not in vain; it gained time
for their comrades in the rear to hold the Cheapside
Line, along the road running north from the west of
Kemmel village, to which the remnants of the 6th
K.O.S.B. had fallen back.	Two companies of the
11th Royal Scots also hastened to this position, which,
though overlooked from Mont Kemmel, was stoutly
held against every attempt of the enemy to capture
it.	Relief came to the hard-pressed remnants of the
27th Brigade at night, and the 11th and the 12th Royal
Scots [1] assembled near Poperinghe on the 26th; the
latter consisted of a mere sprinkling of officers and
men, for the flower of the battalion lay dead on the
disastrous battlefield.

Happily the possession of Kemmel Hill gave the
Germans a smaller advantage than they had hoped.	It

[1] Between the 4th and 21st April the losses of the 11th were : one officer
(2nd Lieut. J. Macgregor) and ten men killed, three officers and fifty-four
men wounded, sixty-nine men missing.	Those of the 12th for the same
period were : thirty-nine men killed, six officers and one hundred and eleven
men wounded, eight men missing.	From the 21st to the 27th April, the
casualties of the 11th were one officer and seven men killed, four officers
and fifty-six men wounded, three men missing ; those of the 12th were :
one officer and three men killed, three officers and fifty-four men wounded,
fourteen officers and five hundred and two men missing.

It was later ascertained that among the dead were Captain W. Skinner
one of the most notable officers in the division, Lieuts. G. G. Callender
W. H. Furley, and 2nd Lieut. H. R. Cunningham.

formed only one of a series of hills, and the discomfiture of our troops in the Salient could not be effected until the enemy carried all the heights of the Kemmel-Mont des Cats Ridge.   Strive as they might, the Boches could make no progress beyond Kemmel, and at the end of April Ypres and the Channel ports were tolerably safe.   The Germans had been lured on by the prospect of substantial prizes, all of which at the last moment were withheld from their grasp.

CHAPTER XXXV

THE TURN OF THE TIDE

May to August 1918

Situation at end of April. 15th and 16th Royal Scots disbanded. German Attack on Chemin des Dames. Location of Royal Scots Battalions. Operations by 2nd Royal Scots near Locon. German gas attack near Locon, 20th May. 4th and 7th Royal Scots in France. Beginning of Allied counter-attack, July 1918. 8th Royal Scots at the Bois de Coutron. 9th and 13th Royal Scots near Buzancy. Action of 1st August.

THE German success in March and April amounted to no more than pyrrhic victories; their positions at the Somme and the Lys formed difficult and expensive salients to defend, and could only prove of value if they could be used as a jumping-off ground for other offensives. Lively fighting near Villers-Bretonneux at the end of April seemed to presage a new attack on Amiens, but the net result of several days' strife in this area was the defeat of the foe and the improvement of our position. Nevertheless the enemy at the beginning of summer still possessed the greater store of reserves, and it was certain that he would continue to attack while the advantage of strength rested with him.

The tendency in Britain was to exaggerate the achievements of the enemy, but though the political leaders exhibited a surprising degree of agitation in extending the scope of the Military Service Act and in introducing conscription into Ireland, the majority of people, to their credit, maintained the national reputation for serenity during a crisis.

In France, the soldierly pride of all ranks in the deeds of their regiments and divisions was a sign that the morale of the army was sound. The British forces, man for man, considered themselves superior to the enemy. The German machine-gunner was never mentioned except in terms of the utmost respect, but the German rifleman was contemptuously spoken of as a poor creature, who dared to advance only when there was nobody to oppose him. This was no doubt an exaggeration, but the belief was general throughout the British Army that all the best soldiers of Germany were in the machine-gun companies, and the experiences of our troops at the Somme and the Lys in 1918 seemed to confirm that impression.

Nevertheless, at the beginning of the summer of 1918, it was impossible for the leaders of the Allies to regard the situation on the Western front with complacence. The Germans were dangerous as long as they had the advantage in reserves, and their nearness to vital strategic centres like Amiens and Hazebrouck demanded unremitting vigilance on the part of our troops. The communications of the Allies had been damaged by the enemy's advance, particularly in northern France, and a scheme of railway construction was undertaken without delay for the purpose of maintaining the mobility of the armies of the Allies. Everywhere along the front, squads of men were busy working on new lines of defences, but in spite of incessant toil few of these at the end of May were comparable in strength with those that had been overrun by the enemy in March and April.

So colossal had been the British losses that virtually every division in France was far below its establishment, and troops from home and from Palestine were hurriedly transported to the scene of danger. Many battalions had been practically demolished and there were not sufficient drafts to restore all to fighting strength. Lowland Scotland had been denuded of men, and was unable to make good the losses of the ten battalions of Royal Scots serving on the Western front. The whole of the Thirty-fourth Division was reduced to cadre strength, a new division being formed later from units that arrived from India and from Palestine. The cadres of the 15th and the 16th Royal Scots and of the other units of the old division were employed for some months near Lumbres in assisting with the training of American levies, and during that period strong friendships were formed between the Scots and the Americans which remain among the cherished memories of the war. When this work was finished, about the end of July, the troops were distributed among the various battalions of the Regiment in France. Officers and men realised that all units could not be kept up to strength and they accepted the order for disbandment with dignity, but their soldier's pride was pierced when they knew that the battalions with which they had linked up their personalities were no longer to fight in the forefront of the battle; their feelings were akin to those which torture a sailor when he sees his well-loved ship swallowed by devouring waves.

The general policy of the British was dictated by circumstances; it was one of active defence. Training and the construction of defences were carried on at the same time, while troops in the line took every precaution to maintain their positions intact not merely by constant alertness but by harrying the enemy by means of raids.

After April the Boches launched no more attacks against the British. The considerations which actuated the German General Staff at this time have not yet been authoritatively disclosed, but on the 27th May the enemy delivered a new attack on the Chemin des Dames.   Hitherto the French had been inclined to attribute our misfortunes at the Somme and the Lys to a lack of tenacity on the part of the British, and seemed by their attitude to suggest that they themselves were unmolested because the enemy was conscious that any attack against them was doomed to disaster.   This feeling of complacent superiority was rudely dispelled by the success of the Germans on the 27th May, when the French abandoned more ground in one day than had hitherto been yielded on the Western front.   Four French and four British divisions were holding the line when the blow fell, and though the latter had been in the very heart of the struggle during March and April they put up a more tenacious resistance than the former.   The loss of what had been deemed an impregnable position covered our Allies with confusion, and so rapid was their retreat that the phrase, " Ils ne passeront pas," meant to indicate the invincible resolution of the French, was chucklingly given a less palatable significance by the British.   The Germans carried their advance up to the waters of the Marne, and stirred us anew with fears for the safety of Paris, but they had in fact shot their bolt.   Americans were now in France in considerable numbers and with their assistance the German rush was stopped.

Thus during May and June the British troops experienced a period of unwonted, if watchful, repose. The battalions of the Royal Scots were scattered along the whole front.   North of the Somme near Aveluy, in undulating country dotted with the ruins of villages, lay the 17th Battalion, which in spite of the exigencies of trench warfare managed to put in a useful spell of training.   There it remained till the beginning of July, when it proceeded north to a sector near Mont Kemmel. In August it was favoured with an opportunity for training and for musketry practice at Eecke, and during this month Lieut.-Colonel Heathcote left for a tour of duty at home, his successor as C.O. being Lieut.-Colonel A. G. Scougal.

The rolling country round Hamelincourt, rather more than six miles south of Arras, was the location of the 5/6th Battalion, which, in a region totally different from the flats of the Nieuport sector, ably sustained its reputation for the execution of daring raids. On the 11th/12th June 2nd Lieut. Veitch and sixteen men, leaving the front trenches at midnight, crossed No - Man's - Land, and regardless of machine - gun fire rushed a hostile post and closed with the garrison; three Germans contrived to make their escape, but two were killed and the other was wounded and captured, while the Royal Scots had only four men slightly wounded. More than a week later a small party of the battalion under Sergeant Macdonald drove some Boches out of a post from which they had inconvenienced our men by persistent bombing. There was general joy when Lieut.-Colonel Fraser, completely recovered from his wounds, returned on the 20th June to command the battalion, which had by this time established a marked superiority over the enemy, who never ventured to do anything more enterprising than throw a few grenades.

The 13th Battalion was in the vicinity of Arras, where the passiveness of the foe gave it an opportunity to recover from the crippling wounds suffered on the 28th March. Its gallant and tried leader, Lieut.-Colonel Hannay, who during his active service had continually to struggle against illness, was obliged in April, through bad health, to relinquish the command, which was taken over by Lieut.-Colonel J. A. Turner, only twenty-six years of age, whose engaging personality and absolute fearlessness had endeared him to all ranks and won him a name that was honoured throughout the Regiment. The battalion's war record from May 1916 to April 1918, during which period Lieut.-Colonel Hannay was in command, was not surpassed by that of any other unit in the British Army, and no small share of the credit is due to the officer whose skill and unflagging attention were responsible for the efficiency of the battalion.

Patrols constantly harassed the enemy, and on two notable occasions the 13th Royal Scots distinguished themselves.   At 3.45 A.M. on the 16th May "A" Company, less one platoon and two Lewis gun sections, led by 2nd Lieuts. Ross and Smith, under cover of an artillery and trench-mortar barrage burst into the German front trenches and killed at least twelve of the enemy, and having sustained comparatively few casualties,[1] returned with seven prisoners to its own lines.   Unhappily 2nd Lieut. P. G. C. Smith, who had shown fine dash during the raid, was cut off and killed.   But on the whole, this was a lucky day for the battalion, for a hostile aeroplane was shot down by a machine-gun.   A more comprehensive raid took place on the 21st June, in which the whole unit assisted by a party of sappers took part.   On a front of 750 yards the German trenches were penetrated to a depth of 500 yards, and as they advanced the Royal Scots and sappers methodically destroyed all dug-outs and machine-gun emplacements.   Many of the Boches were taken unawares and killed before they had time to offer resistance, and several more must have lost their lives in the dug-outs that were demolished ; ten prisoners were brought back, while the Royal Scots lost six killed (including 2nd Lieut. W. A. West), twenty wounded (including two officers), and four missing.

[1] Nine killed, sixteen wounded, two missing.

Brig.-General A. F. Lumsden, D.S.O., The Royal Scots.

[To face p. 640.

On the 1st June the Fifteenth Division was joined by the 9th Royal Scots, whose sojourn near St Venant with the Sixty-first Division was, since the 16th April, mainly uneventful.   The battalion on its arrival in the Arras area was attached to the 46th Brigade.   Within easy reach was its old companion in the Fifty-first Division, the 8th Battalion, which since May had been busy with pick and shovel improving our defences near Roclincourt.

On the 24th June the Regiment as well as the Fifteenth Division sustained a heavy loss, when Brig.-General A. F. Lumsden of the 46th Brigade was killed by a shell.

The 2nd Battalion was established near Locon, where it remained till the beginning of August.   The front line being not entirely satisfactory, it was decided to improve it by advancing it to a hedge near Pont Tournant, which was held by the enemy.   This assault, carried out at 4.10 A.M. on the 2nd May by three platoons of " C," two of " A," and one of " B " Company, was almost entirely successful.   At a small cost[1] the hedge was gained and consolidated, and two prisoners were captured, but a machine-gun post in an orchard baffled the most desperate efforts of " B " Company. This post, established so close to our lines that it could not be dealt with by artillery, caused the Royal Scots intense annoyance, so " A " Company on the right made preparations to attack it on the 4th May.

After the orchard had been bombarded for three hours by Stokes mortars, " A " Company, advancing at 4 A.M., endeavoured to put the post out of action by a bombing attack, but at the same time the Boches put down a violent barrage, causing considerable losses

---

[1] There were two officer casualties, 2nd Lieut. W. T. Philip, killed, and 2nd Lieut. A. M. Scott, wounded.

among the ranks of the centre and left companies. Meanwhile "A" Company was savagely beset in the orchard, and a bitter contest was waged for nearly three hours. In spite of herculean efforts the Germans succeeded in occupying only two posts on the right flank; otherwise the Royal Scots maintained their positions intact. "A" Company, though it failed to clear the machine-gun post in the orchard, had anticipated a Boche operation for the capture of Pont Tournant, and by its rifle and Lewis-gun fire stopped the hostile advance. The garrisons of the two left posts of "A" Company were killed or wounded to a man, but the heap of dead Germans in front of the outpost line was a grisly proof of the effectiveness of the resistance of the Royal Scots, who in killed and wounded lost fifty-one men; one officer, Captain J. C. Myers, was killed.

The revenge of the enemy came on the 20th May, when a gas bombardment incapacitated more than half the battalion while it was holding the line near Oblinghem. The bombardment lasted for just half an hour, during which time the troops wore their respirators, and at first it was believed that nothing untoward had happened, since few men reported at the dressing station. But after 9 A.M. an alarm was roused by the throngs of men that besieged the battalion's medical staff, and Lieut.-Colonel Gillatt immediately issued orders for every man to don his respirator. A personal inspection by the C.O. revealed a most disquieting state of affairs, the trenches being strewn with rifles and equipment, which the stricken men had cast away; all his company officers, except two, were blinded by the effects of the gas and were in consequence wholly impotent. The gas, it was clear, had been absorbed some time after the bombardment, when the men had removed their respirators, and though they had later replaced them, the damage had been done. Fortunately the gas was not lethal, but for the time twelve officers and three hundred and sixty-three men were rendered totally unfit and had to be sent to hospital. Our lines for a space were almost stripped bare of defenders, but luckily the Boches appeared to have no inkling of what had happened, for they made no attack.

After this catastrophe the battalion was relieved, and a large draft of over 500 men, including many from the 16th Royal Scots, restored it to a satisfactory strength. On the 25th May Lieut.-Colonel Gillatt left for a tour of duty at home, and was succeeded at the beginning of June by Lieut.-Colonel J. C. Wemyss, but the latter had to give up the command on account of ill-health, and his successor was Lieut.-Colonel M. Henderson, who had served with the battalion in the first days of the war. Another of its old officers, Captain Strange, also rejoined the unit on the 8th July.

The Locon sector was never an easy one, because it was frequently dosed with gas, but in patrol work the 2nd Royal Scots had the advantage of the enemy, and on the 15th July Lieut. Somerville with Lance-Corporal A. Macdonald, Sergeant Fraser, and Privates MacIver and Wilson silently crawled through a belt of corn and captured four Germans. A rumour having arisen that the enemy had abandoned some of his front posts, the 2nd Royal Scots, on the 5th August, sent forward patrols during daylight to establish contact with the enemy ; but there had been no evacuation, and two men were killed and one wounded before this was discovered. It was now known that the enemy was anxious about his whole position in France, and the battalion was in the best of trim when, on the 7th August, it was transferred to Tangry.

The 11th and the 12th Battalions were despatched

II   2 S

from the neighbourhood of Poperinghe at the beginning of May to Lumbres near St Omer, whence after a spell of rest and training they took over trenches near Meteren. The Germans by their occupation of the high ground were able to scan all the country to the west of the village, so that all movements of our troops had to be carried out during the hours of darkness. The country-side, having come only recently within the war zone, under the glowing summer sun presented an aspect delightfully different from the grim scarred battle-fields to which the men had hitherto been accustomed; up to the horizon spread amber fields of waving corn flecked with the deep crimson of poppies, while red-tiled farmhouses, virtually intact, afforded comfortable, though insecure, company and battalion H.Q. The high corn, almost ready for the sickle, offered scope for enterprising scouting, of which full advantage was taken. The Boches were constantly harried, and during June several prisoners were captured by our men. A patrol, commanded by Lieut. Keen of the 11th Royal Scots, brought in three Germans on the 20th June, and on the night of the 11th/12th July two parties of the 12th Royal Scots under 2nd Lieuts. Driver and Tatham captured five more. A raid planned by the 11th Royal Scots for the 12th had unfortunately to be abandoned, owing to the leader, Lieut. Cavanagh, being killed just when the party was ready to start, but our successes far outnumbered our failures.

The nervousness of the enemy was increased when he was driven out of Meteren by the Highland and South African Brigades, and early on the 25th July he endeavoured to balance matters by raiding our lines, which were then manned by the 6th K.O.S.B. and the 11th Royal Scots; but the net result of this effort was that the Germans left two corpses and two unwounded prisoners with the Royal Scots. Another hostile raid followed early on the 26th July, but though the Germans got a footing in the trenches of the Royal Scots, they were expelled by an immediate counter-attack, nine prisoners being taken. After this rebuff the enemy contented himself with a passive defence.

Among the battalions sent to the Western front from the East were, as we have seen, the 4th and the 7th Royal Scots, who arrived at Marseilles on the 17th April. On leaving the port the battalions near the end of April assembled in the vicinity first of Abbeville, then of Aire, where they were given an opportunity for training. Officers and men listened with great interest to lectures by staff officers on conditions in the Western front, but they would not have been human had they not been slightly amused when one staff officer admonished them to devote their time to the practice of open warfare tactics, since for months they had been engaged in one of the few theatres where open warfare was a matter of performance and not merely of instruction.

After the ceaseless sunshine and burning heat of Palestine the troops suffered severely at first from the rigours of the French climate, and though the season was verging on summer, the men, accommodated in tents, passed cold, shivering nights, but as they gradually became acclimatised, their health remained more consistently good than it had done in the hot lands of the Near East. On the 13th May the long and successful service of Lieut.-Colonel Peebles with the 7th Royal Scots in the field came to an end; he had had a longer experience of continuous command of his battalion during the war than any other C.O. of the Royal Scots, and he had more than earned the relaxation of a tour of home duty to enable him to recover from the strain on his health caused by thirty-four months' front-line service. His departure was a personal loss not merely to his battalion but to the brigade and the division. Reluctantly the 7th Royal Scots bade him farewell, but they found consolation in the fact that his successor was another old friend, Lieut.-Colonel W. T. Ewing, who had already demonstrated sterling qualities of leadership in the Palestine campaign.

At the beginning of May the Fifty-second Division took over a sector on the Vimy Ridge near Mont St Eloi, the ruined tower of which remained a familiar landmark until the war was approaching its conclusion. Here the 4th and the 7th Royal Scots underwent their first spell of trench warfare in France, and they found that though the bombardments were heavier than those to which they had been normally subjected in the East, this was counterbalanced by the better protection of the trenches.

Foiled before Paris in July by the resistance of French and American troops, the Germans sheered off in the direction of Rheims, on which they opened a violent attack on 15th July. They succeeded in crossing the Marne, but there they were firmly held, and on the 18th July, General Mangin, delivering the first blow of the counter-offensive, hurled them back across the river.

The pressure of the Allies was not relaxed, and four British divisions, including the Fifty-first and Fifteenth, were sent south to assist the French; all four divisions were in the XXII. Corps under Lieut.-General Sir A. Godley. In the sector concerned, the Germans were caught in a salient with its front facing south-west, and the Fifty-first and Sixty-second Divisions were detailed to attack on the east side of this salient, while a few days later the Fifteenth and Thirty-fourth Divisions were despatched to operate on the west side of it.

In accordance with these plans the Fifty-first Division left the southern portion of the Vimy Ridge sector on the 11th July, and the men found unusual entertainment in a journey which took them through the outskirts of Paris. On the 15th the 8th Royal Scots, who vastly enjoyed their railway trip round Paris, detrained near Romilly, whence they marched to Chantemarle. For men carrying full kit, the march along switchback roads under the intense heat of a glorious French summer was a severe test of stamina and will-power, and the pioneers had cause to plume themselves on the fact that in four days, during which they covered 100 kilometres, not a single man fell out. On the 19th May they bivouacked at cross-roads near Brugny; setting out next morning at 4 o'clock they marched through Epernay to a point north of Bellevue, a total distance of 20 kilometres. They were now within the trough of the Ardre river, a wide and shallow valley studded with thick copses on both sides, where clustered numerous villages and farmhouses, many of which were improvised into defence-posts by the enemy's machine-gunners.

The position of the Germans was extremely precarious. The chord of the salient stretched approximately from Soissons to Rheims and its nose lay near Château Thierry. The aim of the French was not merely to flatten out this salient, but by attacking it from its eastern and western angles to cut off all the enemy between the Rivers Vesle and Marne. Accordingly, on the 20th July, the Fifty-first Division on a front from Pourcy to Paradis, with the Sixty-second Division on its right and French troops on its left, was set to advance along the Ardre and take a line which included the Bois de Coutron and the Bois des Eclisses. The Bois de Coutron formed the chief obstacle; its tough undergrowth clung to one like the tentacles of an octopus

II   2 S 2

and made it easy for the defenders to lay ambuscades for their assailants.

The news received on the 19th that the Germans in this neighbourhood were on the point of retiring turned out to be fallacious ; the enemy could not afford to give ground here until his troops, withdrawing from the nose of the salient, were within safe distance of the Vesle. Thus on the 20th the Fifty-first Division met with a hot reception, but though it could not secure its final objective, it made good progress by establishing itself along the road from La Neuville through Les Haies to the Ardre. Fighting continued during the next two days without leading to any material change in the situation.

The 8th Royal Scots on the 21st July were brought up under heavy shell fire to a wood just west of Nanteuil, and on the following morning the whole of the battalion, with the exception of " B " Company, took over the front line in the Bois de Coutron under the direction of the 153rd Brigade. " B " Company was temporarily attached to the 7th Argylls, and along with the sappers laboured till midnight cutting tracks through the wood. It was then ordered to take part in an attack by the 154th Brigade at 6 A.M. on the 23rd, the object of which was to clear the Ardre valley from the Bois de L'Aulnay to the hamlet of Espilly, and the task of " B " Company of the 8th Royal Scots, sandwiched between the 7th Argylls and the 4th Gordons, was to assist in sweeping up the western defences of Espilly near the Bois de Coutron.

The operation was an uncommonly difficult one, for the valley bristled with copses, coombs, farms, mills, banks, and sunken roads from which hostile machine-guns covered every approach. Our portion of the Bois de Coutron was daily drenched with gas, and the shell fire was as devastating as it had been at High Wood in 1916 and the Chemical Works in 1917. It is therefore

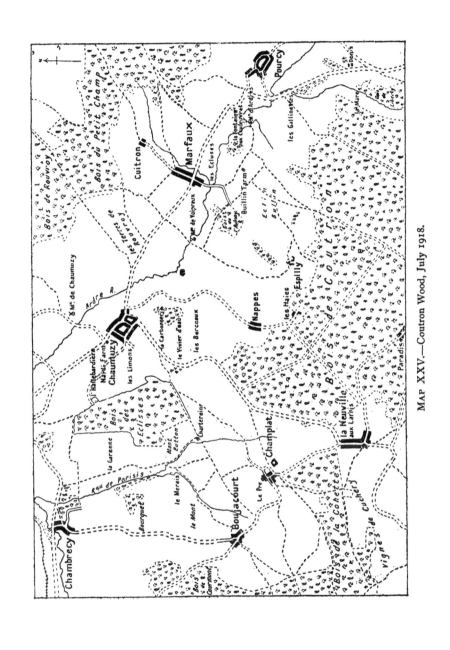

MAP XXV.—Coutron Wood, July 1918.

not surprising that the attack, which imposed enormous physical hardships on the men, was not entirely successful. After stiff fighting the 152nd Brigade carried the Bois de L'Aulnay, but Espilly defied all our efforts. In a day of mixed fortune, " B " Company of the 8th Royal Scots won deserved renown by being the only unit to reach its objective on the left of the attack. The two centre platoons were smashed by the German barrage, but the right platoon under 2nd Lieut. R. P. Fraser and the left under 2nd Lieut. J. F. Crawford broke through the zone of shell fire, and undeterred by the fact that they had no friends on their flanks, reached their objective in the Bois de Coutron to the west of Espilly ; during their advance they outflanked and destroyed two machine-gun nests, capturing twenty-eight prisoners. They clung to the position that they had so gallantly won for some time, but when Captain Pringle realised that the Germans were in force on his rear and that there was no hope of the Argylls and the Gordons arriving to assist him, he withdrew his small force to its original position to prevent it from being cut off. Eighty casualties, including two officers,[1] left him with only the skeleton of a company.

During the night our positions in the forest were violently bombarded, and hostile aeroplanes, flying low, added to the discomfort of our troops by dropping bombs and firing through the trees. The 153rd Brigade was relieved by French troops, and the 8th Royal Scots were moved back to a wood near Bellevue. Ordinary pioneer work was resumed but was interrupted on the 26th, when the battalion was sent to hold the spur of the Forêt de la Montagne de Rheims, and it was in reserve during an attack by the division on the 27th. By that date the

---

[1] Lieut. J. O. Chisholm died of wounds, and 2nd Lieut. J. Oliver was wounded.

Lieut.-Colonel J. A. TURNER, D.S.O., M.C., 13th Battalion, The Royal Scots.

[To face p. 650.

enemy had begun to decamp, and the division made such rapid progress that by the 30th it was established near Chambrecy. Once the Germans commenced to retreat the pioneers were not required for ordinary infantry work, and from the 28th till the 30th July they were employed in constructing roads to Chaumuzy. The division was relieved on the 1st August and was sent back to the Arras area. For the 8th Royal Scots the adventure in Champagne had been full of interest and proved not to be unduly costly, the total casualties of the battalion amounting to one hundred and nine.

The main pressure on the Soissons-Rheims-Château Thierry salient came from the attack on the west side, in which the Fifteenth and Thirty-fourth Divisions took part. The 13th Royal Scots, leaving the Arras sector on the 16th July, were taken by train to Liancourt. After sampling the billets of the hinterland they relieved, on the 22nd July, American troops in the front line in the hilly country to the south-west of Soissons. The movements of the 9th Royal Scots were similar, and on the 22nd they relieved a battalion of the United States Army in support near Chazelle. Both battalions were in the district which had been traversed by the 2nd Royal Scots in September 1914.

The first attack of the division was made on the 23rd July, but neither the 9th nor the 13th Royal Scots were engaged in this action in which the Germans resisted with great stubbornness. Both battalions took over parts of the front line on the evening of the 23rd; their positions were subjected to very heavy shell fire, and the 13th Royal Scots had to mourn the loss of their brilliant young C.O., Lieut.-Colonel Turner, who with Lieut. Shaw was killed on the 26th by a shell which dropped into battalion H.Q. The superstitious no doubt would accept it as confirmation of the evil luck attaching to the number 13, that the 13th Battalion lost more commanding officers by death than any other of the Royal Scots.

The 9th and the 13th Royal Scots went into action on the 1st August in an attack on the German positions near Villemontoire. Zero was fixed at 9 A.M., when the barrage was to open, and five minutes later the infantry assault was to begin. The 9th Royal Scots had French troops on their right, and in order to preserve liaison a platoon from " B " Company was detailed to act along with these. The enemy was strongly entrenched on wooded hills, which " D " and " C " Companies were to take, after which " A " was to pass through " C " and carry another wood to the rear. " D " Company and the liaison platoon assembled behind a hedge, and the remaining companies formed up in a quarry held by " C " Company.

Unfortunately our barrage was ragged and desultory, and the assailing companies were almost massacred by the storm of shells and machine-gun bullets which deluged their ranks. The French troops on the right never stirred from their positions, and the 9th Royal Scots had no support in their attempt to achieve the impossible. Of the liaison platoon only two men returned. Captain R. M. Murray, the one unwounded officer of " D " and " C " Companies, rallied the few survivors, and with the help of Sergeants J. Fraser and K. M. Baird reformed them in their original positions. The quarry, being under direct hostile observation, was a death-trap, and the enemy's shells, pitching into it, added greatly to the casualty list. The stretcher-bearers, conspicuous among whom were Privates Clougherty and Campbell, frequently braved the enemy's murderous fire to bring in the wounded, and the battalion runners, as usual, allowed no dangers

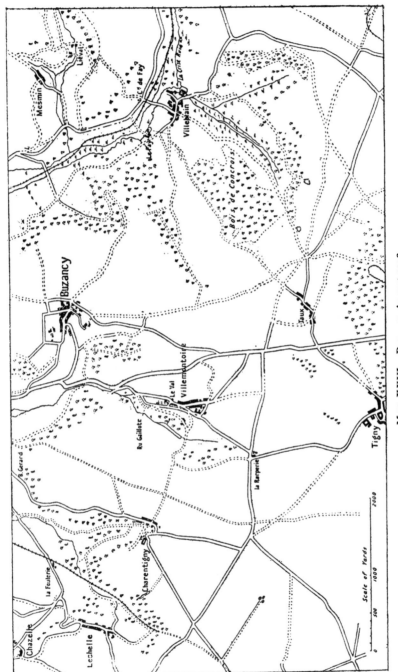

MAP XXVI.—Buzancy, August 1918.

to prevent them from delivering their messages and reports.

The 4/5th Black Watch and the 5th Gordons were hurriedly despatched to reinforce the weak garrison of the Royal Scots in the front line, and at 3.30 P.M. "A" Company was ordered to make another attack. The enemy's machine-gun bullets swept across No-Man's-Land like sheets of driving rain, and once again the Royal Scots, who alone ventured to essay the forlorn hope, were mown down before they had gone forward 100 yards. The casualties of the 9th Royal Scots were appalling, one hundred and twenty killed, three hundred wounded, and thirteen missing, a total which represented about 80 per cent. of the battalion strength, and many of their best officers were slain: of "A" Company, Lieut. F. M. Ross, 2nd Lieuts. T. H. Lawrie, W. M. Robertson, J. C. Jackson; of "C," Lieut. J. D. Willisen, 2nd Lieut. J. M. Black; and of "D," Lieuts. T. Stevenson and D. A. Bannatyne were killed, while five officers were wounded. After nightfall the fragments of "C" and "D" Companies were relieved, but "A" and "B" remained in the line.

This attack was supported in the north by a raid on the German trenches by "B" and "C" Companies of the 13th Royal Scots; at a cost of only nineteen casualties they killed at least fifteen Germans, destroyed four machine-gun emplacements, and captured one prisoner.

It was no small satisfaction to the 9th Royal Scots to learn that the attacks, which had cost them so high a price in life without any apparent result, had not been in vain. By dawn, on the 2nd August, the Germans were in full retreat. The 9th Royal Scots were in reserve, while the 13th pressed on without encountering opposition to a line 500 yards east of Mesnin. On the 3rd August the division was relieved and returned to the familiar haunts of Arras.

The French were profoundly impressed by the magnificent fighting qualities shown by the Fifteenth Division, and have given graceful proof of their appreciation by setting up on the highest point of the Buzancy plateau a monument which bears the following inscription in French: "Here the thistles of Scotland will bloom for ever among the roses of France."

The French assaults on the salient served their purpose. In a difficult situation the Germans conducted their retreat with admirable skill, but they lost many prisoners to the Allies, and their organisation was beginning to break down when on the 3rd August they retired across the Vesle. With the enemy obviously weakening, the time had come to tighten the pressure, and Sir Douglas Haig, who had carefully prepared for this opportunity, delivered on the 8th August a crushing blow on the forces in front of Amiens.

CHAPTER XXXVI

THE ADVANCE TO VICTORY

August and September 1918

Opening of British Attack, 8th August. Action of 5/6th Royal Scots. 11th and 12th Royal Scots at Meteren. Attack of 2nd Royal Scots, 21st August. General British Attack, 23rd August. Action of 5/6th Royal Scots. Action of 2nd Royal Scots. Gallantry of Private H. McIver. 2nd Royal Scots at Noreuil. Action of 4th and 7th Royal Scots. Storming of Drocourt-Quéant Switch. Work of 8th Royal Scots. Result of operations from 23rd August to 2nd September. Development of the Offensive. Advance of 5/6th Royal Scots. 2nd Royal Scots at the Canal du Nord. 4th and 7th Royal Scots at Mœuvres. Task of 9th and 13th Royal Scots. Situation near end of September. Arrangements for Renewal of Offensive. (See Maps XXII., XXIII. and XXVIII.)

THE result of the attack of General Rawlinson's Fourth Army on the 8th August convinced an astonished world that the power of Germany was on the wane. After five days' fighting, Amiens and the important railways that radiate from it were completely disengaged, and the armies of the enemy were in process of disorganisation. The morale of the enemy was undermined; after July 1918 the German soldier, harbouring the corrupting maggot of despair, was a feeble foe compared with what he had been in 1916 and 1917, and those who encountered him only during the triumphant progress of the Allies had no adequate notion what he was capable of when he was inspired with hope of victory. German confidence, which was a rock in 1916 and 1917, was, in 1918, a wretched cockle boat tossing about rudderless amid waves of disaster which finally engulfed it.   On the other hand, the exhilaration of the troops of the Allies rose in proportion to the despair of their opponents, and with renewed zest they threw themselves once more into the battle.

The first phase of the Fourth Army's operations lasted from the 8th till the 21st August, at the conclusion of which time our line ran from Albert across the Somme, west of Bray, through Lihons to Goyencourt.   Only one battalion of the Royal Scots, the 5/6th, served with the Fourth Army during this period.

The Thirty-second Division was attached to the Canadian Corps, commanded by General Currie, and its movements before the opening of the battle gave rise to much speculation among the men.   The 5/6th Royal Scots, for example, on leaving the Ransart area were conveyed by train on the 19th July to one of the most northerly parts of the British front, and were then brought south on the 7th August to Flixecourt, whence they marched to Bourdon.   The purpose of these moves was to prevent the enemy from suspecting that the Canadian Corps was to be employed on the Amiens front, and with a view to checking any leakage of plans, officers and men were not informed of the intended operations until the last possible moment.

These measures were justified by their result, for, on the 8th August, the Germans were taken utterly by surprise.   During the first two days the Thirty-second Division was in reserve, the 5/6th Royal Scots on the 8th August being brought by bus through Amiens to St Nicholas.   On the 9th the battalion halted at nightfall near the village of Beaucourt.   On the following day the division entered into the battle, and, breaking down the enemy's opposition, marched through difficult country to the western outskirts of Damery and Parvillers, but the 14th Brigade being in reserve, the 5/6th Battalion was not called on to fight, though it was obliged to deploy into artillery formation on nearing Le Quesnoy. The units of the 14th Brigade halted for the night in rear of the village of La Folie.

The innings of the 14th Brigade came on the 11th August, and the 5/6th Royal Scots took over the outpost line from the 10th Argylls, preparatory to attacking Parvillers. Lieut.-Colonel Fraser placed "B" Company on the right, "D" in the centre, and "A" and "C" on the left; zero was 9.30 A.M., and the battalion was informed that it would be supported by tanks. A thin and ragged barrage had little effect on the strongly-wired positions of the enemy, who had no difficulty in repelling the attack, while the tanks, which were almost an hour late in arriving, were all wrecked while crossing our front line. Only on the right was any progress made, where 2nd Lieut. Tomlinson and ten men pushed forward in conformity with the Dorsets and held on to the ground that they had won. The battalion's losses were severe and included twelve officers,[1] of whom Captains J. W. K. Darling, A. W. Macrae, Lieuts. W. Brown, R. G. S. Durward, H. W. R. Hine, R. E. Murray, 2nd Lieuts. M. Marshall, D. B. Pait, M. Veitch were killed. The division was relieved by Canadian troops on the 12th August, and the 5/6th Royal Scots were not engaged in battle again till near the end of the month.

The sweeping advance of the Fourth Army inspirited our troops in other parts of the front, and in every sector the Boches were being constantly harassed by raids. Several local enterprises, too, of some importance were engineered, and prominent among these was the capture of Hoegenacker Ridge on the 18th August by

---

[1] The wounded officers were Lieut. J. H. Walker and 2nd Lieuts. W. H. Loch and D. Sinclair.

the Twenty-ninth and Ninth Divisions. In the operation against this ridge, which overlooked the ruins of Meteren, the 11th Royal Scots took part, having on their right the 6th K.O.S.B. and on their left the 9th Scottish Rifles. With a view to effecting a tactical surprise, zero was fixed at 11 A.M., and in order to screen the assembly of the troops from the prying aeroplanes of the foe, the trenches were covered with cocoanut-fibre matting, along which a broad black streak was painted, the general effect of which gave to the trenches, when viewed from the air, the appearance of being unpopulated. The assembly position was a trench parallel to the road in front of Meteren, and the objective of the 27th Brigade was the ridge east of the Meteren Becque, the attack on the other side of the stream being the task of the Twenty-ninth Division. To move along packed trenches shut in by the stuffy fibre matting was a most exhausting business, as Major Boyd, who commanded the 11th Royal Scots on this occasion, found before he reached his battalion H.Q. in the assembly trench.

The operation was wholly successful, the ridge being carried almost at a rush. The 11th Royal Scots, brushing aside all opposition, swarmed up the hill close on the heels of a very effective barrage, and captured nearly 300 of the enemy, who made but an abject effort to meet the attack. Most of the casualties in the 27th Brigade were caused by the hostile shell fire, which made the work of the carrying parties, supplied by the 12th Royal Scots, as dangerous as it was fatiguing. A counter-blow was confidently expected, but the Germans did nothing more than shell the ridge after it was in our possession. Without any hope of recovering the initiative, the enemy had no reason to cling to the Lys salient, and on the 22nd August he

II   2 T

began to retire. This step had probably been decided on before the 18th, but it was undoubtedly precipitated by the loss of Hoegenacker Ridge. A few days after this action the 11th and the 12th Royal Scots were relieved and sent to the neighbourhood of St Omer for a course of training.

In their offensive in March the Germans had failed to maintain the original frontage of their attack, whereas in August Sir Douglas Haig was able, when their resistance showed signs of hardening, not merely to continue the pressure on the forces opposed to General Rawlinson's army, but to extend the battle northwards by bringing into the fray first the Third then the First Army. On the 21st August a pre-liminary operation was to be carried out by the Fourth and Third Armies, for the three-fold purpose of gaining the line of the Arras-Albert Railway, clearing the valley of the Ancre, and capturing Albert. These objects were all achieved ; the line of the railway was gained, the north bank of the Ancre was cleared about Beaucourt, and our line between the Somme and the Ancre was advanced east of the Bray-Albert Road.

The 2nd Battalion of the Royal Scots partici-pated in this operation. Since its relief from the Locon sector it had been training first at Tangry, then at Sambrin. On the 19th August the battalion marched up to trenches near Monchy au Bois, and although none of the soldiers had been warned about the impending attack, they realised from the number of tanks and big guns that were being transported along every available road that they were destined to take part in some important enterprise. The battalion was to be in brigade reserve. On the 20th, Lieut.-Colonel Henderson summoned his company commanders, and, having told them what was afoot, gave them their instructions. Since the country to be traversed was open and without any conspicuous landmarks, all took compass bearings.

A sticky mist settled down at night, and the atmosphere was still thick when the attack opened at 4.55 A.M. on the 21st. The Royal Scots began their march at 5.15 A.M., Lieut.-Colonel Henderson with the help of his compass guiding the battalion in the direction of Courcelles. A few shells caused some casualties among "B" Company, but the chief trouble came from the mist, which instead of clearing became so dense that it outrivalled even a London fog. The companies faded away from Lieut.-Colonel Henderson's vision in a manner similar to that of the Cheshire cat in *Alice in Wonderland*, but he plodded steadily eastwards, bumping every now and then into tanks, cavalry, and parties of infantry, all groping for some landmark or road in order to find out where they were. At last he reached the Courcelles le Comte road in the valley just west of the village, from the direction of which bullets were scudding across the road. Happily, after 9.30 A.M., the sun's rays pierced the mist, and he was able to collect his companies with comparative ease.

Anxious to ascertain the situation in front, he ordered Captain Gordon to take "C" Company forward and gain touch with the 7th King's Shropshire Light Infantry, who had been detailed to seize the line of railway. A report being received that the latter, having lost two companies in the mist, were making the attack with only half a battalion, Lieut.-Colonel Henderson also sent "D" Company forward to assist if necessary. Meantime "A" and "B" Companies were halted under the shelter of a convenient high bank. There was some brisk fighting near the railway embankment, but ultimately "C" and "D" Companies co-operating with the King's Shropshire Light Infantry forced back the enemy and gained the objective. While the assault was going on, the men of "A" and "B" Companies were amused by an incident that might have had very unhappy consequences; a tank, which must have become utterly lost in the fog, suddenly appeared and opened fire with all its guns on a carrying party of the Guards, fortunately without causing any damage.

After the railway was gained "C" and "D" Companies rejoined the rest of the battalion, which remained in reserve behind Courcelles. All our positions were heavily shelled on the 22nd, but there was no counter-attack, and the 76th Brigade, advancing at night, carried the line of the Third Division forward to the vicinity of Gomiecourt.

The satisfactory result of the operations on the 21st August cleared the way for the general attack of the Fourth and Third Armies on the 23rd. Success liberally befriended our efforts, and on the 26th August, our advance having formed a salient of the hostile positions opposite Arras, the First Army was flung into the battle with disastrous consequences to the foe. On the 2nd September the famous Drocourt-Quéant switch line was stormed, and our troops set foot on territory which had been in possession of the enemy since 1914. On the evening of that day the British line from Quéant ran south to Péronne and along the line of the Somme Canal; Bapaume and the chief centres of the old Somme battlefield were once more in our possession.

Five battalions of the Royal Scots were involved in the fighting between the 23rd August and the 2nd September; of these the 5/6th was in the Fourth Army, the 2nd, 4th, and 7th were in the Third Army, and the 8th was in the First Army.

The Thirty-second Division returned on the 18th August from the hinterland to a sector of the Fourth Army front near Harbonnières, and on the 23rd attacked and captured the village of Herleville. The 5/6th Royal Scots were in reserve, and their share in the action was confined to furnishing carrying parties. Near Herleville there was comparative inactivity for three days, but on the afternoon of the 27th "C" Company on the right of the 5/6th Royal Scots made an advance of nearly 700 yards, while two platoons of "A" shared with Australians the glory of storming Foucaucourt. During this advance a gap developed between "C" and "A" Companies, but "B" Company filled the space, and, though twilight was deepening into darkness, the whole battalion continued to press eastwards until the line was established about 1400 yards west of Soyécourt. With the Germans now in full retreat our advance on the 28th was a procession. The 5/6th Royal Scots encountered only a trifling opposition, and when they halted and consolidated a line nearly 1000 yards north-east of Soyécourt, the 15th Highland Light Infantry passed through them and continued the pursuit. Following in reserve, the Royal Scots halted for the night near Berny-en-Santerre, and on the following morning marched through the outpost positions of the 1st Dorsets, and without meeting resistance, reached the high ground on the west side of the Somme Canal near Briost, where "B" Company formed an outpost line.

The Somme Canal with its broad marshy banks was a line on which the enemy might hope to make a prolonged stand, particularly as he had taken care to demolish all the crossings. The volume of shell fire which greeted the Royal Scots was a warning of the enemy's intentions. On the 30th August two platoons of the Royal Scots, having discovered a bridge 200 yards

II   2 T 2

to the north of Briost, crossed the canal by means of this gangway, but became bogged in a marsh which was impassable even for infantry. The Germans, moreover, did not neglect to rake the canal banks with machine-gun bullets and shells, and the Royal Scots could do no more than establish posts along the west side of the river. On the same evening they were relieved by the 10th Argylls and went back to the brigade reserve line, about 1000 yards west of Villers-Carbonnel.

The 2nd Royal Scots, who took over the front line on the Arras-Albert Railway opposite Gomiecourt on the 22nd August, were given some high ground immediately to the east of their position as their objective. The 23rd, being the anniversary of Mons, was regarded by the battalion as an auspicious day, and the men went into the battle inspired with the utmost confidence. From the start, at 4 A.M., there was never a hitch, and skilfully controlled by their officers the men brilliantly sustained the reputation of the battalion. "C" Company at one time seemed to have the prospect of a stiff fight, but the extraordinary daring of the company runner, Private H. McIver, converted a potential resistance into an absolute rout. Early in the fray he singled out a German and chased him for 150 yards. The hunted man jumped for refuge into a machine-gun nest, but Private McIver, who gave no thought to his own safety, immediately followed him and fought like a man possessed against the occupants of the trench. After six Germans had been shot or bayoneted by the daring runner, the remainder of the garrison, about twenty in number, although they were armed with two machine-guns, surrendered. After this exhibition of dare-devilry the task of "C" Company was plain sailing. Along the rest of the line the despairing resistance was of no avail against the ardour of the attack, and fifteen officers, two hundred and sixty-nine other ranks, and numerous field-guns, howitzers, and machine-guns formed the handsome "bag" of the Royal Scots. When the objective was secured, another division passed through and carried on the attack, and the Royal Scots, after consolidating their position, stood ready to move up in support if required.

Between the 21st and the 23rd August the battalion lost four officers (Lieut. W. K. Strachan, 2nd Lieuts. C. Irvine, L. K. Macfarlane, and J. M. Stewart) and twenty-seven other ranks killed, twenty-eight other ranks wounded and missing, three officers[1] and one hundred and ninety-five other ranks wounded, and eleven other ranks missing. An interlude of a few days followed to allow of recuperation, the battalion moving back to trenches east of Adinfer. On the 29th it moved forward to Boiry-St Martin ready for action, and on the 1st September it entered trenches at Hamelincourt. Orders for a new attack were received, and after midnight the men, under a fusillade of gas-shells, which forced them to don their respirators, passed through Ervillers and Mory and assembled in trenches just west of the village of Noreuil.

The front of the 2nd Royal Scots fringed a ridge facing another ridge, which was the principal object of their attack. The latter, with the fortified ruins of Noreuil at its northern end, was separated from the Royal Scots by a deep and forbidding valley, after descending into which our men would have to scale the coverless slopes of the far side, practically every inch of which would be swept by the enemy's fire. Thus the task of the battalion was beset with difficulties, and was rendered even more hazardous by the fact that its attack was to be launched at 5.30 A.M., thirty minutes

[1] 2nd Lieuts. W. A. Cunningham, J. G. Reid, and R. Thomson.

later than that delivered by the Corps on its flank; the consequence was that for half an hour the men had to suffer the enemy's shelling before they made a move.

The encroaching rays of the sun were scattering the early morning darkness, when " A " and " D " Companies began their descent into the valley. At the same time the German machine-gunners and riflemen opened fire with deadly effect, but failed at first to stop the charge of the Royal Scots. Though every officer of " A " Company was either killed or wounded, the N.C.Os. proved worthy of their rank, and the Royal Scots continued to progress till they reached a railway line that skirted the eastern slope of the valley. Beyond this a flood of whistling lead, forming a barrier which no mortal man could hope to penetrate, skimmed every yard of the stretch that lay between the Royal Scots and their goal. From a trench (Macaulay Avenue), half-way up the eastern incline, the Boches commanded every approach by their fire and pinned the survivors of " A " Company to the ground along the railway.

At the start of the attack the German fire caused " D " Company to veer to the left, a space being thus formed between the two attacking companies, so Lieut.-Colonel Henderson sent up Captain Gordon with " C " Company to close the gap and move straight on Noreuil. Never wavering, the company reached the tumbled ruins of the village, and mastering two machine-gun nests captured the entire garrison of Noreuil, which consisted of one officer and thirty men. With a view to assisting " A " Company, Captain Gordon directed Lieut. Morrison to take two platoons and clear the ridge to the south-east of the village. By a dashing advance this small party reached Macaulay Avenue at a point where it was cut by another trench (Lagnicourt Trench) running across it at right angles, but here the Germans were in great numbers and violently assailed the Royal Scots. For nearly two hours the latter held their ground, but by that time they had been reduced to a pitiful handful and were forced back to Noreuil; among the slain was Lieut. Morrison.

Meantime the village was being battered by an intense fire which prevented the other two platoons of "C" Company, scattered amid the ruined houses, from being reorganised. In the absence of support the remnants of "C" Company were held in a prison from which it was dangerous to attempt to escape.

"D" Company on the left, after struggling through the northern outskirts of Noreuil, reached the line of the railway beyond the village, where several prisoners and a number of machine-guns were secured, but all its endeavours to advance beyond this point were checked by the German fire. One platoon, entering Lagnicourt Trench, began to move in the direction of Macaulay Avenue, but it was abruptly halted by the galling machine-gun fire that smote its left flank.

At an early stage of the attack even part of the reserve company, "B," became involved in the fighting. Two platoons, having been detailed to maintain liaison with the 7th King's Shropshire Light Infantry on the right, advanced with that battalion, which veered off towards the right, and along with it succeeded in crossing the ridge. There was, however, a wide space between this force and "A" Company of the Royal Scots, and the King's Shropshire Light Infantry and the two platoons of "B" Company were compelled by the volume and accuracy of the German machine-gun fire to retire for protection to a trench near the railway.

Lieut.-Colonel Henderson, anxious for news, went

forward to a spot in the assembly trenches, from which the battlefield stretched before him like a map. The situation, as he first saw it, was anything but promising, and he realised that a speedy death would almost certainly be the fate of any runner who attempted to cross the valley, where innumerable spouts of earth were dancing to the unceasing crack of machine-guns. The tanks, from the assistance of which much had been expected, could do little ; near the front line three had been knocked out by the enemy's fire and one was blazing furiously. There was only one matter, the successful storming of Noreuil, that could give Lieut.-Colonel Henderson any measure of satisfaction.

He rendered a full report of the situation to the brigade, which thereupon issued orders for a company of Suffolks to enter Vraucourt Trench and work along it towards the left in order to clear Macaulay Avenue, which appeared to be the key of the hostile position. At 11 A.M. "B" and "C" Companies assisted this turning movement by a frontal attack, and the enemy's resistance suddenly collapsed. The greater part of the ridge was cleared, and the line of the Royal Scots was carried forward to the junction of Macaulay Avenue and Lagnicourt Trench, many prisoners and machine-guns being taken.

No immediate effort was made to advance farther, because the terrain east of the junction bristled with hostile machine-guns, and the left flank of the Royal Scots was still in the air. As far as opportunity permitted the companies were reorganised. At 8 P.M. a forward move was made by "C" Company, which, working eastwards from the trench junction along Macaulay Avenue, reached a sunken road to the north of Lagnicourt village. Two machine-gun posts made a show of resistance, but these were cleverly rushed, and in addition to the guns twenty-one Germans were taken. With the arrival of the 1st Northumberland Fusiliers all apprehensions with regard to the battalion's left flank were allayed, and in the small hours of the 3rd September the Guards passed through the Royal Scots to carry on the attack. Thus at the end of a day of difficult fighting the German line was once more in flux; screened by the darkness the enemy stole away from his positions, and the opposition to our advance on the 3rd September was negligible.

The losses of the 2nd Royal Scots were numerous, the casualties being two officers (Lieuts. A. S. Robertson and W. F. O. Morrison) and twenty-five other ranks killed, four officers[1] and one hundred and thirty-two other ranks wounded, and six other ranks missing; among the fallen was Private McIver, who had so greatly distinguished himself on the 23rd August. The enemy lost more heavily still, for three hundred and eighty-four prisoners were captured by the battalion. The material booty was considerable, and included thirty-nine machine-guns. After the action the 2nd Royal Scots returned on the 3rd September to the vicinity of Hamelincourt, where a spell of training in the hinterland ensued, and the battalion did not return to the front line till the 16th.

The 4th and the 7th Royal Scots took part in their first major operation on the Western front on the 23rd August. The sojourn of the Fifty-second Division at the Vimy Ridge was not marked by any striking incidents, but the 7th Royal Scots had to lament the loss of Lieut. I. M. Molyneaux, who after two and a half years' service with the battalion died from the effects of wounds received while on patrol duty on the 9th July. From the 19th

[1] Lieut. W. R. McNiven, 2nd Lieuts. D. M. Aitken, R. W. Cresswell, and J. Munro.

till the 30th July the division was in reserve near Béthune, returning to the line near Oppy on the last day of the month. Between the 14th and 16th August it was again relieved and sent into reserve near Villers Chatel and Aubigny. On the 21st the 4th Royal Scots moved up to Wanquetin and the 7th gathered at Berneville. The latter place received more than its fair share of bombing at night, but the 7th Royal Scots, whose rest was thus brutally disturbed, were to some extent mollified when one of the obnoxious German aeroplanes was brought down in flames.

The 4th Royal Scots, temporarily commanded by Major J. M. Slater in the absence of Lieut.-Colonel Mitchell on leave, formed the right battalion of the Fifty-second Division, which on the 23rd August was to attack over the rolling country north of the Cojeul river; the Fifty-sixth Division was on their right flank and the 7th Royal Scots on their left. The assembly point of the 156th Brigade was near Mercatel, and the journey to this position was extremely harassing owing to every road and path being choked with traffic.

Arrangements had been made to convey the men close to the assembly point by bus, but only about half the requisite number of these vehicles turned up, with the result that the 4th Royal Scots did not arrive at the assembly position till 3 A.M., which allowed them scant time to reach the point of deployment where they were due to be at 4 A.M. The extra ammunition, grenades, and flares necessary for the operation were issued to the men at the roadside, but owing to the time that had been lost "C" and "D" Companies were obliged to move up to the battle without receiving the additional supplies. Troubles during this night were gregarious; the guides detailed by an English battalion to lead the Royal Scots to the front line completely lost their way, so that it was 4.35 A.M. before the first company, "A," arrived at the jumping-off position. The 7th Royal Scots were also beset by difficulties, and they had the misfortune to come under a heavy mustard-gas bombardment before they reached their allotted positions, yet they were able to settle all their dispositions some time before zero, which was at 4.55 A.M.

When the battle began, "A" Company was the only one of the 4th Royal Scots in position, and "B" and "C" Companies, which followed it, had to extend as they attacked. "D" Company could not possibly get up in time, and it was ordered to take shelter in a trench near the front line. Tempers were short and nerves were raw because of the spurt that had been made in order to be ready for the assault, but once the advance started everything went smoothly. The three attacking companies smashed all resistance and easily reached their objective, about a mile ahead: one hundred melancholy prisoners and fifteen machine-guns fell into the possession of the battalion during the advance, which brought it to a position just north of the hamlet of Boiry. Then, with the assistance of a section of tanks, "B" Company exploited the ground in front of the objective for a distance of 300 yards and within thirty minutes all this space was cleared of every living foeman. A platoon of the same company advanced some time later for another 500 yards in order to conform with the movements of the Fifty-sixth Division on the right.

An equal measure of success attended the attack of the 7th Royal Scots who, with No. 1 and No. 2 Companies leading, brushed aside the enemy's feeble opposition and arrived at their goal on the heels of the barrage; twenty-five Germans including one officer, three machine-guns, and two anti-tank rifles formed the booty of the battalion. In their final position the 7th Royal Scots were established along a line facing the village of Hénin.

When the advance was resumed on the 24th August, the 4th Royal Scots were in reserve, while the 7th Royal Scots reached their objective opposite the Hindenburg Line without experiencing any determined resistance. Patrols went out and examined the strong German entrenchments and brought back valuable reports about their condition. No operations were carried out by the 7th Royal Scots on the 25th, on the night of which " D " Company of the 4th took up a position on the right of Lieut.-Colonel Ewing's battalion, occupying four platoon posts in the Cojeul valley, just south of the village of St Martin.

On the 26th August the 155th and 157th Brigades of the division carried on the attack, forcing a lodgment in the outer fortifications of the vast Hindenburg system, and next day the 156th Brigade again came into action with the 4th Royal Scots on the right and the 7th on the left. The jumping-off position of the former was a trench about 100 yards to the east of the derelict houses that formed the village of Héninel, and following an exploration of the ground by the battalion Intelligence Officer, Major Slater sent three of his companies forward to this position after dark on the 26th and established his reserve company about 300 yards behind the others. By thus anticipating his instructions, he had his attacking companies in position before daybreak on the 27th, and he had good reason to plume himself on his foresight, for the official instructions to move arrived only one hour before zero, which was fixed for 10 A.M.; moreover, his forethought saved lives as well as time, since all approaches to the assembly position were savagely shelled for an hour or two before zero. In spite of

short notice the assembly of the 7th Royal Scots was
also satisfactorily accomplished, the position of the
battalion being almost due east of the southern portion
of Héninel.   The directing flank of the attack, which,
it was hoped, would take the 156th Brigade up to the
village of Hendecourt, was the left, for it was on this
wing, where the Canadian Corps was posted, that the
strongest opposition was expected.

The general line of the assault was in a south-easterly
direction, and since the battalions were crowded in their
trenches, the men were required to fan out as soon as
they sprang over the parapets.   An intricate manœuvre
of this description, however, was a mere bagatelle to
troops bubbling over with assurance, and there was no
hitch.   The Boche resistance was devoid of sting, and
there seemed to be almost more sport than danger in
hunting the enemy in his fastness; even the doughty
German machine-gunners were less dour than usual,
and most of the casualties sustained by the 4th Royal
Scots were due to shell fire, which was at its fiercest
during the first hour of the contest.   In former years
the village of Fontaine les Croisilles, girt with trenches
and pill-boxes, near the Sensée river, would have been a
tough nut to crack, but it fell into the hands of the
4th Royal Scots with astonishing ease; many Germans
threw down their weapons with a readiness that was
almost indecent and gladly surrendered in order to get
out of a war from which they no longer expected profit
or victory.   "D" Company, in addition to securing
many prisoners and much miscellaneous loot, found in
a pill-box near the Sensée a hot meal and coffee, left
behind by the absconding garrison; the pleasures of
the table are rarely enjoyed by soldiers during a battle,
and the men of "D" Company, taking advantage of the
opportunity, fell to and devoured the adversary's dinner

with keen relish. Fontaine les Croisilles was taken by
1.30 P.M., but the position was not consolidated till
thirty minutes later, since the battalion was required to
extend to the right in order to gain touch with the
157th Brigade, which had met with a stiffer resistance.
Ten trench-mortars and guns, twenty-five machine-guns
and an immense quantity of ammunition fell into the
hands of the 4th Royal Scots, while the prisoners taken,
three hundred and forty-four in number including four
officers, were more than half the fighting strength of
the battalion.

The resistance experienced by the 7th Royal Scots,
who attacked with No. 2 and No. 3 Companies in front,
was equally feeble, clusters of Germans surrendering
after doing little more than making a pretence of
fighting. Near the river, however, the opposition was
of sterner stuff, and the Boche machine - gunners,
splendidly sustaining their reputation for tenacity,
succeeded in bringing the advance to a halt at the
Sensée about noon. Against the Canadians on the
left the Germans were stubbornly disputing every
fraction of ground, and until a deeper advance had
been made in this area it was impossible for the
156th Brigade to push on to Hendecourt. The 7th
Royal Scots therefore consolidated a line near a path
which led in a north-easterly direction from the tumbled
masonry of Fontaine les Croisilles. The spoils of victory
were substantial and varied; two hundred and fifty-five
prisoners, including two officers of whom one was a
battalion commander, two field-guns, twenty machine-
guns and other material made up a list of which the
7th Royal Scots were justly proud.

A brief and well-earned rest rewarded the efforts of
the 156th Brigade. Both the 4th and the 7th Royal
Scots were relieved on the night of the battle, and were

concentrated near Mercatel, where they made themselves ready for the important attack on the Drocourt-Quéant Switch, arranged for the 2nd September.   The 4th Royal Scots accordingly moved up on the 31st August to the neighbourhood of Bullecourt, and on the evening of the 1st September took over trenches to the east of that village.   The entire district had been a storm centre for months, and was a chaos of broken and battered trenches ; during darkness it was a matter of the utmost difficulty to maintain direction, and the task of the 4th Royal Scots was rendered no easier by the fact that, owing to our communications having been cut by hostile artillery fire, orders were late in reaching Lieut.-Colonel Mitchell, who had rejoined his battalion.   The assembly trenches lay far forward in the area of the 155th Brigade, and Lieut.-Colonel Mitchell had only time to show his company commanders their objectives on the map.   Fortunately he had arranged to have scouts posted at intervals along the route, but even with this precaution the battalion had not quite reached its jumping-off position when our barrage opened at 8.45 A.M.   On this occasion the unit was on the left of the 156th Brigade, the 7th Royal Scots, posted between Bullecourt and Hendecourt, being in reserve. The general objective of the 4th Royal Scots was a road running from the Moulin Sans Souci to the north of Quéant.

The famous Drocourt-Quéant Switch was a system so strongly fortified that even a faint-hearted enemy might be expected to put up a tremendous resistance. The 4th Royal Scots were well aware of this, and putting on a spurt the three leading companies, " B," " C," and " D," caught up the barrage.   " D," on the left, finding the ground in front of it comparatively unencumbered, cut right through to the Moulin Sans

II   2 U

Souci without serious difficulty, but the other two companies were for a time stopped by a vast stretch of uncut wire. If the hostile machine-gun fire had been directed with its usual accuracy, the attack might have been shrivelled up, for the Royal Scots could make no appreciable impression on the thick wire with their puny hand wire-cutters, but fortunately the enemy's aim was wild, and though the Royal Scots stood exposed in the open their losses were fewer than they should have been in the circumstances. Lieut.-Colonel Mitchell, on discerning the cause of the stoppage, immediately instructed his reserve company, " A," to veer to the left so as to clear the wire obstacle, and then turn southwards along the two lines of trenches in front of " B " and " C " Companies. This flanking movement, backed up by the fire of machine-guns and Stokes mortars, fulfilled its purpose, and " B " and " C " Companies were enabled to press on to their objectives. Considering the tremendous strength of their position, the resistance of the Germans was wretchedly weak, and only eleven of the 4th Royal Scots were killed during the fighting on the 2nd September. Such opposition as there was came chiefly from isolated machine-gun nests and was of a local character, and by 3 P.M. the 4th Royal Scots were on their final objective, having collected four prisoners, three field-guns, ten machine-guns, and other material. Patrols were at once sent forward in the direction of Quéant, and these returned with the information that the village was unoccupied.

After the capture of the objective, orders were issued to the 7th Royal Scots to advance and roll up the switch system to a depth of 800 yards to the north of Quéant. Led by No. 1 Company, they set out at 8.30 P.M., and since the enemy was in retreat, were able to occupy and consolidate the position without any more difficulty than that incidental to all night operations. On the morning of the 3rd September the 4th and the 7th Royal Scots were withdrawn to the western slopes of the high ground lying west of Quéant, where they had the unexpected pleasure of an alfresco concert by Sir Harry Lauder. On the 7th the 156th Brigade retired to a rest area near St Leger, and it was not till the 16th that it turned its face once more towards the line. The casualties sustained by the 4th and the 7th Royal Scots during the operations from the 23rd August till the 2nd September were by no means unduly heavy: the 4th had three officers (Lieuts. J. G. Mylne, S. Macdonald, and 2nd Lieut. T. J. Turner) and thirty-five other ranks killed, six officers [1] and two hundred and forty-nine other ranks wounded, and seventeen other ranks missing: the 7th lost one officer (Captain K. Mackenzie) and sixteen other ranks killed, eight officers [2] and three hundred and eighty-eight other ranks wounded, and one other rank missing.

The only battalion of the Royal Scots with the First Army was the 8th, to which a battle meant little more than that it had to perform its work under more violent shell fire and under rather more disagreeable conditions than usual. The repair and construction of roads were matters of vital importance, and on this indispensable work the 8th Royal Scots were employed in the wake of the advancing infantry, so that there might be no delay in the delivery of rations, stores, and ammunition to the assailing troops. Road construction and repair were at least as fatiguing as fighting, and imposed an immense strain on the pioneers and sappers, who were responsible for the preservation of communications

---

[1] Captain W. M. Carmichael, Lieuts. G. Gardner, J. Halley, 2nd Lieuts. A. E. Abbott, A. W. Bannerman, and J. S. Marsland.

[2] Captain W. Hunter, Lieuts. C. A. Cole, J. C. McCulloch, T. McLauchlan, J. MacNab, S. V. Spence, and 2nd Lieuts. D. McLennan and J. S. Weir.

between the front line and the depots. The 8th laboured near Fampoux till the 13th September, on which date they were relieved and sent back for a much-needed rest till the 23rd, when they returned to the Rœux-Greenland Hill district, where they were engaged in the construction of cross-country tracks and in the building of a light railway.

The success of our operations from the 23rd August to the 2nd September, particularly the storming of the Drocourt-Quéant Switch, created a profound depression in Germany, but though the Hindenburg system had been punctured in the north, the Germans had still some strong defences, behind which they might hope to keep their foes at bay during the winter, and to these they now retired. To tanks broad waterways were more formidable obstacles than trenches, and in the Canal du Nord the enemy had a very useful protection for such notable centres as Douai and Cambrai; behind this barrier the Boches held their ground for some time, but north and south of it our advance continued, progress being made both in the Lys salient and on the French and Fourth Army fronts. By the 18th September the Lys salient had been flattened out, and our line extended south from Lens to the west of St Quentin. Much of the fighting during September was of a most vigorous character, but though the season was growing late for offensive campaigning, our pressure was not suffered to relax, and by the 27th September Lens was in our hands and the enemy on the Fourth Army front was pinned behind the Hindenburg system.

The battalions of the Royal Scots engaged in this fighting were the 5/6th, 2nd, 4th, 7th, and 8th.

The 5/6th Royal Scots returned from the vicinity of Villers-Carbonnel to the front line near Briost on the 3rd September. On the 30th/31st August the brilliant exploit of the Second Australian Division in storming

Mont St Quentin led to the capture of Péronne and weakened the German defence on the Somme Canal. The Royal Scots, who spent the 4th September in reconnoitring the canal and in repairing foot-bridges, crossed the Somme on the 5th, and with "C" and "D" Companies in front advanced against Brie. The Boche machine-guns made a considerable din, but their aim was unsteady, and the Royal Scots, passing through the village without losing a single man, formed a line about 2000 yards to the east of it; about forty or fifty German corpses were seen during the advance, and three prisoners and five machine-guns were taken. Driven from the canal the enemy now retreated rapidly towards the Hindenburg Line, and the battalion for the rest of the month was engaged in no further fighting. On the 14th the Thirty-second Division was drawn back into Corps reserve and did not return to the line till the end of the month.

The 2nd, 4th, and 7th Royal Scots were allowed just sufficient leisure to enable them to reorganise and to assimilate reinforcements. After a few days at Hamelincourt, the 2nd Battalion, on the 6th September, moved forward to the vicinity of Ransart, and on the 11th it was accommodated in dug-outs in the railway cutting near Courcelles; the next step was to Beaumetz on the 15th September, and on the following day the battalion entered familiar territory when it took over trenches in the front-line system north of Havrincourt, near which place it had put in one of its quietest spells of trench duty in 1917. With 1100 yards of the front and support trenches of the original Hindenburg Line to guard, the whole battalion, except "A" Company, which was in reserve on what had been the British front line prior to the Battle of Cambrai, was posted east of the Canal du Nord.

II 2 U 2

There was no excitement on the 17th September, on the evening of which the Royal Scots Fusiliers took over a part of the front on the left of the Royal Scots. The 18th September dawned wet and cloudy, and in the morning the German heavy guns were busy for a short period. Then followed a quiet interlude which lasted till the late afternoon, when the Boche guns spoke again. Our battery and reserve positions were plastered with shells, all communications between battalion H.Q. and the brigade being shattered, and our guns retaliated by putting down a barrage on the S.O.S. lines. Danger threatened when the German fire was switched on to our front trenches, and soon after 5 P.M. Lieut.-Colonel Henderson received a report from Captain Main of "D" Company that the Boche infantry were about to attack. The S.O.S. signal was immediately sent up, and "A" Company was despatched from reserve to guard the crossings over the canal.

The German attack was no kid-glove affair. Supported by low-flying aircraft, Boche infantry, using bombs and *flammenwerfer*, rushed an outpost, the garrison of which had no time to recover from the shock of the bombardment, and burst through the front trench on the right of the battalion. The surge of the Germans carried them into the support trench, where our men were ready and stood firm; then, wheeling rapidly north, the Boches cleared the front trench for a distance of fully 500 yards, while on the left a strong party which had entered the front trench of the unit on the left of the Royal Scots began to bomb southwards. Thus the Royal Scots were subjected to a dangerous converging attack, and "C" Company on the left, commanded by Lieut. Gunn, was at one time almost surrounded.

Lieut. Gunn's men rose to the heroism that the

gravity of the situation demanded and stood fast against the northern group of the foe, while Captain Main with "D" Company magnificently assisted them by preventing the Boches from forcing a passage along the support trench. Every attempt of the Germans to push home the attack by a dash across the open was frustrated by the steady fire of the Royal Scots, and they were obliged to confine themselves to operating along the trenches. Even the low-flying aeroplanes, with their sputtering machine-guns and occasional bombs, could not unnerve the Royal Scots, and "C" and "D" Companies, taking the offensive, steadily pressed the Germans back from the battalion trenches on the north. The menace from the left flank having been thus warded off, Lieut. Gunn, reinforced by two platoons of "D" Company, organised a counter-attack to the right, and step by step the Royal Scots rid the front trench of the Boche intruders. The drive was extended even beyond the battalion's sector, and over sixty prisoners, including two officers, were gathered in. After 7 P.M. "A" Company crossed the canal, and assisted by two platoons of "D" Company attacked along the old German communication trench connected with our front line, and established a strong outpost in advance of our positions. The reserve position was taken over by two companies of the 7th King's Shropshire Light Infantry, who became responsible for the protection of the crossings over the canal.

It was largely due to the stonewall resistance of the Royal Scots and their brilliant counter-attacks that our foothold east of the canal was maintained. "C" Company, particularly, covered itself with glory, but every officer and man in the battalion had shown the most praiseworthy devotion to duty and thoroughly deserved the heart-felt encomium uttered by Lieut.-

Colonel Henderson, "Everyone has done splendidly!" The casualties suffered, fifty-nine[1] in all, amounted to less than the number of our prisoners (eighty-five, including two officers), while four light machine-guns and a large quantity of grenades were left by the Germans in our trenches. By the 19th the line was wholly restored, and the battalion began to get ready for a big engagement which was to commence on the 27th September.

From their trenches north of Havrincourt the 2nd Royal Scots could see the brooding shadow of Bourlon Wood, which from another angle caught the gaze of the men of the 4th and the 7th Royal Scots. On the night of the 20th/21st September these battalions entered the front line near Mœuvres, with the 7th on the right and the 4th on the left. The line consisted of a series of posts on the forward slopes of a ridge which frowned down on the dry basin of the Canal du Nord. Though annoyed by considerable shelling, the 7th Royal Scots did not experience much difficulty in taking over their positions, and when the move was completed, three companies, each with two platoons in posts in the outpost system, held the front from Mœuvres to a point about 700 yards to the south, while the remaining company was in reserve. The 4th Royal Scots took over a similar series of posts along the eastern and north-eastern outskirts of Mœuvres, with Canadians on their left. The ground was terribly broken, and in the pitch darkness it was easy for small groups to go astray, so that there was considerable suspense at the H.Q. of the 4th Royal Scots when no news was forthcoming from a party under Lieut. Rutherford, which had been entrusted with

---

[1] Including two officers (Lieuts. J. G. Campbell and A. H. M. Moir) wounded.

the duty of taking over one of the most perilous posts
on the front to the north-east of Mœuvres.

All the posts were mere shallow dips, offering no
adequate protection against any serious bombardment,
and were under the direct gaze of the enemy. Every
movement drew a burst of gun fire, so that little could
be done to improve the positions during daylight.
Intermittent shell fire troubled the garrisons till about
3 P.M. on the 21st September, when a nerve-shaking
bombardment commenced and gave the 4th and the
7th Royal Scots probably the worst ordeal that they
ever endured in France. S.O.S. rockets were sent up by
the 7th, and our guns were prompt in answering the
signal, but the terrain offered advantages to the Germans
of which they were not slow to avail themselves.

Crawling along derelict trenches and saps, the
Boches, undetected, came close to the lines of the Royal
Scots, and when their barrage lifted they swooped
down on the posts. Each platoon of the 7th was
attacked simultaneously on front and flanks and all
fell back for about 100 yards; then, ré-forming, they
delivered a counter-blow. Lieut. A. S. Miller, leading
No. 2 Company on the right, scattered the Germans
on his front and reached the line of the posts; then,
supported by 2nd Lieut. A. E. Watson and C.S.M.
Fleeting, he attacked a pill-box, from which a machine-
gun was firing, and after a brief and lively fight captured
it; two machine-guns were unhoused from it and on
its muddy floor lay the bodies of thirteen Germans.
No. 3 Company, in the centre, also succeeded in
fighting its way back to its original position, but the
left company, No. 4, was more heavily punished. The
two northern posts of the battalion were the most
difficult to defend because of the multiplicity of the
approaches; these enabled the Boches to form a

cordon round the posts, and as soon as the barrage lifted they overwhelmed the garrisons.

The enemy's success, therefore, was greatest at the junction of the 7th and the 4th Royal Scots, and on ascertaining the situation Lieut.-Colonel Ewing sent forward his reserve company, No. 1, under Captain W. Robertson, to close the gap. Captain Robertson was severely wounded, but Sergeant D. Hook proved himself a resolute leader, and the company stopped the enemy's charge by rifle and Lewis-gun fire. As far as the 7th Royal Scots were concerned the danger was now at an end, and under the supervision of Captain Ballantyne the original line, with the exception of the two northern posts, was reoccupied. The losses were the heaviest that the battalion had yet suffered in France; three sterling officers (Lieuts. L. Muirhead, T. A. Herdman, and 2nd Lieut. R. P. Innes) and eleven other ranks were killed, one officer and twenty-eight other ranks were wounded, and one officer[1] and forty-five other ranks missing.

The ground in front of the 4th Royal Scots did not afford so many opportunities for a secret approach, and the ranks of the German infantry were mown down by the concentrated rifle and Lewis-gun fire of the Royal Scots. "D" Company, on the left, escaped without an infantry attack, but along the battalion front all the trenches were terribly battered, and under the circumstances the losses of the battalion (two officers, Lieuts. Thomson and Hudson, killed, and eight men wounded) were surprisingly low.

On the night of the 21st/22nd September, "C" and "D" Companies of the 4th Royal Scots were ordered to advance their lines, the former to take a trench running between the north of Mœuvres and the

---

[1] Lieut. W. F. R. Macartney, wounded and captured.

canal basin, and the latter to secure the important tactical post (E 14), which Lieut. Rutherford had been sent to take over. A report from an aeroplane indicated that British troops, which might be Lieut. Rutherford and his party, were already within the ground to be attacked by "D" Company, so the barrage arrangements were altered to keep this spot free from fire. The advance started at 8 P.M. "C" Company, on the right, was held up by the withering fire of the enemy's machine-guns and could make no progress, but "D" Company triumphantly achieved its object; the post, consisting of a fortified ditch, which was connected with the Canal du Nord, was taken at a rush, three Germans and three machine-guns being captured. Then, pushing out to the left, the company was rejoiced to discover Lieut. Rutherford and his men, who, having been unable in the darkness to find out the exact position of the post, had on the approach of dawn settled themselves in a few shell-holes situated quite close to the post.

There was little diminution in the volume of shell fire on the 22nd September, but the only infantry action was a German attack on the post that "D" Company had captured and it was decisively repulsed. Next day another and more desperate attempt was made by the enemy, consisting of troops of the 1st Guards Reserve Regiment, to rush this post, but it too was thwarted by the pluck and steadfastness of the garrison. This particular spot was a veritable Tom Tiddler's ground, and the 4th Royal Scots had the proud satisfaction of being the only battalion to keep the post against all attacks. Relief came to the 4th[1] and the 7th Royal

---

[1] The fighting near E 14 cost the battalion seventy-nine casualties, including four officers (Captain Harrison, Lieuts. Elliott, Grant, and Richardson) wounded.

Scots on the night of the 23rd/24th September, when the 156th Brigade went back for two miles into divisional reserve.

Five battalions of the Royal Scots, the 9th, 13th, 11th, 12th, and 17th, had so far not been involved in the British offensive that began on the 8th August. The 17th Royal Scots, as we have seen, were stationed in the Salient during August, and there they remained, and took part in the Flanders offensive at the end of September. The 11th and the 12th Battalions after their profitable spell of trench duty near Meteren, enjoyed a long period of training first near St Omer and later in the vicinity of Esquelbecq; on the 11th September they came under the II. Corps, and they, like the 17th, were earmarked to take part in the Flanders offensive.

The 9th and the 13th Royal Scots after their experiences near Buzancy returned, as we have noted, to the Arras sector, and they were not a little disgusted when, on the eve of the operations of the First Army, they were transferred to the Mazingarbe district, which was well known to the 13th, and was now one of the dullest spots on the front. The 13th Battalion was at this time commanded by Lieut.-Colonel Sir Ian Colquhoun, and the 9th, on the 3rd August, received as C.O. Lieut.-Colonel Stephenson, who had well established his reputation as the leader of the now disbanded 16th Battalion. No general offensive was planned for the Loos salient, because, as the British High Command rightly conjectured, the pressure on other parts of the front would induce the Germans to withdraw from the Loos sector as well as from the Lys salient. At the same time, by a policy of "peaceful penetration," the enemy was to be encouraged to make up his mind to retire; this meant that our troops concerned would experience most of the discomforts and dangers of war without any of its glories. There were to be no "set" battles, and consequently the advances made by units in this area passed almost without notice either in British official bulletins or in the Press, though the hazards of a "peaceful penetration" enterprise were frequently more nerve-trying than those involved by participation in a pitched battle. The troops, who were expected to test continually the enemy's lines, without any adequate artillery preparation, never knew what lay in store for them; they might find a deserted trench, or they might be brought to a sudden halt by a storm of bullets. The nervous tension inherent in this type of war was greater than that arising from the usual organised battle.

The 9th Royal Scots took over the line in front of La Philosophe, and since there was a suspicion that the enemy had only weak patrols in his front trenches, a party of the 9th Royal Scots sallied forth one night to secure definite information on this point; it encountered a large Boche patrol and after a bout of firing each side returned to its own lines. On the 3rd September "A" Company, under the command of Captain T. W. Bennet Clark, was instructed to ascertain the Boche dispositions and to secure an identification, but unfortunately the officers concerned received very short notice of the enterprise and had just time to make a hurried reconnaissance before darkness fell. Before dawn the platoons gathered at Captain Bennet Clark's H.Q., where they were shelled, and later they moved to their assembly positions 100 yards out in No-Man's-Land. At daybreak, covered by a barrage, the company advanced and explored the hostile front system of trenches without meeting a single German, so that it had to return empty-handed; six raiders were missing, and it was ascertained afterwards that these had been caught in our own barrage.

After being in reserve at Mazingarbe from the 8th to the 14th September, the battalion in two groups again entered the line on the latter date. In order to facilitate a raid which was to be carried out by another unit, the brigade front was held by three composite battalions: the right consisted of a company of the 10th Scottish Rifles and "C" and "D" Companies of the 9th Royal Scots under the command of Major W. C. S. Lindsay; and on the left were "A" and "B" Companies of the 9th Royal Scots and a company of the Scottish Rifles under the command of Captain Bennet Clark. The raid took place with the same result as that which had attended the effort of "A" Company on the 3rd September; no touch with the hostile infantry was obtained.

On the 20th September the 46th Brigade changed over with the 45th, and after a brief sojourn in the commodious but excessively damp tunnels at Vermelles, the 9th Royal Scots occupied trenches that had recently been taken from the enemy. The route from the tunnels led through a long communication trench, the latter part of which, being underground, was used as the H.Q. of the company in reserve, and also provided the cooking accommodation of the battalion. The approach ended with a good communication trench across the old No-Man's-Land, and then the battalion entered the battered remains of a German communication trench. There were several dug-outs, but as it was feared that these might contain traps no one was allowed to occupy them until they had been certified as safe by the Tunnelling Company; the entrances, of course, faced the wrong way and only the top portions of the stairs leading into the dug-outs could be used for resting accommodation. Moreover, much required to be done in the matter of consolidation, for the enemy was vindictive and gave the front companies a lively time. Quite a number of communication trenches ran into the new German positions and the blocks in these were gradually pushed forward; sentry duty at these dangerous forward posts was most exacting, our men suffering from lack of sleep and of regular hot meals, and it was with a keen sense of relief that officers and men left the line on the 28th September for a rest.

Very similar were the experiences of the 13th Royal Scots at this time. Opposite the battalion front at the beginning of September were the Quarries, which acquired a grim fame during the Battle of Loos in 1915, and at 5 A.M. on the 12th "D" Company moved forward into them and established a line of posts. This occupation was vigorously disputed by the Boches, and at 2 P.M. Captain Kelly and his company, finding that they were working round the flanks, were obliged to fight their way back to their original lines, bringing with them two prisoners. Next day "A" Company took the Quarries and held them against a series of German bombing attacks during the night. On the 14th September "C" Company relieved "A" and was kept busy repelling three desperate bombing assaults. Neither rest nor sleep was possible for the occupants of the Quarries, consequently reliefs were frequent, and on the 15th September "B" Company took over from "C." It was the intention of "B" Company to drive the enemy farther back, but the latter struck first, and at 5.25 A.M., in a furious charge, succeeded in establishing a post on the lip of the Quarries; there ensued some grim and desperate fighting, which reminded the veterans of the 13th Royal Scots of old times at the Hohen-zollern Redoubt, and ultimately the Germans were dislodged. In this *mêlée* 2nd Lieut. W. F. Forsyth was killed.

" D " Company was the next to occupy the Quarries, and attacking at 5 A.M. on the 16th it carried forward the line for some distance and held its own against a number of attacks. Thus though there was no big battle the experience of the 13th Royal Scots in the line during September was not devoid of risk or adventure. They were relieved on the night of the 16th/17th, and after another tour of trench duty, from the 20th till the 24th, they remained out of the line till October.

During September 1918 the forces of the Allies in France went on from strength to strength; after each slight lull the attack was resumed on a vaster scale. Near the end of the month the Germans still held Cambrai, Douai, and other important centres, and their position, particularly opposite the front of General Rawlinson's Fourth Army, was exceedingly strong, but the sound decision had been made that there was to be no halt on account of the lateness of the season, and plans were drawn up for a renewal of the attack on a scale which virtually made the battle extend from the Alps to the English Channel. The Americans were to assault the southern flank of the German line west of the Meuse in the direction of Mézières, and the French were to co-operate with them by an attack west of the Argonne; the task of the British was to break through the last of the Hindenburg defences and press on towards Maubeuge, while a combined force of Belgians and British was to attack the northern flank of the enemy in Flanders. The British attacks were arranged to begin on the 27th and 28th September. But before dealing with these it is necessary to turn our attention to the Balkans.

CHAPTER XXXVII

THE COLLAPSE OF BULGARIA

1st Battalion The Royal Scots, 1918

Position in the Balkans. 1st Royal Scots transferred to the Vardar. Plan of General Franchet d'Esperey. Task of 1st Royal Scots. Collapse of Bulgaria. Advance of 1st Royal Scots. Capitulation of Turkey.

THE decision to continue and even to extend the offensive on the Western front was supported by our dramatic victories in the Near East, where during September there was a sudden collapse of Bulgarian and Turkish military power. Quiescence was the normal state of affairs on the Balkan front till almost the close of the war, and people had ceased to expect important developments in that area. But Bulgaria had staked her fate on a German victory, and when, on the 8th August, the British troops began the drive that the Boche armies seemed impotent to arrest, she realised that she would be involved in the humiliation of her patron and ally. And while a feeling of hopelessness pervaded the Bulgarian armies, a new confidence awoke in the armies of the Allies, now commanded by the French General, Franchet d'Esperey. The offensive of the Allies was launched on the 15th September; on the first day the hostile line was broken on a front of 16 miles, and after a few days the Bulgarians made scarcely a pretence of resistance. The advance became a route march; on the 25th September the enemy requested an armistice and five days later accepted the terms of General Franchet d'Esperey.

In a campaign so brief there were few battles that provoked attention, and indeed the 1st Royal Scots always felt, that in being sent to a region so devoid of military incidents as the Balkans, they were denied a fair chance of showing the worth of the battalion. Their home throughout the winter of 1917-18 was the Struma valley, and during this period the command of the battalion was taken over by Lieut.-Colonel J. M. Mackenzie on the 18th October 1917, when Lieut.-Colonel Forbes was transferred to his own regiment. At the beginning of April 1918 the Royal Scots were relieved by a Greek unit and passed into Corps reserve. Lieut.-Colonel Mackenzie went to France on the 28th April, and the new C.O. was Lieut.-Colonel A. M. Ritchie of the Argylls.

Then followed a period of training of the most intensive description till the end of June, and on the 1st July the battalion with the other units of the division was transferred to the Vardar front. The move took nine days to accomplish, the troops proceeding to their destination by rail, by motor lorries, and by route march, and on the 10th July the Royal Scots took over the Slop sub-sector, on the west bank of the Vardar river, from the 148th French Regiment. This position was about 800 yards from the Serbian frontier immediately south of Dzeovo and was guarded on the right by the Vardar. Except for the riverine area the terrain consisted of steep, rocky hills and valleys, the British holding the south and the Bulgarians the north side of the valley of the Slop, a tributary of the Vardar.

The Bulgarians in this area were more daring than their comrades at the Struma; they had apparently been

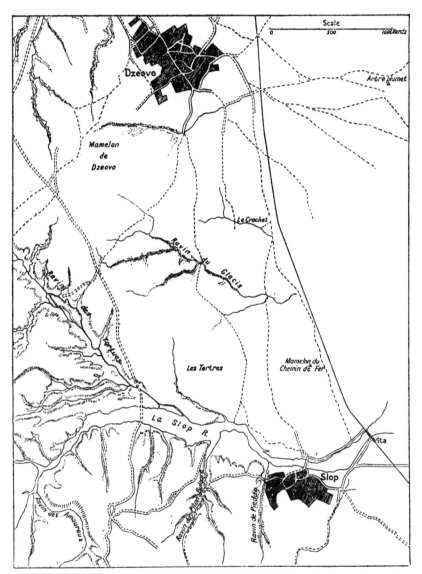

Scale

0   500   1000 Yards

Dzeovo

Arbre plumet

Mamelon
de
Dzeovo

Le Crochet

Ravin du Glacis

Ravin des Tertres

Les Tertres

Mamelon du
Chemin de Fer

La Slop R.

Ravin des Amoureux

Ravin de Pieddre

Ravin de Pied Bougre

Sta.

Slop

MAP XXVII.—The Vardar Valley.

allowed by the French to roam at will over No-Man's-Land, and two days before the Royal Scots took over, they had seized a Frenchman from a post on the railway which ran along the Vardar valley. One of the first patrols sent out by the 81st Brigade was attacked and bombed before it had proceeded ten yards beyond its own wire. Naturally there was a brisk struggle for the domination of No-Man's-Land after the arrival of the British troops, and the Bulgarians were soon convinced that they had opposed to them a foe more tenacious and enterprising than themselves. Thus a Bulgarian raid on a post of the Royal Scots, situated in the north-west side of Les Tertres, was smartly repulsed by "C" Company on the 30th July, the enemy leaving two corpses in our wire, while a month later, on the 30th August, the same company under Captain Storrar made a successful raid on Arbre Plumet in which it killed three Bulgarians and took one prisoner. Within a remarkably short space of time our troops enjoyed almost complete freedom of movement in No-Man's-Land. The enemy, having a plentiful supply of guns and ammunition, kept our trenches under almost continuous shell fire, and our men were grateful to the French for the excellent shelters which they had hewn out of the soft rock. Some of the deeper ravines and the caves on the reverse slope of the steep hills were absolutely safe, but many of our trenches were faulty, and most of the lateral and forward communications, though screened from view, offered no protection against shells.

Nightly raids were an item in the ordinary routine till the 1st September, when the Twenty-seventh Division began to play its part in the preparations for the general offensive that had been planned by General Franchet d'Esperey. The design of the division was to induce the Bulgarians to believe that we were about to launch a grand offensive on the Vardar front and so encourage them to crowd their reserves in this spot, while our main effort was made elsewhere. The more successful the Royal Scots were in the performance of their task, the worse would they make conditions for themselves; for while our guns were being sent to where they were required for the offensive, the Bulgarians were to be incited to increase the number of their guns on the Vardar front.

The deception of the enemy was skilfully engineered. The number of guns was temporarily increased, dummy camps were pitched, gangs of men were set to work on the roads, numerous screens, apparently to conceal our preparations for the offensive, were erected, patrols and raids were on a more ambitious scale, and gaps were cut in the hostile wire by artillery fire. These measures proved entirely successful; judged by the increase in the volume of his artillery fire the enemy was making ready to meet a thrust along the Vardar valley.

The Royal Scots carried out their part in the business with whole-hearted zest. No night passed without patrols being sent out, and though the men were fatigued by a sojourn of two and a half months in the line, they showed great enthusiasm in harassing the Bulgarians. On the night of the 1st/2nd September the whole of the 81st Brigade attacked and held the enemy's outpost line; the share of the Royal Scots in this enterprise was a small one, consisting of a raid by a patrol of "B" Company, led by Lieut. A. Wemyss, which cleared two advanced posts of the Bulgarians. On the following night the Royal Scots carried on the work by storming and holding a strong post known as Le Crochet.

The maintenance of this new line for twenty-one days after its capture was an arduous duty bravely

II   2 X 2

carried through by officers and men. In the hard rocky ground it was impossible to dig to any satisfactory depth, and our men consequently occupied the actual posts that had been used by the enemy. But their precise position was known to the Bulgarians, and their gunners directed gusts of shells on our posts, especially on Le Crochet, with the result that fairly heavy casualties were sustained by all the units of the 81st Brigade. Ration parties and reliefs were also often disturbed by heavy bursts of shell fire. But our men drew substantial consolation from the knowledge that their diversion had fulfilled its purpose; for by the 21st September the news was received that Serbian and French troops had pierced the Bulgarian front near Sakol and Veternik, and were advancing on the enemy's main line of communications.

In the mountainous fastnesses near the Vardar it was apparent that no general offensive could be under-taken without a gigantic cost in life, and this was borne out by the check which the Bulgarians administered to an attack by the British on the east side of the Vardar on the 18th September. It was confidently expected, however, that the advance of the Serbians would compel the adversary to abandon his present positions on the Vardar front, and this turned out to be the case. Ever since the beginning of September the hostile lines had been nightly tested by patrols, and at last, on the evening of the 21st/22nd, it became evident that something was happening. " The glare of fires could be seen all over the enemy's back lines, and constant explosions told of ammunition dumps being blown up, while their artillery fire gradually slackened and then ceased altogether, but not before my Staff Captain and my Galloper, Lieut. R. L. Gorrie of the Royal Scots, had been severely wounded by nearly the last shell fired in our direction."[1]

---

[1] From a description by Brig.-General Widdrington.

At 11.30 P.M. a patrol of the Royal Scots found that a hostile strong-point immediately south of Mamelon de Dzeovo (Ghevghueli) was vacant, and at daybreak on the 27th every unit of the Twenty-seventh Division was moving forward in column of route.

As far as the 1st Royal Scots were concerned, fighting in the Great War was at an end, for the pursuit of the Bulgarians was carried on by the Serbian and French troops, and by the British and Greek forces on the east of the Vardar. Thus the battalion enjoyed an untroubled march, and on the 29th September it arrived at Izlis on the Bulgarian frontier. There could be no doubt about the genuineness of the enemy's debacle; the road bore unmistakable traces of a defeated foe, and the gorges that skirted it on each side were choked with derelict transport of every description— guns, shells, and field kitchens. While the Royal Scots were in bivouac at Izlis on the 1st October, the tidings came in that Bulgaria had capitulated. Seldom has an overwhelming victory been accepted in so matter-of-fact a manner; there were no organised rejoicings, and for some days, under pouring rain, the units of the Twenty-seventh Division were kept hard at work mending the road, an uncommonly disagreeable method, the men thought, of celebrating a great victory.

The casualties sustained by the Royal Scots in the Vardar operations were considerable; Lieuts. W. A. Carruthers, G. Fyson, L. Scott, and seventeen men were killed, while four officers[1] and about one hundred men were wounded. But many more had succumbed to malaria, and so weak were all the units of the 81st Brigade that they were formed into a composite battalion. This arrangement was maintained for only a brief period, and then the battalions resumed their separate identities.

[1] Lieuts. N. A. Baines, R. L. Gorrie, G. E. M. Gore-Langton, and R. Scott.

Turkey had yet to be accounted for, and on the 16th October the Royal Scots began an advance on Adrianople. The battalion had reached Klisura, when orders were received for the Twenty-seventh Division to go back to Salonika, and the return march was commenced on the 3rd November. Turkey also had been compelled to capitulate.

The line reached by General Allenby after the series of victories resulting from the capture of Gaza lay north of Jaffa, Jerusalem, and Jericho, and while it was being consolidated during the summer, preparations were being made for the final humiliation of Turkey. The offensive began on the 19th September, and a series of admirable manœuvres, carried out by the cavalry, crumbled the Turkish forces to pieces; and ultimately the Ottoman power, impotent to stem the British advances from Palestine and Mesopotamia, accepted our armistice terms on the 30th October.

The elimination of Teutonic power in the Balkans and in Asia Minor had a potent effect upon the situation in France; when a substantial portion of the German structure fell in ruins, what remained standing was deprived of stability. It was obviously sound policy to deny the enemy time to repair the damage, and, as we have seen, arrangements were made by Marshal Foch and Sir Douglas Haig to extend our front of attack from the Alps to the sea. At the end of September the curtain was rung up on the final act of the drama.

CHAPTER XXXVIII

THE FINAL BLOW

September to November 1918

Attack of the British Fourth, Third, and First Armies, 27th and 29th September. 5/6th Royal Scots at Sequehart, 1st to 5th October. Action of 2nd Royal Scots, 27th September. Further operations of 2nd Battalion. Attack of 4th Royal Scots, 27th September. The Flanders offensive. Action of 17th Battalion, 28th to 30th September. Action of 11th and 12th Battalions, 28th September to 1st October. Continued success of Allied offensive. Operations of 17th Battalion, 14th to 31st October. Operations of 11th and 12th Battalions, 14th to 24th October. Advance of 9th and 13th Battalions. Battle of the Sambre, 1st to 11th November. Work of the 8th Royal Scots. 2nd Royal Scots at Vertain, 23rd October. 5/6th Royal Scots at the Battle of the Sambre. Last operations of the 4th and 7th Royal Scots. (See Map XVIII.)

THE general operations were commenced on the 26th September by the Americans and French on the right of the Allied line and immediately yielded successes, but the issue of the campaign, which was to determine whether the war would be concluded before the end of the year or was to stagnate throughout another weary winter, hinged upon the British attack in the centre delivered by the Fourth, Third, and First Armies. Protected by the colossal fortifications of the main Hindenburg Line, which represented all that German industry and skill could achieve in the art of defence, the enemy, fighting with the desperation of a man with his back to the wall, was certain to offer the most stubborn opposition of which he was capable.

Incomparably the strongest part of the Hindenburg system was on the Fourth Army front, where the keystone of the German defence was the St Quentin Canal, extending approximately from the village of Bantouzelle to St Quentin, and so formidable was this section of the hostile entrenchments that no infantry, however gallant or skilful, could hope to carry it until it had been weakened by a fierce and sustained bombardment. In order to give sufficient time for this to have its effect, it was arranged that the assault of the Fourth Army should take place two days after the attack on the 27th September of the Third and First Armies, which were confronted by entrenchments not quite so strong. The success attained surpassed our most sanguine hopes, and after many lively encounters the Germans were turned out of the last remaining sectors of the Hindenburg Line by the 5th October.

The 5/6th, 2nd, 4th, and 7th Battalions of the Royal Scots were all engaged in this phase of the offensive.

In the Fourth Army the Thirty-second Division was brought up from the hinterland to take part in the grand attack on the 29th September, when it assaulted the village of Le Tronquoy and the high ground in the vicinity of Levergies, and though it failed to carry the whole of its objectives the division made sufficient progress to secure the bridge-head which was established across the St Quentin Canal near Bellenglise. The 5/6th Royal Scots were inactive as far as fighting was concerned, since they were in reserve during the first two days of the battle. On the 30th, when the battalion was near Le Haucourt, "C" Company was sent up to the firing-line to fill a gap on the left of the 1st Dorsets.

After the Hindenburg Line was breached, there was

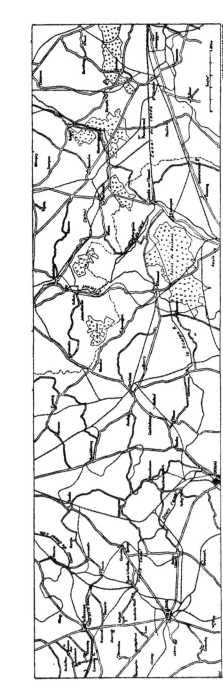

Map XXVIII.—The Final Advance (9th, 13th, 4th and 7th Battalions), September-November 1918.

(*See also* large scale Map at end of volume.)

a noticeable acceleration in the rate of our advance, but for several days on the front of the Fourth Army the fighting was of a desperate character, because other trench systems, the Beaurevoir-Fonsomme Line, had also to be carried; these defences were particularly strong near the village of Sequehart, perched on commanding ground.

Sequehart was the objective of the 5/6th Royal Scots in an attack at 4 P.M. on the 1st October. Advancing from Levergies with "B" Company on the right and "A" on the left, the Royal Scots swept through Sequehart in a rush and captured over one hundred and fifty Germans and numerous machine-guns. But the Boches in the evening revealed some of their old form, when, counter-attacking on both flanks at 8.30 P.M., they compelled the Royal Scots to evacuate the village and withdraw to a line from 100 to 200 yards to the west of it. In a second attempt, on the 2nd October, the battalion recaptured Sequehart after furious fighting, and with a view to parrying the expected counter-thrust, two companies of the 15th Highland Light Infantry were sent to guard the left, and another company the right, flank. Even these measures were not sufficient, as the enemy showed, three hours later, when he fell with overwhelming force on the left flank, driving it in again, and causing the Royal Scots to retire. The latter succumbed only to sheer weight of numbers, and a glorious effort to preserve the captured position was made by 2nd Lieut. A. Davidson Smith, who was in command of a company and had not allowed a nasty wound in the knee to deter him from remaining with his men till the objective was gained; on the news reaching him that the Germans were pouring through Sequehart, he tore himself free from the minis-trations of an orderly who was dressing his knee, and, making for the village, was striving his utmost to rally his men when a bullet brought his brave life to an end. The 5/6th Royal Scots lost other sterling officers in 2nd Lieuts. D. M. Duncan and J. Woltherspoon. The German losses must have been very heavy, for during the day's fighting two hundred and eighty prisoners, thirty machine-guns, and three field-guns were taken by the Royal Scots, but Sequehart was of such importance that the enemy seemed willing to make any sacrifice to keep it. In addition to the officers killed, the Royal Scots lost five officers [1] wounded, and more than one hundred other ranks in killed, wounded, and missing.

On the 3rd October a third attack met with better fortune. The Thirty-second Division was engaged in a general assault, and at the request of Lieut.-Colonel Fraser, Sequehart was again allotted to the Royal Scots as their objective. At 9 A.M. "C" and "D" Companies advanced with the fixed determination to carry and keep the village, and a glorious charge took them right through Sequehart, on the east side of which they consolidated a line; forty-five more prisoners were gathered in, and the hostile attempts to concentrate were all shattered by artillery and machine-gun fire. For two days the Royal Scots clung grimly to their shell-swept position, and having by this time secured a firm grasp on the village they beat off two counter-attacks with great loss to the enemy. The cost to the battalion was light, there being only one officer casualty (2nd Lieut. A. R. Mitchell wounded), and on the night of the 5th/6th October it was relieved and enjoyed respite from battle till the end of the month.

[1] Captains G. Benholm and T. Russell, Lieut. W. R. Graham, 2nd Lieuts. A. Hunter and P. Macarthur.

The sector occupied by the Third Division lay to the north of Havrincourt, and after a spell of duty in the rear lines the 2nd Royal Scots, on the 24th September, entered the front line a little to the north of the trenches which they had so gallantly and successfully defended on the 18th. Lieut.-Colonel Henderson was warned of the impending attack as early as the 24th, the objective assigned to his battalion being a very strong system of hostile trenches running north of Flesquières. So reduced in number was the battalion by this time that all four companies had to be used for the assault, which was timed to begin at 5.10 A.M. on the 27th September.

A gentle drizzle of rain, which began about 10 P.M., and the unusual darkness of the night did nothing to ease the muster of the troops, and the difficulties of the assembly were multiplied when about an hour before zero a heavy gas H.E. bombardment crashed upon the trenches of the Royal Scots. "C" and "D" Companies were caught by this barrage while on the move and suffered several casualties, but they recovered quickly from a momentary confusion and took up their allotted positions in good time. The shelling gradually died down, and the German guns were silent at zero when our barrage opened with telling effect. In a trice the Royal Scots were over the parapet, following in its wake. The first German trench, abandoned by its tenants, was crossed without incident; a second strip of trench was also passed, and still the opposition was negligible. But beyond this point was a ridge looking down on the objective, and as soon as the Royal Scots topped it, they heard the long-expected rattle of machine-guns. Some men dropped, but the line of bayonets surged on with the steadiness of a wave, and after a short struggle the whole objective was captured by 6.30 A.M. It was during the final stage of the attack that the battalion sustained most of its casualties ; Captain McLaren was wounded ; Captain R. D. Crossman, hit in the arm by a bullet, was waiting to have the wound dressed when a second bullet pierced his skull, killing him instantly.

To their great surprise the Royal Scots now saw behind them large parties of Germans, who must have hidden themselves in the dug-outs of the trenches that had been passed, and who, noticing how few in number their assailants were, plucked up courage to attack them from the rear. Bombing squads of the Royal Scots, organised by Lieut. Gunn of "C" Company, promptly advanced to engage the Boches, and while directing his men from the top of a parapet Lieut. Mitchell was killed by a rifle bullet. The Royal Scots rapidly closed in on the Germans, and were giving them a warm reception, when the sudden appearance of the leading troops of the 76th Brigade, who were to pass through the battalion, brought the resistance of the enemy to an inglorious conclusion ; the hostile force which comprised seven officers and two hundred and sixty men at once surrendered to "C" Company, which numbered less than one hundred men in all.

No counter-attack interrupted the work of consolidation, and though "A" and "B" Companies on the right had the misfortune to lose their senior officers, the subalterns on the spot proved themselves competent to deal with the situation and soon had everything in shipshape order. Posts were pushed out to a sunken road east of the captured trenches and were held despite the harassing machine-gun fire that was directed on them from the north-west. Lieut.-Colonel Henderson, who kept in close touch with the development of the battle, exposing himself too freely while reconnoitring the road, nearly fell victim to this machine-gun, which fortunately was mopped up by the Guards Brigade on the left when it continued its advance early in the forenoon. After this the situation was appreciably easier.

With the opening of the second phase of the battle, which commenced at 9.15 A.M., when the Sixty-second passed through the Third Division, all the anxiety of the 2nd Royal Scots was ended. No longer disturbed by hostile fire, parties collected the bodies of the fallen, which were sent back for burial in the cemetery at Morchies. Besides the officers mentioned, Lieuts. Craw, Dickson, Maconochie, and Thomson were wounded, and of the men twelve were killed, one hundred and nine wounded, and three missing. On the 30th September the battalion was transferred to dug-outs near Flesquières; next day it occupied trenches some distance west of Marcoing, and, while there, was instructed to take over trenches in brigade support to the east of Masnières.

Before this move was begun, Lieut. - Colonel Henderson was ordered to send a company to assist the Gordons, who were to attack Rumilly at 6.30 P.M., and for this purpose he selected "B" Company, commanded by Captain Maxwell, at the same time reporting to brigade that it could not possibly reach Rumilly till 7.30 P.M. Captain Maxwell thereupon led his men off, and had the satisfaction of arriving in time to clear the village after it had been captured; the houses and cellars were thoroughly combed out by searchers, but only two Germans were discovered.

The other companies set off an hour after "B" and were lucky to reach their positions without loss, since the bridge by which they had to cross the St Quentin

Canal at Masnières was being shelled by a heavy gun. Lieut.-Colonel Henderson was searching for some catacombs in the village, where he had been told to establish his H.Q., when he observed several men in the distance and hailed them. To his intense astonishment they rushed towards him with arms in the air and waving handkerchiefs that had once been white; these were Germans, whose immediate anxiety was to find someone to whom they could surrender. The catacombs eluded the most exhaustive exploration, and after satisfying himself about the dispositions of his companies, which were entrenched near the Crêvecœur Road, just east of Masnières, he set up his H.Q. in dug-outs on the Masnières-Rumilly Road. On the evening of the 4th October the battalion relieved the Royal Scots Fusiliers in the front line, "D" and "A" Companies manning the firing-line trenches on a ridge 2000 yards east of Rumilly. But the strength of the battalion was such that this arrangement had to be slightly altered, all four companies going into the line and disposing their platoons in depth.

This line was maintained till the 8th October, in the early morning of which the 76th Brigade and the Second Division were to resume the attack, a brigade of the latter having to pass through the lines of the Royal Scots. To facilitate the operations, Lieut.-Colonel Henderson withdrew "A" and "C" Companies on the night of the 7th/8th to Rumilly, while the others spread out so as to cover the whole front. Prior to the attack the two front companies were also withdrawn, and on the 8th October the 2nd Royal Scots were taken from the battle to Hermies, and did not return to action till the 23rd October.

The 4th and the 7th Royal Scots near Mœuvres were

II   2 Y

ready in good time for their share in the great attack
on the 27th September. The task of the 156th Brigade
was uncommonly difficult, seeing that no assistance
could be given by tanks, owing to the impassable
barrier presented by the deep dry fosse of the Canal
du Nord, and the infantry would have to accomplish
their object with the help of such support as could be
given by the artillery. The hostile defences formed
part of the main system of the Hindenburg Line,
which was here exceptionally strong, since the ground
on the east side of the canal stood higher than that
on our side, while the banks of the canal formed a
forbidding-looking rampart of an average height of
20 feet. Moreover, the terrain was a confusion of
trenches, barbed wire and strong-points, the legacy
of the terrific conflicts during the Battle of Cambrai.

The 4th Royal Scots, the leading unit of the
156th Brigade, had first to secure the line of the
canal, and then a trench to the east of it, cut by
the Mœuvres - Graincourt Road. From this stage
the 7th Cameronians were to carry on the advance,
and after they had accomplished their task, the Fifty-
second Division was to be squeezed out of the front
line by the divisions on both sides extending their
flanks after the crossings of the canal were secured.
The 7th Royal Scots were in brigade reserve.

An excellent barrage heralded the assault, and at
5.30 A.M., on the 27th September, "A" and "D"
Companies, having formed up in front of their shelter
trenches, spread out into the waste of No-Man's-
Land. After a few steps, the Royal Scots, like
poachers surprised by hidden snares, were struggling
in a ganglion of rusty wire, concealed by the jungle-
like growth of long rank grass, and by the time they
tore themselves free, leaving fragments of skin and

clothing on the wire, the barrage had lifted beyond protecting distance. Their losses were heavy, and the men were slightly shaken by the violence of the German fire, but rallying at the call of their officers and N.C.Os., they regained cohesion and captured a shallow trench lying immediately west of the rampart of the canal.

Against so formidable a barrier even a victorious frontal assault would cost many lives, so Major Slater, who commanded the battalion in this action, ordered groups of bombers to endeavour to work round the left flank. These advanced northwards along the trench, until they were separated from the canal embankment only by a short strip of trench, guarded by a tiny pill-box and two machine-guns. The tactics so often employed with success against these fortifications were once more adopted; while his comrades engaged the pill-box with fire, Corporal Foggo, dashing forward, flung two bombs into the post, then, being joined by the others, speedily cleared the pill-box and scaled the wall of the canal just south of the Graincourt-Mœuvres Road. The resistance of the enemy, apparently surprised and disheartened by the sudden appearance of this small party, thereupon collapsed; "A" and "D" Companies, hastily swarming up the western embankment, slid down into the dry bed of the canal and clambered up the eastern wall. After this triumph there was nothing to stop the Royal Scots, who by 10.30 A.M. were in possession of the whole of their objectives, and the tide of battle, rolling onwards, left the battalion unmolested. Lieut. A. M. Wood Hawks, 2nd Lieut. G. W. Sinclair, and twenty-three men were killed; eight officers[1] and eighty-

---

[1] Captain Bolton, Lieut. Archurch, and 2nd Lieuts. Barnetson, Leiper, Liston, Philp, Rutherford, and Smart.

seven men were wounded. These losses were heavy in proportion to the total strength of the battalion, but were a mere bagatelle compared with what they would have been had the operation not been against a demoralised foe. Over two hundred prisoners and a litter of all sorts of war material formed the spoils.

With no hitch of any consequence in the attack, the 7th Royal Scots were not required to do more than take up a series of positions in readiness to act if called upon.

For both battalions there now ensued a period of comparative ease. After a short sojourn on the ground captured by it on the 27th September, the Fifty-second relieved the Sixty-third Division in the line near Cambrai, where the German resistance was conducted with determination and skill. On the 1st October a courageous attack by the 155th Brigade failed to carry the hostile defences at the Faubourg de Paris. The 156th Brigade, in reserve, was not involved in the action, and the men of the 4th and the 7th Royal Scots were employed in numerous disagreeable fatigues, mostly performed under shell-fire. In this part of the battlefield indeed the conflict equalled in fury the murderous struggles of 1916 and 1917, and every night was rendered hideous by the bombing activities of German aircraft. Consequently the Royal Scots were glad to turn westwards on the 5th October, when the whole division was relieved. Comfortable billets awaited the battalions at Izel le Hameau, and they did not return to the line until the 28th October.

The brilliant victory of the British Fourth, Third, and First Armies in the centre of the Allied line removed all possibility of the Germans protracting their defence beyond the winter, and their position was rendered even more hopeless by the successful attacks of the Americans and French on the right flank, and of the British and Belgians on the left flank, of the Allied line. The Flanders offensive opened on the 28th September, and in its first phase, extending till the 1st October, carried the line approximately to the Menin-Roulers Road. The 17th, 11th, and 12th Royal Scots were engaged in these operations.

The ground traversed during the battle was familiar to many of the officers and men. Superficially the landscape had undergone a vast change since the struggles of 1917, when there was not a vestige of greenery to gladden the eye and the country was a wilderness of water-filled shell-holes and mud. During the unwonted tranquillity with which the Salient had so far been blessed during 1918, an amazing trans-formation had been wrought. The silent processes of nature buried the scars of war beneath a fresh green mantle, and what had been a chaos of mud and water now presented itself as a broken prairie land clothed with long rank grass. But the thick groves of pre-war days were beyond revival; only a few forlorn stumps, protruding here and there from the earth, marked their sites.

The 17th Royal Scots took over a portion of the line south of Ypres at the beginning of September. The hostile shelling was fairly vigorous, and on the 18th Lieut. - Colonel Scougal, one of the original officers of the battalion, was killed by a shell; no one had been more intimately associated with the battalion than he, and his death, virtually on the eve of the operations, cast a gloom over the whole unit. He was succeeded by Lieut.-Colonel W. A. Murray.

Except for the great discomfort of marching over

II   2 Y 2

difficult country, the opening day of the battle brought no particular trouble to the battalion, which was in reserve to the 12th and the 18th Highland Light Infantry. During the night of the 27th/28th September it was near Zillebeke, and on the 28th, under a steady downpour of rain, it moved at 6.50 A.M. to positions south-west of Zillebeke Lake. Then, after advancing to a point near Shrewsbury Forest, it received orders at 11.45 A.M. to support the left flank of the 18th Highland Light Infantry by occupying the slight ridge crowned by the ruins known as Alaska Houses. This was accomplished without a hitch, and by means of patrols touch was eventually established with troops of the Twenty-ninth Division on the left.

The Alaska Houses Ridge was maintained till the afternoon of the 29th, when instructions arrived for the 106th Brigade to advance in support of the 105th, and thereafter assist it to attack a line extending north-east from Tenbrielen, the advance being in the general direction of Wervicq. While the Royal Scots were moving forward, they were ordered to make an attack on the left of the North Staffords, and at 3.10 P.M. the battalion, passing through Zandvoorde without encountering opposition, set out on its mission with its right flank on the Zandvoorde-Tenbrielen Road. Shells began to fall and, on reaching the forward slope of a rise, the battalion came under vigorous machine-gun fire which appreciably retarded progress. By a skilful use of fire and movement, it continued to creep onwards until the rate of advance was suddenly accelerated by the arrival of a company of the 12th Highland Light Infantry on the right flank. The Boches were forced to abandon a counter-attack, for which they had been obviously preparing, and two companies of the Royal Scots, under Captain Craig and Captain Matley,

Lieut.-Colonel A. G. Scougal, M.C., 17th Battalion, The Royal Scots.

[*To face p.* 712.

stormed and captured the enemy's machine-gun posts. There was little diminution in the volume of fire, but the German opposition was worn down by the tenacity of the Royal Scots, and by nightfall the battalion was established on a line about 500 yards to the north of Tenbrielen, facing south-east.

On the following day, the 30th September, the 12th and the 18th Highland Light Infantry passed through the outpost positions of the 17th Royal Scots and pressed on towards Wervicq.   For the first 1500 yards our progress was unimpeded, but then heavy machine-gun fire broke out on the front and both flanks of the brigade.   The left flank was the critical one, and Lieut.-Colonel Murray with sound judgment sent forward two companies to safeguard this wing. These, crossing a deep belt of wire, reached a position to the north of Wervicq, while the remainder of the brigade bore down on the village, but the resistance of the enemy markedly hardened, and the other two companies were called on to advance in support of the forward companies. Harassing fire scourged the Royal Scots not merely from the left flank but from the left rear, where the enemy still held some pill-boxes, one of which was daringly rushed, an N.C.O. and six Germans being captured.

The casualties of the Royal Scots were mounting rapidly, and the battalion had to brace itself up to meet a dangerous counter-attack, in which the Germans displayed some of their old-time skill and perseverance. The support companies were forced to give ground, and two platoons of the forward companies were overwhelmed, but after much stern fighting the battalion succeeded in forming a firm line along a road to the north-west of Wervicq, in touch with the 18th Highland Light Infantry.   All the trouble had sprung from the fact that liaison with the troops on the left had been lost, and in spite of every effort it had not been restored, when at the end of the month the 17th Royal Scots were relieved by the 7th Royal Irish Regiment of the Thirtieth Division and returned to the vicinity of Zillebeke. During this period Captain S. McKnight, Lieut. W. Gairns, and 2nd Lieut. A. Bennie were killed, one officer was missing and nine were wounded[1]; in other ranks the casualties in killed, wounded, and missing totalled three hundred and nine. The stubbornness of the enemy's opposition may be gauged from the fact that only thirteen prisoners were brought in.

The Ninth Division, lying near "Hell-fire Corner," had to traverse a series of ridges, Frezenberg, Anzac, and Glasgow Spur, before it reached its final objective near the Polygone de Zonnebeke. On this occasion the 27th Brigade was in reserve, and its action would depend upon the situation at the close of the day. Brig.-General Croft was expected to be prepared for any one of three courses : to assist either of the attacking brigades if necessary, to advance north from Broodseinde to help the Belgians on the left, to exploit the victory by storming the village of Becelaere.

Fortified by a course of training extending over five weeks, the 11th and the 12th Royal Scots were in the best possible trim for a difficult campaign, and they returned to the battle line with a keen desire to join in the chase of the Boches. Previous to the 28th September they were in camps behind the line, and early on the morning of the battle they followed up the 26th and 28th Brigades, which led the attack. Rain was falling in torrents, and Ypres loomed through the dun light like a spectral shadow as the battalions skirted

---

[1] 2nd Lieut. A. I. Grant missing ; the wounded were 2nd Lieuts. A. S. Asquith (who died from the effects of his injuries), J. R. Craig, P. Bourhill, L. Hamlet, J. Kennedy, C. Mann, A. Ruston, A. G. Syme, and A. T. Tait.

the city and marched along the Menin Road. A sense of uncanniness was produced by the total absence of shell fire ; on the Western front there was no highway which had earned such a sinister reputation as the Menin Road, yet not a casualty was sustained by the Royal Scots as they trudged along that desolate route in the grey September morning. Physical endurance was tested when the men turned north from this highway and at each step sank, ankle-deep, in the broken, unstable soil. A plank track led to the Frezenberg Ridge, but it was in such a state of disrepair that horses, hauling up field-guns, slipped through the spaces in the boarding and were extricated only with enormous trouble. But the hostile guns were still silent, and the Royal Scots continued to advance, without human molestation, over ground which a year ago the Boches had defended so obstinately that every inch gained had represented a heavy cost in life.

The 26th and 28th Brigades secured all their objectives, and the Royal Scots moved steadily onwards till they reached the unsightly mound of the Polygone Butt. By this time it had been decided to employ the 27th Brigade against Becelaere, and at 2.30 P.M. the 12th and the 11th Royal Scots deployed from the Butt to attack the village. The left flank of the latter battalion was strenuously opposed, the chief resistance coming from German gunners who pluckily brought up three batteries near the north of Becelaere and opened fire at point-blank range. But the hostile infantrymen were little more than spectators, and the Royal Scots, covered by the fire of machine-guns, were allowed to approach close to the guns, when they silenced two of the batteries and captured the other. Meantime the 12th Royal Scots, driving the Boche infantry before them like sheep, entered the ruins of the village just before dusk, and at this point a halt was called. The Germans beyond Becelaere were evidently in considerable strength, for a fairly heavy shell and machine-gun fire was directed upon the 11th Royal Scots; the right flank was quite satisfactory, being linked with the Twenty-ninth Division, but the left was in the air and it was, therefore, politic to press the advance no farther that night.

Making themselves as comfortable as circumstances permitted, the men passed the night on the ground that they had captured, and they were enormously cheered by the arrival of their rations, which, in spite of stupendous difficulties, the brigade had contrived to bring up on pack-mules. Dawn, on the 29th September, broke quietly without any indication of a German counter-stroke, and at 9.30 A.M. the Ulster Division marched through the outposts of the Lowlanders to attack the village of Terhand.

With the Irishmen on the right and the Belgians on the left, the Ninth Division resumed its attack with the 28th Brigade in the van. There was a momentary check when the leading men reached a strongly-wired line of defences running east of Moorslede and Waterdamhoek, but the 27th Brigade had followed on the heels of the 28th, and two companies of the 11th Royal Scots and two of the 6th K.O.S.B., being thrown into the battle, gave our attack the necessary impetus to burst the defence; the Germans hurried eastwards in disorganised groups, and our advance was carried up to the Menin-Roulers Road. Darkness was falling, and the evening air vibrant with the rattle of countless machine-guns indicated that considerable reinforcements had reached the enemy. Our tired troops were rapidly reorganised, and an outpost line was formed along the road,

The 30th September dawned wet and disagreeable, and the Ninth Division, resting on its gains, hoped that Hill 41, a slight rise dominating the whole of the country round Dadizeele and Ledeghem, would be captured by the division on its right; but this had not been done when the 27th Brigade was ordered to resume the attack on the 1st October.

The village of Ledeghem, which had not been within the zone of the war since 1914, was the objective of the brigade, and after a farm, standing on high ground about 1000 yards north-west of the village, had been carried by a company of the 11th Royal Scots, the attack was to be launched by the K.O.S.B. and the 12th Royal Scots at 5.30 A.M. A heavy hostile barrage before zero betokened the intention of the Germans to fight, but providentially it fell behind the brigade, and at first it seemed as if the assault would carry all before it. Several farm buildings were quickly cleared, and Ledeghem itself was seized within a few minutes of the opening of the attack, but the Germans, recovering from the first effects of our onslaught, began to hold firm, and, secure in the possession of Hill 41 and the high ground south of the village, they were able to rake the entire front of the 27th Brigade with deadly enfilade fire. Thus, though the 12th Royal Scots advanced 1000 yards beyond Ledeghem, the K.O.S.B., on the right, were forced to form a defensive flank. Unfortunately the left flank of the division, where the 26th Brigade was attacking, was in the air, as well as the right, and the Germans commenced a dangerous counter-attack. Led by mounted officers, they advanced in close order from the south-east at 10.30 A.M., but they were stopped by the concentrated fire of composite groups of the K.O.S.B. and 12th Royal Scots, stationed near the village cemetery. Two hours later a second attack, delivered both from the north-east and the south-east, drove the remnants of the 27th Brigade out of the village, but a prompt counter-assault by the 11th Royal Scots recovered the station buildings, and enabled the brigade to maintain its grasp on the northern portion of Ledeghem. The opportune arrival of a battalion of the Ulster Division removed all apprehension as far as the right flank was concerned, and at nightfall the position of the 27th Brigade, holding the line of the railway and the northern half of Ledeghem, was thoroughly secure. After the action the brigade was relieved, and from the 2nd till the 13th October there ensued a lull in the operations.

The collapse of the German centre and northern flank precipitated the withdrawal of the hostile garrisons holding the Loos and the Lys fronts. The Boches in front of the Fifteenth Division commenced to retire on the 2nd October, and the 13th Royal Scots, who relieved the 8th Argylls on the 3rd, did their utmost to accelerate the backward movement of the enemy. The ground traversed during the pursuit brought back memories of 1915, for the village of Vendin, entered on the 4th October by patrols of the battalion, had been looked on as one of the prizes of the Loos offensive. The Germans momentarily rallied, and though the Royal Scots, acting in co-operation with the Camerons, worked through the village in the course of the evening, they could not keep all the ground that they had gained. A quiet day on the 5th was followed by a Boche raid which forced an advanced post of the 13th Royal Scots to retire about 150 yards, the energy of the adversary being probably due to his anxiety to shake off our pressure in order that he might have an opportunity of withdrawing

without interruption across the Deule Canal. This
suspicion was confirmed by observers of the 13th Royal
Scots, who noticed that many of the enemy were
accoutred in full marching order, while aeroplanes
returned with information that most of the bridges
across the canal had already been demolished. No
change occurred, however, while the 13th Royal Scots
remained in the line. On the 10th October they were
relieved by the 9th Royal Scots, who had been training
near Vermelles since the 28th September, and returned
to the vicinity of Mazingarbe.

At the end of the first week of October there was
barely a flicker of hope to comfort the Germans.
Driven from almost the whole of their carefully prepared entrenchments, which had hitherto proved so
effective as bulwarks, they were now compelled to base
their defence upon such natural obstacles, particularly
the rivers, as were presented by the lie of the ground ;
they had no time to do more than erect hasty artificial
obstacles. But it could not be expected that hurriedly
improvised barriers could stop an enemy that had
broken through the most formidable entrenchments on
the Western front, and as a result of the Second
Battle of Le Cateau, lasting from the 8th till the
12th October, the Germans lost Cambrai and were
forced back to the line of the River Selle. Moreover,
the difficulties of re-establishing and constructing new
communications across the wastes of Flanders were
speedily overcome by the Belgians and British, and
a new offensive, beginning on the 14th October,
pushed the enemy to the eastern bank of the River
Scheldt. The 17th, 11th and 12th Battalions of the
Royal Scots were concerned in these operations.

Having moved forward from Zillebeke to a camp at
Gheluvelt, the 17th Battalion on the eve of the battle

was in divisional reserve about 3500 yards to the east of Gheluvelt; it had little to do during the first part of the action. On the 15th it was near Kezelberg on the west side of the Menin-Roulers Road, when it received orders to support an attack by the 106th Brigade on the 16th October at 5.30 A.M. The battalion was in support, but even its assembly position, approximately south of Gulleghem, was indicated on a map which the Allies had never had occasion to use since 1914. Nothing could be done during daylight on the 17th October, since sufficient artillery was not available to support the crossing of the Lys south of Courtrai, but it was arranged that at 10 P.M. the 12th Highland Light Infantry and the sappers would cross the river and establish bridge-heads; after this was done the 17th Royal Scots, passing through, were to seize the railway north of Marcke, and, if possible, secure the village. All the bridges arranged for could not be set up, owing to the enemy's opposition, but a foot-bridge was thrown across the Lys and two platoons of the 17th Royal Scots, under Lieuts. Harvey and Inman, crossed to the east side after midnight and rushed a German post, capturing three of the garrison. Other posts were also vacated by the enemy, and after killing six Boches the patrol returned at dawn on the 18th, its only casualty being Lieut. H. R. Harvey, who was wounded.

On the 18th October the battalion was asked to carry out a night operation for the purpose of seizing Marcke. With "Z" and "Y" Companies leading, the battalion could only reach its assembly position by the slender foot-bridge, but the darkness facilitated its approach, and, advancing at 10 P.M. under a barrage, it secured all its objectives with little difficulty, and the loss of three men wounded. Marcke was full of civilians, who to some extent handicapped the movements of the men, who could not be absolutely certain of the attitude of the Belgians towards the foe; twenty-four Germans and four machine-guns were captured. On the 19th October the 104th Brigade carried on the attack, and the 17th Royal Scots passed into divisional reserve.

At 7 A.M., on the 20th October, the battalion set out on a march to Evangelie Boom, but before it reached the main highway leading south-east from Courtrai, word arrived that the brigades in front had been checked by machine-gun fire. At 10 A.M. it was ordered to move forward to the vicinity of Geeteknok, where it remained till 4.30 P.M., when instructions were received to proceed to Kreupel in reserve to the 12th and the 18th Highland Light Infantry. Then came news that these units had pressed on to Molente Claere, and the battalion was accordingly instructed to clear a ridge extending from this place to Hoogstraatje, and drive the enemy from the west side of the Courtrai Canal. Early on the morning of the 21st October the 17th Royal Scots, reinforced by a section of the Machine-Gun Battalion, set off on this mission, two platoons of "Z" Company forming the van and main guard, and the remainder of the company and "Y" forming the main body. Lieut.-Colonel Murray's plan was to continue the advance along the road leading from west of Kreupel to west of Zonnebergen until resistance was encountered, and then deploy and attack the ridge.

There was no opposition until the battalion had gone about half-way along this road, when a Very light was sent up and a machine-gun opened fire. Supported by machine-gun fire, a platoon under Lieut. Inman routed the Boches, and the battalion, deploying, advanced and made good its hold on the ridge. There was no sign of any foeman in Hoogstraatje, but a patrol which was sent to explore the canal bank was stopped by machine-gun fire. A few pockets of the enemy had been over-looked, but the clearing parties of the Royal Scots had no difficulty in dealing with them, one German being killed and two others captured. The flanks were secure, as the battalion was in touch with the 12th Highland Light Infantry on the right, and at 9 P.M. another division passed through; on the 22nd October the unit returned to the comfort of billets at Courtrai.

There were no other events of note in the war career of the 17th Royal Scots. On the 24th October they were at Sweveghem, and on the 26th they had a spell of front-line duty near Avelghem. On the 31st they supported an attack of the 104th Brigade with two companies, after which they were withdrawn to billets near Kreupel. The dearth of exciting incident is borne out by the brevity of the casualty list during October; Lieut. H. R. Harvey was wounded and thirty-six other ranks were killed or wounded.

The 11th and the 12th Battalions, like the 17th, were in reserve on the 14th October, when the general objective of the Ninth Division was the Courtrai-Lendelede Railway. The advance was carried without any outstanding episode as far as a low ridge near Steenen Stampkot about noon, but from this time the German resistance became more determined, and though the Highlanders of the 26th Brigade gained a footing in Laaga Cappelle Wood, they could make no more progress owing to the heavy fire which was brought to bear upon them from Hill 40, a low-lying ridge about 500 yards east of the wood.

On the following day, the 27th Brigade, with the 11th and the 12th Royal Scots in front, advanced through the outposts at 9 A.M., and under cover of a smoke-screen doubled forward towards Hill 40. The 11th Royal Scots cleared Laaga Cappelle Wood of the enemy, but on leaving the shelter of the trees they came under a fire so intense and accurate that the men dropped to the ground for cover, and it seemed for a time as if the whole advance would be stopped by two machine-gun posts which the enemy had stationed on the hill. At this juncture Corporal Elcock, in what seemed an act of daring folly, dashed forward with a Lewis gun, and, ignoring the gusts of hostile bullets, opened fire, and with his first burst killed the two men who were working one of the German guns; then leaping into their shelter, he turned his gun on the other Boche team and by splendid shooting put it out of action. The obstacle to their advance having thus been adroitly and opportunely removed, the 11th Royal Scots moved rapidly over the hill. Meantime Lieut.-Colonel J. Murray and the 12th Royal Scots, who had followed the 11th through the wood, had swung to the south and driven the Boches from Steenbeek and the southern portion of Hill 40.

After hasty reorganisation the two battalions pressed eastwards, with the 12th Royal Scots on the right, and only a feeble opposition was encountered at Heule Wood, where the 12th Battalion secured a number of prisoners, of whom twelve were killed by one of our 6-inch howitzer shells which dropped short. At Snephoek Road there was a brief halt to make sure that touch was maintained with the troops on both flanks. From this point till the objective was reached, the resistance of the enemy developed in strength, and it was due to the dexterous and enterprising manœuvres of sections and platoons that progress continued to be made. On arriving at the Heule-Ingelmunster Railway the Royal Scots were harried for a time by the fire of two hostile field-guns, but these on being located were cleverly stalked by Captain Brock and some of the 12th

II   2 Z

Royal Scots, who shot the crews and secured the guns as trophies.

After some hesitation it was decided to carry on the advance, for the risk of pressing on with both flanks in the air was negligible in view of the obvious demoralisation of the enemy. Cyclists indeed had already passed through the ranks of the infantry, and were in close pursuit of the Boches. On the right flank, where the 12th Royal Scots and the 6th K.O.S.B. followed the cyclists, nothing happened to occasion any anxiety, and the 12th Royal Scots entered Cuerne on the Lys between 3 and 4 P.M., while the K.O.S.B. relieved the cyclists in the posts that they had taken up near the river. The left flank gave more cause for uneasiness, for the Germans, having forced the Belgians to yield some ground, were in a favourable position to pour enfilade fire into the 11th Royal Scots as they passed Heetje. Tough fighting ensued before the village was cleared, and the autumn sun was westering when the 11th Royal Scots were free to resume their advance. The Germans appeared to be in considerable force on a slight ridge between Abeelhoek and the Lys, and they checked an attempt of Lieut.-Colonel Campbell's men to disperse them by a rush, but they evacuated their position in the course of the night. The situation on the left wing was now so obscure that there was no justification for pushing on, and the 27th Brigade formed an outpost line with the 6th K.O.S.B. and the 11th Royal Scots near the Lys, while the 28th Brigade was diverted to Cappelle St Catherine to protect the exposed northern flank.

The Lys looked a nasty obstacle; it was at least 70 feet wide, and for an immediate crossing there was just one partially destroyed bridge near Harlebeke, which was strongly guarded by machine-guns. From the houses bordering the Courtrai-Harlebeke Road the Germans commanded every inch of the glacis slope leading up to it from the river, and the only possibility of securing a lodgment on the east bank was by a night operation, which Brig.-General Croft arranged to carry out at 8 P.M. on the 16th October. By means of two slender bridges, constructed under tremendous difficulties by the sappers, the K.O.S.B. slipped across, but the 11th Royal Scots, entrusted with the task of rushing the semi-ruined bridge near Harlebeke, could do nothing against the heavy fire that raked every approach.

The bridge-head formed by the K.O.S.B. had not sufficient depth to be safe, and shortly after dawn, on the 17th October, the Germans, turning every available gun on the rickety bridges, made a violent counter-attack. The situation became so grave that two companies of the 12th Royal Scots were despatched to reinforce the K.O.S.B. The bridges straddling the river were already giving way when the Royal Scots began their perilous crossing; men were gripped by the foot in the broken boarding, and spouts of water, thrown up by bursting shells, drenched them to the skin and prevented them from seeing where they were going. Several were drowned in the Lys, but the survivors, inspired by the courageous leadership of Lieut. Georgeson, went through this ordeal of fire and water as steadily as if they were on an ordinary parade, and their arrival averted any immediate danger of the bridge-head being rushed.

Nevertheless the position of the garrison on the east bank of the river was not satisfactory, for when the hostile fire had reduced the bridges to a few fragments of splintered timber, the men were entirely cut off from their comrades in Cuerne. Rations and ammunition were sent to the garrison by means of aeroplanes, while two platoons of the 12th Royal Scots rendered conspicuously gallant service; one by one, leaping from plank to plank, and occasionally up to the neck in water, the men, every yard of whose progress was made under unnerving machine-gun fire, ultimately succeeded in reaching the far side, and conveyed precious supplies of ammunition to the firing-line; it was an ordeal which the most hardened Indian fakir might have shirked without shame. But the Germans had lost heart for infantry clashes, and comparative quietness prevailed till night, when new bridges were hastily thrown across the river and the K.O.S.B. and the two companies of the 12th Royal Scots were brought back to the safety of the west bank. Relieved by a brigade of the Twenty-ninth Division, the Lowlanders retired to the neighbourhood of Laaga Cappelle Wood.

The passage of the Lys had still to be forced, and on the night of the 19th/20th October this operation was brilliantly achieved, the 26th and 28th Brigades on the front of the Ninth Division carrying the line forward on the 20th to the station at Vichte. The 27th Brigade came on the heels of the others, and, spending the night near Harlebeke, moved up on the following day to some farms on the west side of Vichte. The whole of the district was overlooked by the high ground east of that village, and gusts of shells periodically burst on the farms where the men were sheltering. The 12th Royal Scots were most unfortunate. Three shells, landing in rapid succession, inflicted mortal injuries on Captain S. McKinley, than whom no more loyal and efficient Adjutant ever breathed. During the black days of March and April his unfailing cheerfulness, when foot-sore and racked by an asthmatic cough, endeared him to the men of his battalion, and earned for him a high prestige in a division where gallant men were numbered by hundreds. The loss of such an officer spread a gloom that was not easily dispelled.

The 22nd October witnessed the resumption of the advance. The 11th Royal Scots at 9 A.M. went forward to clear the village of Vichte and to carry the height beyond it known as Hill 50. A dense mist and a heavy concentration of gas caused a certain amount of delay and confusion, but the Royal Scots penetrated the village without much trouble. Their difficulties started when they were clear of the houses and began to mount the rise. The German machine-gunners on Hill 50 and Klijtberg were in their most stubborn mood and checked the advance, but the attack of the 11th Royal Scots so far weakened the enemy that the K.O.S.B., who followed them, were able with the support of some forward guns to carry Hill 50, where a line was established, the 11th Royal Scots and the K.O.S.B. forming the outposts, with the 12th Royal Scots, who had not been involved in the fighting, in brigade reserve. This line was held till the night of the 24th/25th October, when the 27th Brigade was relieved by the 26th and 28th Brigades, which on the 25th drove the Germans back to the line of the Scheldt. On leaving the battle-front the 11th and the 12th Royal Scots concentrated first at Harlebeke and later at Cuerne. They were not destined to be involved again in active operations.

The collapse of their positions at Cambrai, and their defeat in Flanders, caused the Germans in front of the Fifteenth Division to hasten their retirement.

II   2 Z 2

The 9th Royal Scots at Vendin lost no time in bustling the enemy and on the 12th October delivered a very successful attack. "A" and "C" Companies, advancing with great dash, turned the Germans out of every post that they held on the west side of the Deule Canal, and captured thirty-five prisoners and a considerable number of machine-guns. Much of the fighting that occurred was of an isolated character. One concrete emplacement gave promise of trouble, but a skilful attack, engineered by Sergeant W. Allan and assisted by the covering fire of a Lewis gun worked by Private G. Briggs, speedily humbled the Germans, fourteen of whom surrendered. Private S. G. Salberg, Lance-Corporal W. F. Clark, Lance-Corporal J. Hynds, Private J. McGregor, and Private J. Todd all played a prominent part in contributing to the humiliation of the foe, and there was no officer more prominent in the attack than Lieut. W. S. Leslie who led "A" Company with fine courage.

By this victory the 9th Royal Scots secured the most important tactical feature on the divisional front, and Major-General Reid, in congratulating them on having captured the key of the hostile position, concluded his message with the inspiring phrase, "Well done, 9th Royal Scots." The battalion was now in a position to put the screw on the enemy, and it did not neglect to do so. The advance was continued on the 14th, and a Boche machine-gun post, which threatened to hold up the attack, was outmanœuvred by the skilful tactics of 2nd Lieut. J. Haig, supported by Sergeant T. Macdonald, and forced to beat a hurried retreat. On the 15th October "A" and "C" Companies crossed the canal, and reached Epinoy Wood on the following day, after carrying the villages of Epinoy and Carvin. The enemy's attempts at resistance were almost pitiful;

the machine-gunners alone sustained their reputation, some of them fighting with the utmost gallantry till they were captured or killed. On the 17th October, the Argylls, taking up the chase, passed through the positions of the 9th Royal Scots, who remained in reserve till the 27th.

The 13th Royal Scots were not allowed to stay long at Mazingarbe when it was realised that the Boches were on the run, and early on the 17th October, after marching through Carvin, they went through the lines of the 44th Brigade, and without meeting any opposition chased the Germans eastwards for 3 miles. By this time the Royal Scots were in territory almost unsoiled by war. Most of the houses were intact, and from their chimneys smoke, soothingly suggestive of home comforts, wriggled skywards. The liberated civilians were almost overwhelming in their gratitude to the troops whose arrival proved beyond doubt that the tyranny of Germany was being ended. But the Boches did not quit the haunts where for five years they had been the lords without doing some mean tricks, and from nearly every place they took away as much of the furniture as they could carry. The 13th Royal Scots fell back into divisional reserve on the 20th, and at La Croisette were employed for several days in repairing the roads, which the foe had torn up in the hope of delaying our pursuit. Never again did the battalion exchange shots with the enemy, and it was billeted at the village of Blicquy when the armistice came into force.

On the 27th October the 9th Royal Scots were brought up from reserve to the outpost line near Hollain and Jollain Merlin, where they remained for three days till they were relieved by the Black Watch and returned into reserve. A spell of duty on road repair ensued, but the battalion had the mixed pleasure of being in the front line when the order to cease fire came. There was considerable satisfaction in being in contact with the enemy in the last act of the war, but the knowledge that in a few hours hostilities were to be suspended naturally did not dispose a man to run any risks. Returning to Jollain Merlin on the 9th November, the battalion on the 10th followed the enemy through Antoing. Flooded ground in front of the village could not have been easily passed if the Germans had been in the mood to fight, but they, too, were not anxious to take chances when the end of the war was in sight, and the advance of the Royal Scots was not hindered. The pursuit was now nothing more than a triumphal procession; all the villages were profusely beflagged in honour of the rescuers, and the 9th Royal Scots moved on through throngs of grateful French people till they reached Pipaix where the night was spent. On the 11th the progress of the battalion was quietly continued as far as Blicquy, where the glad news was received that hostilities had ceased.

The series of rivers provided no refuge for the beaten foe, and in the Battle of the Selle River, the Germans between the 17th and the 25th October were driven back by the British to the line of the Sambre and Oise Canal. Disasters continued to crowd upon them, and the surrender of Austria on the 3rd November left Germany without an ally. The result of the Battle of the Sambre (1st to 11th November) crowned the discomfiture of the foe, who was obliged to bow to defeat. The battalions with which we are concerned during these operations were the 2nd, 4th, 7th, 8th and 5/6th.

The chief task of the 8th Royal Scots was to clear the communications behind the advancing infantry, and in this respect they accomplished much excellent work.

They left the Greenland Hill sector on the 3rd October, and after spending a few days at Neuville St Vaast, marched through the Hindenburg Line to the neighbourhood of Cambrai. Though the roads were for the most part in a fair condition, all the bridges and cross-roads had been demolished, so there was no lack of labour for the pioneers. The battalion was particularly proud of the work accomplished by "A" and "C" Companies in repairing bridges at Iwuy and Thiant respectively, and by "B" Company in filling up the craters on the main Valenciennes Road. "One job was estimated by the Corps as likely to take the company nine days; it was done in three." After performing these necessary tasks, the battalion tramped through Avesnes le Sec and Douchy le Maing, where it was relieved on the 31st October, and it was at Estrun on the 11th November.

The 2nd Battalion, after moving from Hermies to Ribécourt on the 13th October, advanced to Quiévy on the 21st, and in the late afternoon of that day went forward to Solesmes; it was now in country where it had been operating during the retreat from Mons, but on this occasion its rôle was not defensive but aggressive. It was detailed to attack on the 23rd the southern portion of the village of Vertain, and Lieut.-Colonel Henderson, who was thoroughly familiar with the district, took up his company commanders on the afternoon of the 22nd to reconnoitre the terrain.

Zero being at 3.20 A.M., the battalion had to set out shortly after midnight for its assembly position, which was a sunken road between Solesmes and Vertain. Unfortunately the troops in the line, unduly suspicious of a German patrol which had been observed, sent up the S.O.S. signal and in a moment pandemonium broke out; shells, many of them filled with gas, sprayed every approach, and "D" and "C" Companies between them had thirty-eight casualties, but the situation became more tolerable as the front line was reached. " D " and " C " Companies, which led the attack, were not finished with their misfortunes, for our barrage dropped right on their assembly trench and caused many losses. Refusing to be shaken by their evil luck, the men comported themselves with the greatest courage and drove straight through to their objective, capturing two hundred prisoners on the way. Lieut. R. Maxwell, commanding " A " Company, was killed by a machine-gun bullet at close range, but his men rounded up the gun team and forced it to capitulate. After Vertain was captured the Royal Scots Fusiliers passed through and carried on the advance. Lieut. Maxwell was the only officer slain but five were wounded,[1] while twenty-two men were killed and one hundred and twenty-five wounded ; the loot consisted of eleven machine-guns, five anti-tank rifles, and two trench-mortars.

This proved to be the battalion's last fight. On the 24th it advanced to Escarmain, and remained in brigade reserve till the 27th October, when it took over the line of resistance from the Royal Scots Fusiliers. Relieved from the outpost line on the 29th, it returned to Vertain, and on the 3rd November Lieut.-Colonel Henderson led the men to Audencourt, where a memorial service for those who had fallen in the battle fought there in August 1914 was held. This ceremony was attended by Major-General F. J. Duncan, who addressed the men and presented company banners. The battalion was soon ready to take part in another attack, but the war terminated before it was due to return to the firing-line.

The 5/6th Battalion, still under the command of the

[1] 2nd Lieuts. W. Caldwell, S. Forbes, P. Mackenzie, L. K. Underwood, and R. H. Westley.

Fourth Army, had a considerable share in the final struggles of the war. Le Haucourt, Bouvencourt, Bellenglise, Bohain, and St Souplet formed in turn its quarters from the 5th till the 31st October, by which time the Germans had been forced back to the Sambre Canal, and on the 31st the battalion entered the front line, occupying posts west of the canal between the villages of Catillon and Ors.

An appraisement of the terrain showed that the defence had many advantages. The first barrier was the canal; the distance between the banks was 75 feet, and its width at water-level varied from 35 to 40 feet, except at certain locks, where it was no more than 17 feet; its depth, from 6 to 8 feet, was such that the Sambre could not be crossed except by bridges or boats. Moreover, the natural difficulties of the crossing were augmented by the pools with which the enemy had inundated the low-lying land on both sides of the canal. Then the ground to the east of the Sambre provided the Germans with numerous facilities for defence; it was scored by a series of roughly parallel valleys, formed by the tributaries of the river, each separated from its neighbour by forbidding ridges. Off the roads the soil was raddled with wire and hedges, and in the valleys nestled villages consisting of houses of a more substantial and opulent appearance than those with which our troops were familiar in Picardy.

The 5/6th Royal Scots, who formed the right attacking battalion of the Thirty-second Division, were required to establish part of a bridge-head over the canal from Catillon, and then to advance to a position east of Mezières. The vital and most hazardous part of their task was the forcing of the Sambre, and in order to avoid any loss of time the Corps arranged for complete bridges to be carried up to the bank of the river. This critical operation was timed to begin at 5.45 A.M. on the 4th November.

The direct route of the battalion to the river led through a swamp that had been created by inundation, and it was commanded by a hostile strong-point known as Le Donjon. Two platoons of "A" Company were detailed to deal with this fort, but their attack was checked by very heavy machine-gun fire, and even the arrival of a third platoon failed to make any impression on the German defence. Happily the Dorsets on the left succeeded in crossing the river south of Ors by a bridge which was then put at the service of "C" Company and the remaining platoon of "A," while "D" Company managed to reach the east bank of the Sambre by a bridge north of Catillon. Thus the Germans in Le Donjon were isolated, and when "B" Company of the Royal Scots advanced to the attack, they signalled their surrender. In this way the most difficult part of the battalion's task was accomplished, and the Royal Scots, after crossing the canal, made rapid progress, reaching Rue Verte village by 8.15 A.M. Boche machine-gunners continued to put up a praiseworthy resistance, and were so far successful that the battalion had not quite reached its objective when darkness came down.

Though the rolling and enclosed country east of the Sambre offered many opportunities for defence, which a determined opponent could have turned to good account, the Germans were so utterly dispirited by their failure to prevent us from crossing the river, that they put no sting into their resistance. The maimed and broken roads and the driving rain troubled our men more than did the enemy. Thus, on the 5th November, the Royal Scots reached their objective

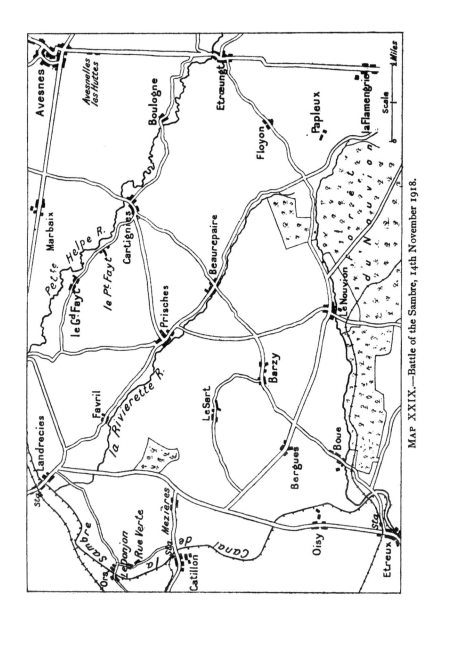

MAP XXIX.—Battle of the Sambre, 14th November 1918.

without encountering any opposition, and shortly afterwards a unit of the Forty-sixth Division passed
through them and took up the advance. The battalion's
casualties had not been heavy, and it had taken eighty-
nine prisoners (including two officers), thirteen guns,
twenty - one machine - guns, and one trench-mortar.
There was no longer any organised opposition to the
British advance, and the 5/6th Royal Scots were not
again sent into action. On the 6th November the
battalion was at Favril, on the 7th at Grand Fayt, and
on the 9th at Avesnelles, where it remained until the
armistice.

In their last experiences of active service the 4th
and the 7th Royal Scots must have felt that they were
almost playing at war. Invigorated by rest and training
at Izel le Hameau, the men were anxious to be in
"at the death," and satisfaction was general when, on
the 19th October, the Fifty-second Division began to
push eastwards. The route led through Camblain
l'Abbé, and what had been the old No-Man's-Land for
so many years of conflict, to the town of Auby just
north of Douai, where the troops halted for two days.
The billets were excellent, containing not merely
comfortable furniture, but luxuries such as pianos and
other musical instruments, and the troops thoroughly
enjoyed their brief sojourn there. The trek was
then continued through a chain of liberated villages,
the inhabitants of which gave a most cordial welcome
to the Lowlanders. For some days the 4th Royal
Scots were quartered at Molinel and the 7th at
Coutiches, where the men were employed in repairing
roads.

They entered the danger zone on the evening of
the 28th October, when the 7th Royal Scots took
over the outpost positions on the Jard Canal. On

the 1st November the battalion was relieved by the Scottish Rifles, and shortly after this date the campaign developed into the pursuit of a thoroughly demoralised foe, for on the 8th November the Boches slipped silently away from the canal. After the Scottish Rifles had established themselves on the east side of the canal, the 7th Royal Scots took up the chase and carried on the advance for two miles. Next morning, the 9th November, the battalion acted as advanced guard to the brigade, and, encountering no resistance, proceeded east to the line of the Antoing-Pommerœul Canal. On the way the French villagers gave them an unrestrained welcome ; at every hamlet the troops were not only greeted with tempestuous ovations, but were loaded with gifts of flowers, cigars, and coffee.

On the 10th November the Scottish Rifles became the advanced guard, and when the brigade reached Sirault word was received that the Germans were holding the village of Erbaut about 4 miles away. The Scottish Rifles were sent forward to clear this place, while the 7th and the 4th Royal Scots pressed on to Herchies, little more than a mile from Erbaut. With the knowledge that fighting was to end on the following day the men naturally had no desire to run into unnecessary danger, but unfortunately as the Royal Scots were nearing the village they were shelled by the Germans and four men of the 7th were hit, one of whom died from the effects of his wounds. Erbaut was cleared without difficulty by the Scottish Rifles, and the Royal Scots spent the night near Herchies. On the next day, the fateful 11th November, another brigade took the lead, and shortly afterwards came the glad tidings that fighting was at an end.

CHAPTER XXXIX

THE 2/10TH ROYAL SCOTS IN NORTHERN RUSSIA

August 1918 *to May* 1919

Reasons for Expedition to Northern Russia. History of the 2/10th Royal Scots. Importance of the Dwina. Operations between the Dwina and the Vaga. Adventures of Major Skeil's Company. Limit of Royal Scots' advance, September. Operations from October 1918 to May 1919. Winter conditions. Return of 2/10th Royal Scots.

THE armistice, which came into force at 11 A.M. on the 11th November, was an act of mercy on the part of the Allies, for had hostilities been allowed to run their course, the world would have had the spectacle of the greatest military disaster in the annals of history. "The strategic plan of the Allies had been realised with a completeness rarely seen in war. When the armistice was signed by the enemy his defensive powers had already been definitely destroyed."[1] No small part in the consummation of this happy ending had been played by the British forces, which had been responsible for attacking the Germans on the most vital parts of their front.

Our success in arms was as complete as could be desired except in Northern Russia, where our hopes of a popular rising against the Bolshevik regime were destined to be disappointed. The peoples of Western Europe were reluctant to believe that the rule of the Tsar had utterly forfeited the confidence of the Russian nation, and they hoped that a diversion by troops of the

---

[1] Sir Douglas Haig's Despatches, p. 298.

Allies on the Murmansk coast would enable Admiral Koltchak, who was operating from Siberia, to overthrow the Bolshevik Government, which was considered to be nothing more than the docile instrument of Germany. Accordingly a British expedition was sent to Northern Russia in 1918 and included in it were the 2/10th Royal Scots.[1]

The previous history of the battalion may be briefly indicated. After the sanction of the War Office for the raising of second-line units was received, Lieut.-Colonel E. Peterkin, V.D., who had formerly been Major in the 8th V.B.R.S., raised the 2/10th Royal Scots by the 24th September 1914, after a recruiting campaign of less than a week. The battalion was accordingly mobilised at Bathgate on the 13th October, but it was not till the 11th January 1915 that uniforms and the necessary military equipment began to arrive. With Berwick as their centre, the 2/10th Royal Scots, a cyclist battalion, became responsible for a share in the defence of the East coast, and from May 1916 furnished drafts for overseas service. The battalion went into camp at Coldingham in June 1916, and its chief thrills were caused by air raids and by reports of hostile landings. Throughout its sojourn on the East coast a high standard of discipline and training was maintained, and more than once the battalion received a well-earned compliment from inspecting Generals, including Lord French.

On the 18th January 1918 Lieut.-Colonel Peterkin, having reached the age limit, was obliged to resign his command and was succeeded by Lieut.-Colonel H. H. Sutherland, D.S.O., of the Black Watch. The battalion's

---

[1] An excellent account of the work of the 2/10th Royal Scots in Russia is contained in *John Buchan's Annual*, "The Long Road to Victory," Chap. XII.

II   3 A

tour of duty in Scotland terminated in June, when it was transferred to Ireland, where it continued to function as a cyclist unit. By this time the battalion was composed of men most of whom had already seen considerable service abroad, and it was officered chiefly by war-worn officers who had been sent home from France for a six months' rest. But while rich in war experience it contained many who were no longer fit for active service. Man-power, however, now constituted such a serious problem that when the unit was prepared for the Russian expedition "B1"[1] men were retained for service, and the necessary strength of 1000 was reached by bringing in troops from all battalions quartered in Ireland at that time.

On the 31st July the recognised 2/10th Royal Scots left Ireland for Aldershot, and on the 8th August they embarked at Newcastle on the *City of Cairo*. After a few hours at sea the ship had to return to port owing to engine trouble and did not resume its voyage till the 17th. The men were equipped with everything except rifles, but Russian rifles were discovered on the boat and these were issued to the troops. Without any untoward incident, Murmansk, a village of wooden houses on a splendid harbour, was reached on the 23rd August, and two days later the vessel arrived at Archangel, where the Royal Scots landed, and, headed by a band of American marines, marched through the town, passing *en route* the G.O.C., Major-General T. C. Poole, C.B., C.M.G., D.S.O. Afterwards they returned to the *City of Cairo*.

From Archangel to the south there were two possible routes of advance, the railway between the port and Vologda, and the River Dwina. The operations of the Royal Scots were concerned almost entirely with the

---

[1] Men certified as fit for garrison duty only.

River Dwina from Bereznik, near the junction of the Dwina and the Vaga, to about 50 miles south of that village.

The date of their arrival allowed the Royal Scots little more than two months of summer conditions. From May to October the Dwina is navigable for at least 500 miles, and during this season it furnishes the only comfortable means of progress inland. The width of this fast-flowing river astonished troops familiar only with the tiny streams and burns of Scotland; at no place was it less than a mile wide, and where the banks were low it spread out to two or three miles. The greater part of the riverine area was marshy, and observation was blocked by extensive forests on both banks. Land-routes in summer were consequently almost non-existent, and no large force could venture to wander far from the river. It was, in short, a country which severely circumscribed the possibilities of manœuvre, for troops were chained to the Dwina, which formed the only reliable means of communication with Archangel. At frequent intervals hamlets and villages of log-huts bordered the river and its tributaries, and the people who dwelt in them roused admiration by the magnificence of their physique, and despair by their abysmal ignorance. The attitude of the Russian peasants was a terrible disappointment to the Allies; they were utterly indifferent to the war. "They showed no enthusiasm for, nor did they display any antagonism against, our forces."[1] Hospitality, supplies, and a certain amount of manual assistance in felling trees were the most that could be expected from them.

Three companies of the Royal Scots, " A," " B," and " C," under Major C. W. Whitaker, the Second-in-Command, embarked on barges on the 26th August,

[1] "The Long Road to Victory," p. 289.

and five days later reached the village of Bereznik. "D" Company was stationed at Archangel. On the 4th September it sent a platoon under Lieut. Anderson to join a small force of marines and Russians, afterwards known as "D" Force, which was put under the command of Captain F. M. Scott of the Royal Scots.

The three companies at Bereznik formed two-thirds of "C" Force, the remainder consisting of small detachments of Russian scouts, Poles, marines, and a British monitor (M25), with a few launches. A party of 100 Royal Scots under Captain A. R. Rowland-Thomas went by boat up the Vaga on a propagandistic expedition, but though it was favourably received by the inhabitants of Shenkursk the Russians committed themselves to nothing more than polite assurances. Meantime reconnaissance revealed that there were Bolshevik troops in the triangle formed by the Dwina and the Vaga, and the first task of "C" Force was to clear all this territory of the enemy. A column of 500 Bolsheviks was reported to be advancing along the right bank of the Dwina, and 200 of the Royal Scots, supported by a detachment of Poles and two 18-pounder guns, advanced to engage it, while on the left bank of the river a company of Royal Scots assisted by a Russian gunboat was entrusted with the task of clearing the triangle.

These preliminary operations were entirely successful, and the result of the first brushes with the Bolshevik troops inspired our men with the utmost confidence. "A" Company, commanded by Major A. P. Skeil, was the most hotly engaged, and, after breaking an attack delivered by the Bolsheviks in vastly superior numbers on the night of the 11th September, it pushed on and occupied Prilutski the following day. The discomfited enemy began to fall back, and on the

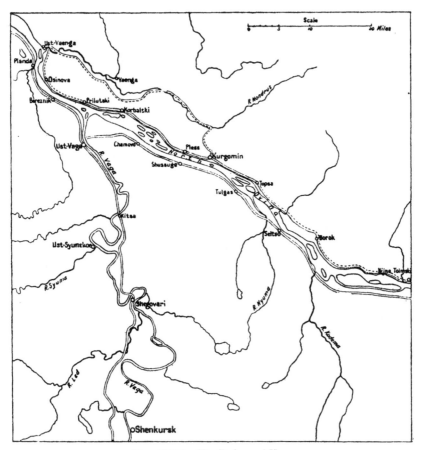

MAP XXX.—The Dwina and Vaga.

14th the Royal Scots pressed on in pursuit. "A" Company, most effectively assisted by the guns of the monitor, harried the Bolshevik rear-guard, and in carrying the village of Korbalski acquired a damaged 3-inch gun; other captures of the company included a staff-officer, who supplied useful information about the strength and dispositions of the enemy. Meantime "B" Company, under Captain J. A. Edwards, starting from Ust-Vaga at 2 A.M. on the 14th, marched to Maly-Bereznik, about 16 versts[1] away. At 10 A.M. the company, less a small group under 2nd Lieut. H. Braham, crossed over to the right bank of the Vaga and advanced against Chamovo. The route took the Royal Scots through an immense tract of forested marsh. So unstable was the ground that in many places trees had to be felled by a Russian detachment, which acted with the company, to form a track or bridge, and it was 6.30 P.M. before the eastern edge of the forest belt was reached. A platoon under 2nd Lieut. Orr, assisted by the Russian detachment, then advanced on Chamovo, and in the first assault cleared half the village. An attempt of the enemy to remove a 3-inch gun was frustrated by rifle and Lewis-gun fire, and only the descent of darkness prevented the work from being finished that night. Three platoons formed a cordon round the village, and early on the 15th Chamovo was entirely cleared, several prisoners being taken, while the material booty, in addition to the 3-inch gun, consisted of three and a half limbers of ammunition, twelve gun-team horses with harness complete, a motor-car, two field telephones, rifles, S.A.A., and valuable papers. With the object of driving Bolshevik stragglers into the hands of an American company that was advancing along the left

---

[1] A verst is equivalent to 3500 feet.

bank of the Dwina, Captain Edwards with two platoons marched to Navolok unmolested, while on the other side of the river "A" Company continued its victorious progress to Rostovskoe.

One of the difficulties of the Royal Scots was that the general flatness of the country and the widespread network of forest precluded observation over a wide area, but it was definitely known that the enemy was as much tied to the river as we were. He was reported to have at Pless a strongly entrenched position, supported by artillery and gunboats. An attack on Pless bristled with difficulties, for by taking the precaution to mine the river the enemy deprived us of any possible assistance from our own boats until the mines had been cleared, and, since a frontal attack seemed a forlorn hope, it was resolved to attempt to turn the hostile position by a flanking movement through the forests. Accordingly, while Lieut. L. W. Shute with one platoon advanced along the river road, Major Skeil with the remainder of "A" Company, at 8.30 A.M. on the 15th September, began the flank march.

The forest-march was a feat of amazing endurance and fortitude, and would certainly have resulted in the utter destruction of the force but for the resolution of the men and the quality of their leader. The path which for the first few hours the troops followed, necessarily in single file, was no better than a quagmire, and when after noon rain descended in torrents the conditions became appalling. The troops started at a rate of three versts an hour, but progress soon slowed down, and long before the march came to an end one verst per hour was a satisfactory speed. Water, usually knee-deep, and never less than ankle-deep, covered the floor of the forest, and deep pools and ditches had to be crossed by means of felled trees.

Hungry and cold the troops plodded on, till at 2 P.M., on the 15th, Major Skeil judged that his men were well beyond the hostile position. The column then veered towards the river, but all progress was suddenly barred by an impassable marsh. "Attempts were made by daring individuals to find a path across, but there was none. Our guide had failed us. He had never been farther, he said, except in winter, and no one had crossed the marsh in summer. The blow to the already exhausted troops was a heavy one Although September, the night was bitterly cold, and as we stood knee-deep in water to consider things, occasional plops would be heard of tired men slipping from trees against which they had been leaning into the icy water. Some hillocks, drier than the surrounding woods, had been passed a short time before, and orders were given to kindle fires on these somehow, and rest round them for two hours."[1]

The rest and a mouthful of tea stirred the troops to new vigour, and they set off at 7 A.M. on the 16th for a mill about 15 versts off in the forest. It was absolutely essential for the column to reach some place where food could be procured. Berries plucked from bushes afforded meagre relief to starving men, and some, from sheer weariness, began to fall out. Major Skeil, realising that the only chance of saving his force was to push on without delay, issued a curt warning that any who fell out would be left behind. This stern but necessary command had the desired effect, and at 3 P.M. the whole force reached the mill, where some food was obtained, but not nearly enough to satisfy the needs of the party. The people, however, said that there was a village about 8 versts away, and while the majority lay down to rest, the hardiest

[1] "The Long Road to Victory," p. 305.

proceeded to the hamlet, from which they brought back a sheep and some Russian bread. At 8 o'clock in the evening the men had their first meal that day.

The night was spent in bivouacs in the woods, and early in the morning Major Skeil and his men set out for Kurgomin, nearly 12 versts up the river from Pless. The enemy, it was learned from the mill-keeper, had been greatly alarmed on hearing that a British army was advancing through the woods, so Major Skeil, in the hope that the Bolsheviks would credit him with a greater force than he actually had, determined on presenting a bold front. The situation indeed was such that audacity formed the only prudent course of action, and his stratagem succeeded. The Royal Scots in the afternoon of the 17th entered Kurgomin, which had been hurriedly evacuated by the foe, who believed that 8000 British troops were advancing against the village. Thus triumphantly terminated one of the most remarkable adventures in the war, in which marvellous endurance had been displayed and almost incredible hardships overcome by men, most of whom were classified as " B1."

Major Skeil's flanking march fulfilled its purpose, for the enemy had withdrawn from Pless, leaving a free passage to Lieut. Shute who occupied the place on the 16th. On the same day an attempt by the Bolsheviks to land some men at Chamovo was defeated, and their boat was sunk by the M25, the crew being either killed or taken prisoner. " C " Company now arrived to swell the force on the right bank of the Dwina, and before the 17th September closed, Major Skeil's gallant band was joined by the rest of " A " and the whole of " C " Company. " B " Company was transferred from the left bank on the 18th, and with " B " and " C " leading, the advance of the Royal Scots was continued to Topsa, while a parallel drive on the left bank was carried out by Americans. With orders to push on as far as possible, both columns advanced to the neighbourhood of Nijne-Toimski, where the enemy held a position of immense strength.

Our small force had not the weight to break through the strong entrenchments, and on the 27th the three companies of the Royal Scots were withdrawn to a cluster of villages at Borok, which was put into a state of defence. On the left bank of the Dwina, Seltso was fortified by the Americans, who, on the 28th, were reinforced by "A" Company of the Royal Scots. Next day all the troops operating on the Dwina became known as the North Dwina River Force, and were put under the command of Major Whitaker of the Royal Scots. Meantime another column of "C" Force, consisting of Americans and Russians, had been established at Shenkursk on the Vaga.

In such a country it was futile to attempt to dig trenches, so block-houses of log and sand were constructed. On the 2nd October the Borok - Seltso garrison was weakened by the transference of the American company to the Vaga, and while the preparations for stationary warfare were going on, the Royal Scots were daily shelled by hostile gunboats, which could use the river with impunity, since on the 4th October the M25 had returned to Archangel. Its withdrawal was necessitated by the fact that in winter the Dwina becomes ice-bound at Archangel a clear ten days before it freezes at its junction with the Vaga, while in spring the river is navigable at the junction for a similar period before Archangel is free from ice. Thus the Bolshevik gunboats could use the river ten days later than we could in autumn and ten days earlier in spring. The enemy endeavoured to make the most

of his advantage, and on the 5th October attacked the
outpost line of the Royal Scots at Borok, but was
driven off by rifle and machine-gun fire, a Vickers gun
falling into the possession of "B" Company. On the
6th when a platoon of the same company advanced to
locate the Bolshevik positions, it was heavily fired on
and retired with the loss of one man killed.

The constant shelling, to which we could not make
any effective reply, destroyed by fire several of our
log-houses, but the Russian peasants fortunately were
adepts in extinguishing fires and gave invaluable assistance. The arrival of a company of Americans from
Shenkursk and a Russian 5.1-inch gun with a British
crew encouraged us to teach the enemy a lesson, and
on the 7th October we attacked the Bolsheviks on the
left bank, routed them, and captured one pom-pom and
two machine-guns. A hostile raid on our outpost line
was decisively repulsed and a counter-thrust by the
Royal Scots drove the foe from the village nearest our
line. In these affrays the Bolsheviks, of whom three
were taken prisoner, lost heavily, while the Royal Scots
had only one man killed. The enemy, however, possessed
the virtue of perseverance, and on the 9th the outpost
line was engaged all day in repelling assaults. Similar
hard fighting in which all the Royal Scots were involved
followed on the 10th and our outpost line was accordingly
slightly withdrawn.

The Bolsheviks had by now at least thirty gunboats
on the river as well as two or three heavy land guns.
Conflagrations were of almost hourly occurrence, and
since the enemy, with his immeasurably greater numbers,
was beginning to threaten the rear of both the left and
the right bank forces, it was deemed expedient to bring
back our line to Kurgomin-Tulgas. The hospital at
Borok, which had been frequently hit, was evacuated on

the 13th, and the wounded of the Royal Scots, about one hundred in all, were safely removed. Determined attacks on Borok that day[1] and on Seltso on the 14th were smartly repulsed. These checks enabled us to carry out our retirement without serious molestation, and after a pause at Topsa-Troitsa the line at Kurgomin-Tulgas was reached on the 17th October.

The Bolsheviks were disconcerted by this withdrawal and followed up our men with great caution. Meanwhile defensive works were in course of preparation, and the Royal Scots had now the welcome assistance of a Canadian Field Artillery Battery. Major Skeil received well-earned promotion, and as Lieut.-Colonel was given command of the force on the Dwina, which was henceforth known as the River Column. The new position underwent its first serious test on the 23rd October, when an attack on the left flank of the right bank force was summarily defeated, while a counter-stroke by a platoon of "A" Company completed the discomfiture of the Bolsheviks, of whom two were killed, five taken prisoner, and many more wounded; on the other hand, the Royal Scots, without losing a man, captured three machine-guns. This triumph unfortunately was offset by the worst reverse which the Royal Scots experienced during their sojourn in Northern Russia. On the 27th October Captain J. A. W. Penman with two platoons of "B," three platoons of "C" Company, and thirty Poles made a flank attack on Topsa at dawn. The march to the assaulting position was performed in a blinding snowstorm, but the enemy was vigilant and the attack was shrivelled up by his rifle and machine-gun fire. The failure cost the Royal Scots about eighty[2] in

---

[1] During the fighting on the 13th October the Royal Scots lost three other ranks killed, and one officer and five other ranks wounded.

[2] One officer, Lieut. W. Bassett, was killed.

killed, wounded, and missing, the survivors returning with great difficulty through the marsh and forest.

Winter was longer in setting in than had been anticipated, and on the morning of the 11th November, the day which brought the war to an end in other theatres, the Bolsheviks delivered their most desperate assault on the River Column. Supported by gunboats, their infantry debouched from the woods and assailed our forward positions on both flanks. The attack on the right bank was easily dealt with, but the enemy on the left was pressing us with considerable dash and determination, when a force of 500 Bolsheviks, suddenly emerging from the screen of the woods, fell upon our rear, stormed the village where the hospital was established, and almost succeeded in rushing the Canadian field-guns. The gunners, assisted by two platoons of "A" Company, swung round to face this new and unexpected foe, and were soon engaged in a grim hand-to-hand struggle against fantastic odds. "Glorious work was done by category men that day, but nothing finer than the work of a Royal Scots sergeant (Sergeant Salmons), who, rushing into the midst of the enemy firing a Lewis gun from the hip, fought till he died."[1] This magnificent defence saved the situation, and the issue no longer remained in doubt when the Canadians switched round some of their guns and fired at point-blank range into the clusters of the enemy.

Meantime the frontal attack on the left bank had driven in our outposts, and the Bolsheviks held possession of the forward village. The force on the left bank was for a time utterly cut off, but despite their most frantic efforts the Bolsheviks could not overcome its resistance, and at nightfall the enemy began to steal

[1] "The Long Road to Victory," p. 317.

away from the battlefield. Following on the heels of the decamping foe, the Royal Scots reoccupied the rear villages. Having consumed all their rations before launching their attack, the rear party of Bolsheviks suffered ghastly agonies in its retreat through the woods ; many died from exposure, while eighty woe-begone wretches who reached the Vaga surrendered to our force there ; barely a hundred survivors remained of the original force that had embarked on the enterprise. Two days later the forward village was also taken by the Royal Scots.

Over 1000 Bolsheviks were engaged in this operation which, we discovered from captured documents, had been expressly ordered by Lenin. The losses of the Royal Scots were trivial compared with those of their opponents, nineteen being killed and thirty-four wounded. After this affair there followed a few more bickerings, in one of which Lieut. J. M. Dalziell was killed, but the Royal Scots had no difficulty in holding their own. In real earnest winter began to set in and the Bolshevik gunboats retired to hibernate, while near the end of November the Royal Scots were brought up to four companies by the arrival of "D" Company.

This last company had not been wholly without excitement. On the evening of the 14th October, Captain Bright with a detachment of "D" Company was despatched to Obozerskaya on the railway line, where he reported to Lieut.-Colonel Sutherland, who was in command of Force "A" operating on the railway. Captain Bright and his men were at once sent forward to Point 444, where they began to construct trenches against an expected attack by the enemy, who was in considerable strength at Point 443. There was no infantry assault, Point 444 being beset only

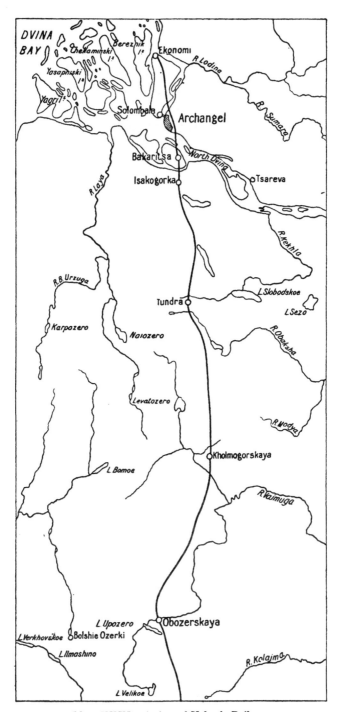

MAP XXXI.—Archangel-Vologda Railway.

by rifle and shell fire. An armoured train, steaming up from Point 447, shelled the enemy, but the Bolsheviks brought up more guns and bombarded the Royal Scots with great violence. When our armoured train was withdrawn owing to the exhaustion of the crew, a Bolshevik train appeared on the line, and supported by the fire of heavy guns, the enemy infantry attacked the flanks of the Royal Scots, but were kept at bay by accurate rifle and machine-gun fire. But our position on the railway was most uncomfortable, and a slight retirement was made which encouraged the Bolsheviks to launch another fruitless attack from the forest. Considering the intensity of the hostile shelling, the losses[1] of the Royal Scots were astonishingly light. There followed a spell of comparative quietness, and on the 20th October the Royal Scots were relieved by French colonial troops and returned to Obozerskaya. Shortly afterwards they went back to the vicinity of Archangel, where they remained till the 4th November, when the company left by river to join Lieut.-Colonel Skeil's force.

Winter brought new conditions and experiences. The marshes froze up, snow fell to a depth of from five to ten feet, and the forest could easily be traversed by sledges and men wearing snow-shoes or skis. The river ceased to be a highway, for its congealed surface was covered by huge hummocks formed by frozen floes. Tracks across the Dwina, however, were broken and kept in order during the period of operations. Normally the people of Northern Russia were wont to hibernate, but their example could not be followed by the Royal Scots. The troops were issued with suitable raiment, and when shod in Shackleton boots, and wearing lumberman stockings, sheepskin coats,

---

[1] 2nd Lieut. K. M. Croal killed, and two other ranks wounded.

fur caps with ear-pieces, and two pairs of gloves, they found the handling of their Russian rifles no easy matter. Block-houses had to be built for warmth as well as for strength, and the gun-pits for Stokes mortars and field-guns had to be heated. Against frost-bite all had to be on their guard, and the men were expected to assist each other in dealing with it.

Training was incessant, but presented many novelties that made it interesting. The management of snow-shoes was easy to learn, but the use of the swifter skis required more instruction and took some time to master. Ultimately special snow-shoeing and ski-ing platoons were formed, and these did much excellent work in keeping No-Man's-Land clear of hostile prowlers. The troops, it need hardly be said, thoroughly enjoyed as recreation the typical winter sports which in peace times are the monopoly of the wealthy. Journeys of any distance were performed by sleighs, each consisting of a small narrow carriage placed low on a couple of wooden runners and packed with hay to give warmth to the body and compensate for the absence of springs. All troops in the forward areas lived in block-houses, and the others were billeted in villages. In both block-houses and billets fires due to overheating were of frequent occurrence, and the Royal Scots were fortunate in securing the help of such expert firemen as the Russians in dealing with conflagrations.

There was always need for vigilance in the forward area, but the greater activity in patrol work was decidedly shown by the Royal Scots, the Bolsheviks during December contenting themselves with scattering propagandistic messages for our troops to pick up —indeed the Bolshevik newspaper, *The Call*, supplied our men with their most regular and accurate news. Christmas and New Year were celebrated with as substantial dinners as could be provided.   At the beginning of 1919, the enemy, who had the advantage in artillery,[1] became more energetic, and on the 25th January word was received to the effect that a hostile assault had led to the evacuation of Shenkursk on the Vaga.   On the next day attacks developed against Tulgas, but though the enemy gained a footing in one of the forward positions, he was driven out on the following morning.   The River Column was not sufficiently strong to hold all the villages in its area, and between 4 P.M. and 6 A.M. on the 30th/31st January, Forward Tulgas, after being cleared of its inhabitants, was set on fire, while an onrush by a strong party of Bolsheviks was sanguinarily repulsed.

The persistent pressure on the Vaga column was most disquieting, but reinforcements, comprising two platoons of "A" Company of the Royal Scots, helped to steady the situation in that quarter, and prevented the need of further retirement.   Stationary warfare continued, with frequent patrol encounters, until signs of spring began to appear.   At this time the Vaga column had the more precarious position, and in February the two platoons of "A" Company set out from Osinova in 40 to 60 degrees of frost for a place nearly 80 versts away.   After a terrible journey of twenty-six hours, during which time the men alternately rode on and ran behind sleighs, they arrived to find to their relief that the place to which they had been sent had been vacated by the enemy.   The Bolsheviks on both the Dwina and the Vaga were clearly gathering strength, and it was as much as we could do to maintain our position, especially on the latter river.   Occasionally

---

[1] Two 4·5 howitzers, which arrived in January 1919, formed an important addition to the arsenal of the River Column, but did not put us on an equality with the Bolsheviks as regards artillery support.

returned prisoners of war (Russians held as prisoners
in Germany and Austria till the armistice) were allowed
a passage through our lines, but near the end of
March these came in such numbers that orders were
issued that no more were to be permitted to pass
through ; several of the so-called prisoners, there was
little doubt, were Bolshevik spies and agents.

In April the left bank of the Dwina was taken over
by "loyalist" Russians, but they were an unreliable
force, and on the 25th the infantry mutinied, killed
most of their own officers and attacked the British
officers attached to them.   Luckily the Russian gunners
remained faithful, and with the British officers they
fought their way back against tremendous odds.   From
the right bank our 18-pounders poured salvos into the
fortified villages occupied by the insurgents, and enabled
the Russian gunners to escape to Shussuga, while a
platoon of "C" Company of the Royal Scots with the
aid of a boat, which was dragged across the frozen parts
and slipped into the spaces of open water, crossed the
thawing river and assisted in the defence of Shussuga.
This Bolshevik triumph was only transitory, for as soon
as the Dwina became navigable, a counter-attack regained
for us all our lost ground.

The men had borne without complaint the hardships
of a difficult and harassing campaign, but they were
puzzled to understand why fighting should continue in
Russia, when the armistice had put an end to hostilities
in all other theatres.   That event had completely altered
the situation.   There was some purpose to be gained
while the war with Germany lasted, for our expedition
in Northern Russia might be expected to keep some
German forces tied to the Eastern front, but with the
defeat of Germany it was difficult to comprehend the
object of the Russian campaign.   It seemed uncommonly

like interference with the internal affairs of another nation. Such doubts had often invaded the minds of the men during the winter months. There was no longer, in fact, any purpose to be served by persisting in the campaign, and none knew better than the 2/10th Royal Scots that there was little prospect of stirring up in the minds of the Russian peasants an active hatred against the new Bolshevik Government. Our interference, as any knowledge of history should have warned us, was likely to produce the very opposite effect.

Such considerations led to the withdrawal of all the American troops in May, but it appeared as if Britain were determined to carry on the campaign to the bitter end, for at the beginning of June two battalions from England landed at Archangel. Their arrival, however, set free the Royal Scots, who assembled at Osinova and were taken in barges to Archangel, which was reached on the 10th June. The battalion, after being paraded to receive the thanks of Major-General E. Ironside, C.M.G., D.S.O., for the heroism and endurance that it had displayed, embarked on the *Czaritza* and arrived at Leith on the 18th June after an uneventful voyage. Redford Barracks formed the quarters of the battalion and an immediate start was made with demobilisation. A civic reception by the Lord Provost of Edinburgh in the Drill Hall, Forrest Road, showed the men that their gallant work and their hardships had been noted with keen appreciation and sympathy. More rousing still was the welcome given on the following day to the cadre of the battalion in Linlithgow, the home town of the 2/10th Royal Scots. There, among the many glowing tributes paid to the battalion, none gave greater satisfaction than the appreciative address of the founder of the 2/10th Royal Scots, Lieut.-Colonel Peterkin.

CHAPTER XL

Movements of Battalions after the Armistice. Demobilisation. Battle Honours. Reorganisation of Territorial Battalions. The Royal Regiment. Activities of the Royal Scots Association. Suggestion of a Club as the Regimental Memorial. Dedication of the Memorial and formal opening of the Club, 12th August, by H.R.H. Princess Mary.

> " They shall grow not old, as we that are left grow old :
> Age shall not weary them, nor the years condemn.
> At the going down of the sun and in the morning
> We will remember them.

> " As the stars that shall be bright when we are dust,
> Moving in marches upon the heavenly plain,
> As the stars that are starry in the time of our darkness,
> To the end, to the end, they remain."   L. BINYON.

THE Armistice was welcomed by our troops in France in a spirit of sober gratitude ; in victory, as in the worst hours of the war, they comported themselves with the inherent dignity of their race. A few could not rise above the temptation to exult frankly and vindictively over the rout and humiliation of the enemy, but the majority were disposed rather to revel in the deep sense of luxury which sprang from the assurance that lives and limbs were no longer to be exposed to the hazards of war. Naturally all, especially the veterans of many battles, were anxious to tread the land of their opponents, but this was a privilege reserved for few. The 2nd, 11th, 12th, and 5/6th were the only battalions of the Royal Scots quartered in Germany : of these the 11th and the 12th had the honour of taking part in the triumphal march to the bridge-head across the Rhine, which they reached on the 15th December, the former being billeted in Haan and the latter in Wald; the 5/6th Battalion, after a sojourn at Bonn, was transferred to Wald on the 13th March to take the place of the 12th, which was being reduced to cadre strength; the 2nd Battalion was established in Buir. All the other units except the 17th were billeted in hospitable Belgium. The 17th Battalion, which remained in the desolate war area, had the honour of marching past H.R.H. Princess Mary, the Colonel-in-Chief of the Regiment, on its return to Ypres on the 28th November.

In training, reviews, presentations of Colours, education, and sport, time was passed pleasantly for a few weeks, but now that the work to which they had dedicated themselves was accomplished, the great majority of officers and men began to find the yoke of military discipline irksome, and were anxious to return to civilian duties. The process of demobilisation was by no means an easy one, but it was managed with remarkable celerity and fairness. Thanks to the tact of commanding officers there was virtually no awkwardness as far as the Royal Scots were concerned, but at some places there were nasty incidents, and the 17th Royal Scots were hurriedly sent to Calais on the 29th January to prevent riots there; the trouble fortunately was remedied without bloodshed. By the end of 1919 the demobilisation of the Royal Scots was practically complete, and the cadres of the various units received sympathetic and enthusiastic welcomes on their return to Scotland.

There is no need to dwell on the achievements of the Regiment during the Great War; the number of its dead and the list of its Battle Honours form the most eloquent testimony of the part that it had played. Five hundred and eighty-three officers and ten thousand five hundred and seventy-nine men lost their lives in the service of the country. The array of Battle Honours contains seventy-one items :—

THE ROYAL SCOTS (THE ROYAL REGIMENT)
THE GREAT WAR—THIRTY-FIVE BATTALIONS[1]

Mons.

Le Cateau.

Retreat from Mons.

Marne, 1914, 1918.

Aisne, 1914.

La Bassée, 1914.

Neuve Chapelle.

Ypres, 1915, 1917, 1918.

Gravenstafel.

St Julien.

Frezenberg.

Bellewaarde.

Aubers.

Festubert, 1915.

Loos.

Somme, 1916, 1918.

Albert, 1916, 1918.

Bazentin.

Pozières.

Flers-Courcelette.

Le Transloy.

Ancre Heights.

Ancre, 1916, 1918.

Arras, 1917-18.

Scarpe, 1917-18.

Arleux.

Pilckem.

Langemarck, 1917.

Menin Road.

Polygon Wood.

Poelcappelle.

Passchendaele.

Cambrai, 1917.

St Quentin.

Rosières.

Lys.

Estaires.

Messines, 1918.

Hazebrouck.

Bailleul.

Kemmel.

Béthune.

Soissonnais-Ourcq.

Tardenois.

Amiens.

Bapaume, 1918.

Drocourt-Quéant.

Hindenburg Line.

Canal du Nord.

St Quentin Canal.

Beaurevoir.

Courtrai.

Selle.

Sambre.

France and Flanders, 1914-18.

Struma, 1918.

Macedonia, 1915-18.

Helles.

Landing at Helles.

Krithia.

Suvla.

Scimitar Hill.

Gallipoli, 1915-16.

Romani.

Egypt, 1915-16.

Gaza.   El Mughar.

Nebi Samwil.

Jaffa.

Palestine, 1917-18.

Archangel, 1918-19.

[1] All battalions which saw active service in a war zone are entitled to have the ten Battle Honours shown in black type emblazoned on their King's Colour.

The raising of service units was an emergency measure, and therefore they were disbanded after the war. None, however, had contemplated any interference with the Territorial Force, but the policy of economy which accompanied peace led to the Territorial battalions of the Royal Scots being reduced in number from seven to four in 1920. The step was no doubt a necessary one, but it was accepted with reluctance in Edinburgh and the Lothians. In accordance with this reorganisation, the 6th, 8th, and 10th Battalions were disbanded. The surviving four functioned for some time as separate units, but these have now been grouped into two battalions, the 4/5th (Queen's Edinburgh) and the 7/9th (Highland).

Peace brought one notable change which gave general satisfaction. The title of " The Lothian Regiment" was in some respects an appropriate one, emphasising as it did the connection of the Royal Scots with the Lothians, but it hardly did justice to the historical pre-eminence of the Regiment, the oldest in the British Army, and its intimate association with Royal service in the past, and the restoration on the 1st January 1920 of the title which had been conferred on it in 1684, "The Royal Regiment," was but a fitting recognition of its historical standing.

The story of the part played by the Regiment in the Great War would be incomplete without a tribute to those who at home sacrificed their time and their means on its behalf. Prior to the war the needs of Royal Scots and their dependents had been looked after by the Royal Scots Association, which was founded in 1893 by Captain, now Major-General, Sir William Douglas. The machinery of organisation was adequate to deal with the two regular battalions, but could not cope in addition with the needs of the

Territorial and Kitchener units which were sent on active service. The Great War consequently led to several auxiliary organisations being formed.

Of these there were three. The first was the Emergency War Fund, to which all the battalions and the general public of Edinburgh and the Lothians contributed. Sufficient funds were raised to enable monetary assistance to be given in over 300 cases of hardship caused by the war, while numerous families received weekly payments upon a more liberal scale than was possible before 1914.

Another fund, the Comforts Fund, was started shortly after the declaration of war, and by means of concerts and private subscriptions a sufficient sum of money was collected to give to each man every month a supply of tobacco and cigarettes and other comforts to cheer him in his weary vigil in the trenches. The Lord Provost of Edinburgh also set on foot a Comforts Fund for all Scottish Regiments, and in order to avoid overlapping, an arrangement was made whereby soft goods, such as mufflers and socks, were provided by the Lord Provost's Fund, while hard goods, such as candles, tobacco, writing pads, trench boots, were furnished by the Regimental Fund.

The hardest worked fund of all was the Prisoners' Fund. Previous to November 1916 food for prisoners was provided in a somewhat irregular manner by private individuals, who were permitted to go into any shop or store and send parcels to their friends. During this period The Royal Scots Association secured several hundreds of subscribers, who transmitted parcels to prisoners in a more or less irregular way. The absence of system led to abuses and overlapping, and in November 1916 the authorities enacted that

Regimental Care Committees should be formed, through whom alone parcels should be sent to prisoners. The Royal Scots Association was the first in Scotland to set up a Regimental Care Committee, which regularly forwarded three parcels per fortnight to each prisoner connected with the Regiment. The work involved was enormous, and large sums of money were required to defray the expenses incurred on behalf of the vast number of prisoners,[1] for whom the Care Committee was responsible. Appeals to the public were issued, signed by Lord Rosebery, who had always taken an active interest in the Regiment, by the Lord Provost, and by the Chairman of the Royal Scots Association, Lord Salvesen, with the result that within the regimental district the sum of £62,000 was collected. Local committees were also established throughout the Lothians, and these were substantially assisted by the patriotism of the workmen in several large organisations, who consented to give a weekly proportion of their pay to the Fund.

Large as was the sum raised by subscription it did not avail to meet the needs of the Regiment, but no prisoners were ever neglected, owing to the patriotism of the officials of the Association, who used their private means to make up deficiencies. It was ascertained that the upkeep of each man required £36 per year, and that the total annual cost of supplying prisoners with food amounted to 1s. 6d. per head of the total population of the regimental district. In many cases the work of the Care Committee was lightened by the generous action of individual citizens who made themselves responsible for supplying the wants of a number of prisoners. These "adopters," as they were called, not only provided

[1] Amounting in 1918 to eighty-four officers and two thousand two hundred and eighty-three men.

for the cost of one or more of these men, but kept up a correspondence with them which did much to relieve the gloom of their captivity.

The Committee was helped enormously by a large and patriotic band of voluntary workers. The depot, where goods were stored, was at 20 Royal Circus, and three times a week the staff of packers and other workers sent off 2283 boxes to the unfortunate captives. The regulations of the Central Committee for Scotland had to be complied with as regards the number of articles in each box and the mode of addressing ; inside was a post - card, with a number corresponding to the number of the parcel, and this card was sent home by the recipient of the box.

All this work necessitated an elaborate system of book - keeping. The ledger account contained full details of every article sent to each prisoner, and the stock book dealt with the stores which passed through the premises and which amounted to an annual value of over £50,000. Moreover, for each man a special file was kept in which all letters about him and from him were preserved and indexed. Periodically the premises were examined by Government Inspectors, whose reports contained unstinted praise for the manner in which the work was done at Royal Circus.

The voluntary workers never grudged time or labour in the service of the Regiment. For over two years the office work of the organisation was transacted by a number of ladies who attended daily from 9.30 A.M. till 6.30 P.M., while in the packing centre there were many retired workers who devoted the whole of their time to the cause, seeking no fee or reward except the gratification of working for fellow-countrymen, spinning out a dreary existence in prison-camps. To these all

Royal Scots owe a great debt of gratitude, but to none more than Mr Campbell Smith and Miss E. E. Duncan, sister of Brig.-General F. J. Duncan, the Honorary Secretaries of the Royal Scots Association, who by example and persuasion recruited the voluntary staff and supervised the organisation.

The names most prominently connected with the manifold labours of The Royal Scots Association during the war period were those of Lord Salvesen, the Chairman, Colonel Lord Henry Scott, Mr and Mrs Campbell Smith, and Miss Duncan, who were mainly responsible for the striking success of all its activities. The Regiment was most fortunate in having citizens of such eminence willing to spend time and money in its service. Nor did their labours cease with the war. They were anxious that the work of the Association should be rounded off by a Memorial that would be worthy of the Royal Scots who fell in the struggle. This matter was the subject of much consideration and correspondence, and the general trend of opinion was that the Memorial should be something of a useful nature rather than a statue or other purely monumental structure. The first definite lead in favour of a Club came from Colonel Lord Henry Scott, and the Association sent out a letter [1] to all battalions advising them that a meeting would be held to consider the proposal. The meeting assembled in the City Chambers on the 11th March 1919, when it was resolved to proceed with the erection of a Royal Scots Club in Edinburgh.

The Association acted with its customary vigour, and an appeal for the necessary funds was at once issued. The response was a generous one, and in 1919 the Association acquired huts in St Andrew Square, which

[1] See Appendix V.

MEMORIAL TABLET.

[*To face p.* 766.

had been the H.Q. of the American Y.M.C.A. during the war, as temporary premises for the Club. Under the direction of Captain W. Clark, who was appointed Secretary, the undertaking was a huge success and vastly encouraged the Association to obtain without undue delay a more worthy shrine for the Regimental Memorial. A stately house in Abercromby Place was secured for the purpose, and little time was lost in removing from St Andrew Square to the new premises.

The Memorial is in every sense a magnificent one, and all Royal Scots are justly proud of what is one of the most compact and comfortable Clubs in the kingdom. But the premises at Abercromby Place would have no especial significance if they represented only a Club; they form, also, the sanctuary of the Regiment, and they are the visible symbol of a new spirit of comradeship. Before 1914 there was a wide chasm between Regulars and Territorials; unity and co-operation were developed by the common sufferings of all ranks and classes during the war. In suggesting the institution of a Club, Lord Henry Scott proposed a form of Memorial which was singularly well adapted to prevent a return to the separation of the old days and to preserve the newly-won sense of comradeship. For the Club is the rallying-point of all Royal Scots, past and present; it is the centre of all the social and benevolent activities of the Regiment. Respect for the dead reaches the loftiest heights when it nourishes harmony and co-operation among the living.

Occupying the place of honour in the Hall is the Memorial Tablet, and beneath it, in a glass case, is the Regiment's Roll of Honour, with each name engraved by hand in Old English.

All was ready for the formal opening by the summer

of 1922, and H.R.H. Princess Mary, who honoured the Regiment by becoming its Colonel-in-Chief in October 1918, journeyed north to unveil the Memorial Tablet on the 12th August.   There was a great rally of past and present members of the Royal Scots to welcome their Colonel-in-Chief.   A Guard of Honour, consisting of 3 officers and 100 men under Captain N. R. Crockatt, D.S.O., M.C., was furnished by the Regimental Depot. In addition, representatives of the battalions, Regular, Territorial, and Service, were formed up in four brigades, composed as follows :—

1st Brigade (1st, 2nd, and 3rd Battalions), commanded by Lieut.-Colonel E. S. Strutt, D.S.O., O.B.E., with Major J. H. Hamilton as his Brigade-Major.

2nd Brigade (4th, 5th, 6th, 7th, and 8th Battalions), commanded by Colonel W. C. Peebles, D.S.O., T.D., D.L., with Captain T. D. Wilson, M.C., as his Brigade-Major.

3rd Brigade (9th, 10th, 11th, 12th, and 13th Battalions), commanded by Lieut.-Colonel P. J. Blair, D.S.O., with Captain E. D. Stevenson, M.C., as his Brigade-Major.

4th Brigade (14th, 15th, 16th, 17th, 18th, 19th, and 1st Garrison Battalions, 1st, 2nd, 3rd, and 4th Volunteer Battalions, and the 1st Territorial Cadet Battalion), commanded by Brig.-General Sir Robert Cranston, K.C.V.O., C.B., O.B.E., V.D., T.D., with Captain H. T. Allwright, M.C., D.C.M., as his Brigade-Major.

The scene formed a setting worthy of the greatness of the occasion.   In the space between the Club and the gardens that fringe the south side of Abercromby Place, the parade of over 2000 Royal Scots, with 17 Regimental Colours floating in a gentle breeze, made an imposing and heart-stirring spectacle.   A tremendous ovation greeted the Princess as she appeared on the raised dais that had been erected in front of the Club. Accompanying her were Lieut.-General Sir E. A. Altham, K.C.B., K.C.I.E., C.M.G., who had been appointed Colonel of the Regiment in January 1919, Colonel Lord Henry Scott, the Chairman of the Club, and the Very Rev. Dr Wallace Williamson. Lord Henry Scott outlined the inception of the Club, and General Altham, in tracing the record of the Royal Scots, showed how gigantic had been the strain on the man-power of the Lowlands during the war, for the number of the wounded alone, between forty and fifty thousand, was nearly sufficient to make up three divisions. Then followed the ceremony of dedication, in which Princess Mary took the chief part, and her address on that occasion forms the most appropriate conclusion to the story of The Royal Scots in the Great War.

GENERAL ALTHAM, OFFICERS, MEN,
    AND FRIENDS OF THE ROYAL SCOTS:

We are assembled here to-day to remember those officers and men of the Regiment who laid down their lives in the Great War, and to dedicate to their memory a Club which will knit together in a close *esprit de corps* and friendship Royal Scots for all time.

That gallant band numbered eleven thousand one hundred and sixty-two, and came from thirty-nine [1] battalions which served overseas and at home during the supreme struggle.

Let all who enter here see to it that the names of these heroes are honoured and handed down from generation to generation as examples of unselfish devotion worthy of the Regiment—worthy even of Scotland itself.

The Tablet that I am about to unveil will ever bear witness to their sacrifice—a sacrifice that calls for a greater comradeship of the living.

One thought is uppermost in our minds to-day: sympathy for the wives, parents, and children of those who were the life and soul of the home, and whose absence leaves a gap that time can never fill.

[1] Including four Volunteer Battalions.

Yet to them, as to all of us, this Club will remain a place of memories and inspirations.

You have heard from General Altham of the great achievements of the Regiment, which make me prouder than ever to be its Colonel-in-Chief.

We owe much to Lord Henry Scott, to his Committee and to the Secretary, Captain Clark, for the successful accomplishment of this scheme in erecting here in Edinburgh so appropriate a Memorial.

It has given me great satisfaction to take part in a ceremony which is a tribute to the dead, and which so closely concerns the life and welfare of Royal Scots.

APPENDIX I.

The Story of The Royal Scots, "Country Life," 1915, by Lawrence Weaver, is a compact history of the Regiment up to 1915.

History of the Fifty-second (Lowland) Division (4th and 7th Battalions) (Maclehose, Jackson & Co., 1923), by Lieut.-Colonel R. R. Thomson, M.C.

History of the Fifty-first (Highland) Division (8th and 9th Battalions) (Blackwood, 1921), by Major F. W. Bewsher, D.S.O., M.C.

History of the Ninth (Scottish) Division (11th and 12th Battalions) (John Murray, 1921), by Major J. Ewing, M.C.

The Thirty-fourth Division (15th and 16th Battalions) (H. F. & O. Witherby, 1921), by Lieut.-Colonel J. Shakespear, C.M.G., C.I.E., D.S.O.

In addition to the above, the *History of the Fifteenth (Scottish) Division* is now in course of publication, and battalion brochures have been printed by the 8th and 9th Battalions. Matters of interest to those who were with the 2nd Battalion in 1915 are related in *On the King's Service* (Hodder & Stoughton, 1917) by the Rev. A. S. Innes Logan. The early experiences of the 5th Battalion in Gallipoli are recorded by Major (now Lieut.-Colonel) A. H. Mure. T.D., in *With the Incomparable Twenty-ninth* (W. & R. Chambers, 1919). Excellent histories of the 4th and of the 7th Battalions have been compiled, but have not yet been printed; those who served with either of these battalions will appreciate *From Gallipoli to Baghdad* (Hodder & Stoughton, 1917) by the Rev. William Ewing, M.C., D.D., and *With the Fifty-second (Lowland) Division in Three Continents* (W. Green, 1920), by Lieut.-Colonel J. Young, D.S.O., R.A.M.C.(T.), An intimate account of the 11th Royal Scots is given in *Three Years with the Ninth Division* (John Murray, 1919) by Lieut.-Colonel W. D. Croft, C.M.G., D.S.O. The experiences of the 2/10th Battalion in Russia are clearly and graphically described by Lieut.-Colonel A. P. Skeil, D.S.O., M.C., in Chapter XII. of "The Long Road to Victory" (*John Buchan's Annual,* 1920).

APPENDIX II.

The description "Home Service" applies in each case to the unit and not to the personnel, for with the exception of a few officers, N.C.Os., and men, the training staff of every battalion consisted, after the first year of the war, of officers and men who, having recovered from the effects of wounds received on active service, were given a spell of duty at home before being sent back to the front. In the last year of the struggle a great proportion of the instructing personnel was formed by officers and N.C.Os. who after eighteen months' or more continuous service at the front were detached from their units to undergo a six months' tour of duty at home. While battalions were always changing in personnel, instructors remained with each in sufficient numbers to preserve continuity, while such changes as took place prevented stagnation and ensured that the training would be kept up to date in the light of the experience gained in the different theatres of the war.

The chief difficulty at the outset arose from scarcity of supplies as regards equipment, and especially affected newly-formed units, but despite every handicap the training carried out by The Royal Scots units was efficient in every particular, and the drafts sent out from home, with regard to the standard of their training and the quality of their equipment, never failed to give satisfaction. Men were sent not merely to units of the Regiment, but also to English battalions.

Training of drafts and guard duties formed the daily round of life, but, periodically, units were called upon to function as complete battalions, when they were visited by Generals, and on these occasions they always earned a word of high praise from the Inspecting Officer for the excellence of their turn-out and the high standard of their drill. But the most convincing testimony to the value of the work performed by the draft-finding units was the magnificent war record of the Active Service Battalions.

A. 3rd (Reserve) Battalion The Royal Scots.

This battalion, stationed at Weymouth at the commencement of the war, under the command of Lieut.-Colonel The Earl of Ellesmere, M.V.O., supplied more drafts to The Royal Scots at the various fronts than any other unit.   It existed principally to make good the wastage in the two line battalions, but as the Army expanded, it also sent considerable drafts to other Royal Scots battalions.   As the training staff of the 3rd Royal Scots consisted of regular officers and N.C.Os., their work, as was only to be expected, was invariably of first-rate quality.

From Weymouth the battalion moved up to Glencorse, near Edinburgh, and in October 1915 went into billets in Penicuik, returning to Glencorse at the beginning of 1916.   In November of the following year the unit was transferred to Mullingar in Ireland. In the summer of 1918 The Earl of Ellesmere vacated the command on promotion to a higher appointment, and was succeeded by Lieut.-Colonel The Earl of Bradford.   After the armistice Lieut.-Colonel McMicking, on liberation from Germany, joined the battalion as C.O. in January 1919.   On the 6th March 1919 the unit entrained for Dublin, whence it embarked for Glasgow, where it was accommodated at Maryhill Barracks.   Thence in May it proceeded to Gailes. By this time demobilisation was in full swing, and the war experience of the 3rd Royal Scots terminated in July, when they handed over to the 2nd Battalion.

B.   Territorial Units.

2/4th Battalion The Royal Scots.—This unit, raised at the beginning of the war, remained in Edinburgh under the command of Lieut.-Colonel (Hon. Colonel) A. Young, V.D., till February 1915. The daily routine consisted of guard duties and training.   In February the battalion proceeded to Penicuik, and in May to Peebles. When Lieut.-Colonel Young left to take command of the 1/4th in Gallipoli, the command of the 2/4th devolved on Lieut.-Colonel S. Cuthbert, V.D.   Leaving Peebles in October the battalion went in turn to Portobello, Edinburgh, and Cambusbarron.   While at the last-named place it was included in the 195th Brigade of the Sixty-fifth Division, the battalion having been brought up to strength by the inclusion of the 2/5th and 2/6th Royal Scots.   With the Sixty-fifth Division the 2/4th proceeded to Essex, where, in addition to training, it was employed in defence work.   Early in 1916 Lieut.-Colonel Cuthbert resigned his command, being succeeded by Lieut.-Colonel Mackenzie. Later, the command was taken over by Lieut.-Colonel W. M. Kay, C.M.G., T.D., under whom the unit proceeded to Fermoy in Ireland at the beginning of 1917.   After more than a year's anxious service in that distracted country, the 2/4th Battalion was disbanded in July 1918.

3/4th Battalion The Royal Scots.—Formed at Peebles at the beginning of May 1915 this battalion was commanded by Lieut.-

Colonel J. G. Simpson, T.D., when, in addition to the C.O., it consisted
of one orderly-room clerk, one groom, and one horse.   From
these small beginnings it slowly grew till it reached in November
a strength of 500.   On the 10th November it moved to Galashiels,
where within fourteen days its numbers ran into four figures.   From
Galashiels the battalion was transferred on the 25th November to
Loanhead, where the space allotted for the training of the unit, now
swollen to 1400 men, consisted of two fields.   In April 1916 the battalion
went into camp at Stobs under conditions that made Lieut.-Colonel
Simpson feel that he was a resurrected Noah.   Stobs, however, gave
magnificent facilities for training.   Between April and July about
500 fully-trained men were despatched to the various fronts, and in
July the "A" group of the Lowland Brigade, consisting of the third
lines of the 4th, 5th, 6th, 7th, and 8th Royal Scots, was formed into
the 4th (Reserve) Battalion The Royal Scots, under Lieut.-Colonel
D. Ballantyne of the 3/8th Royal Scots.

   2/5th Battalion The Royal Scots.—Commanded at the beginning of the war by Lieut.-Colonel (Hon. Colonel) R. Clark, V.D., this
unit was stationed in Edinburgh till May 1915, when it proceeded
to Peebles, where it was split into two groups, a Home Service wing
which was sent to the Fife coast defences, and a Foreign Service group
which was put under the command of Lieut.-Colonel J. H. Cooper.
The latter formed the 2/5th Battalion, and, on leaving Peebles, it
proceeded first to Loanhead and then to Larbert.   Unable to secure
recruits, it was absorbed in November 1916 into the 2/4th Battalion.

   3/5th Battalion The Royal Scots.—Raised at Peebles in May
1915 under Lieut.-Colonel T. Young, this battalion moved to Galashiels
in November.   Edinburgh, Hawick, and Stobs were other stations
occupied by the unit.   Like most of the third line units the 3/5th
was always under strength, and in July 1916 it lost its identity, when
it was absorbed into the 4th (Reserve) Battalion The Royal Scots.

   2/6th Battalion The Royal Scots.—This battalion was organised
in Edinburgh early in 1915, when the 1/6th was detailed for service
overseas, and Lieut.-Colonel (Hon. Colonel) Stuart Douglas Elliot,
V.D., was appointed to the command on the 1st March 1915.   The
headquarters were at London Street School, and half the battalion
kept guard at Inchkeith and the other half had charge of Leith
Docks.   Early in May the battalion was split up; all Home Service
men were sent to Methil under Major R. M. Cameron, the Second-in-
Command, and the Overseas men, after a short stay at the Marine
Gardens, Edinburgh, went into camp at Peebles on the 15th May,
where they remained till October, when they were transferred to

billets in Selkirk. During the sojourn at Peebles and Selkirk several drafts were sent to the first line. Unable for lack of recruits to continue as a separate unit, the 2/6th Battalion was, in November 1915, merged into the 2/4th Royal Scots.

3/6th Battalion The Royal Scots.—With Lieut.-Colonel K. Whitton, T.D., as C.O., this unit was formed at Peebles on the 31st July 1915. From that camp it was transferred in November 1915 to Galashiels, whence after a stay of three weeks it took over on the 27th November the Selkirk quarters which had just been vacated by the 2/6th. More than five months were spent at Selkirk, and on the 7th May 1916 the 3/6th went under canvas at Stobs. In July the battalion was amalgamated with other third line units to form the 4th (Reserve) Battalion The Royal Scots.

2/7th Battalion The Royal Scots.—At the end of August 1914, this battalion was raised under the name of the 7th (Reserve) Battalion The Royal Scots, and was commanded by Lieut.-Colonel (Hon. Colonel) R. G. Wardlaw-Ramsay, V.D. Its duties were to train officers and men, provide guards for Leith Docks, and to supply trained men to the 7th Battalion. It became known as the 2/7th from January 1915, when it was organised in four companies. From Leith it moved to Peebles in March 1915, and after remaining there for six weeks was brought back to Edinburgh. In May all Home Service men were transferred to the 7th Provisional Battalion under the command of Lieut.-Colonel Wardlaw-Ramsay, and Lieut.-Colonel C. Muirhead was appointed C.O. of the 2/7th Royal Scots.

From billets in Edinburgh the 2/7th proceeded to camp at Peebles on the 22nd May 1915, and was posted to the 2/1st Lothian Infantry Brigade under Scottish Coast Defences. Weak in numbers after the Home Service men were taken away from it, the unit welcomed the addition of two drafts of officers and men, who volunteered to transfer from the 8th Highland Light Infantry. At the end of July the battalion furnished a draft of six platoons for the first line in Gallipoli. On the 14th October it was billeted in Innerleithen and Walkerburn, and in November it was posted to the 194th Brigade of the Sixty-fifth Division and moved north on the 23rd to Larbert. It proceeded with the division to Essex in February 1916, and in April rose to a strength of more than 1000, through the addition of nearly 700 recruits from the depots of English regiments. But as the newcomers were unfit for active service, being all B1 and C1 men, their training presented some difficulties. Many were in the course of time brought up to Category A standard; some did not advance beyond B, and those who dropped below that Category were either discharged or transferred to

II

other units. A troublesome but useful element in the battalion consisted of young soldiers, who had been returned from active service on the ground that they were not yet nineteen years of age.

Large drafts from the Sixty-fifth Division went to the Overseas forces in August 1916, the 2/7th Royal Scots contributing 200 men. Four Zeppelins were brought down in Essex; a detachment of the 2/7th and parties of other units, under Lieut.-Colonel Muirhead, were told off to guard and break up the wreckage of one Zeppelin which was brought down at Bittericoy on the 24th September.

All hopes of the Sixty-fifth Division proceeding on active service were dispelled in January 1917, when the division was sent to Ireland, where the 2/7th Royal Scots were accommodated in Richmond Barracks, Dublin. Guard duties and mobile detachments became the commonplaces of life. On the 18th August 1917 the 194th Brigade was transferred to County Galway where it went under canvas, the 2/7th being encamped at Moycullen on Loch Corrib. A most creditable piece of work was accomplished by the battalion when, leaving camp at 8 A.M. one day, it marched $17\frac{1}{2}$ miles, carried through a field-day, and trekked back to Moycullen, arriving there at 1 o'clock the next morning without a man falling out. The weather during the sojourn in Galway was persistently bad, and there were no regrets when, on the 17th September, the brigade was transferred to the Curragh. Prior to leaving Galway the brigade furnished several mobile detachments (each consisting of 300 officers and men) which marched through different parts of Connemara for three or four days, bivouacking at a different place each night, in order to show the inhabitants of this disaffected region that there were British troops in Ireland; two of these columns were supplied by the 2/7th Royal Scots.

At the Curragh the battalion formed part of a large mobile column of mixed arms, which was always held in readiness to move at any time to any part of Ireland. In addition, the unit continued to furnish drafts for active service, 479 men being sent out in 1917. On the 18th January 1918 orders were received for the disbandment of the division, and the infantry units were broken up. A tribute to the battalion, in the form of a letter from the Field-Marshal Commanding the Home Forces to Lieut.-Colonel Muirhead, thanking him for the fine work accomplished by his battalion, had been fully earned by the admirable services rendered by the 2/7th Royal Scots during their brief but strenuous career. On disbandment all Category A ranks were sent to the B.E.F., most of the Category B men were transferred to the 2/10th, while A 4 personnel and low category men were transferred to the 4th (Reserve) Battalion The Royal Scots.

3/7th Battalion The Royal Scots.—This unit owed its existence directly to the tragic railway disaster at Gretna in May 1915, the 3/7th being formed expressly to receive those members of the first line who had been involved in the accident, on their return from leave or hospital. Thus established at Peebles in June 1915 under the command of Major H. Rose, the battalion later became the principal draft-producing unit for the first line. It was too weak, however, to provide from its own numbers the two full companies for active service, which were called for in July 1915, and the demand was only met by the transference of a whole company of the 8th Highland Light Infantry to the 3/7th. This was the largest draft ever sent to the first line, and was distinguished as "The Five Hundred Draft" (see p. 208).

In November 1915 the battalion moved to Innerleithen, and it remained there till May 1916, when it went to Stobs camp, where on the 31st August it was broken up, officers and men being posted in about equal numbers to the 3/8th and 3/9th Royal Scots.

2/8th Battalion The Royal Scots.—This battalion was raised in the autumn of 1914, and on the first line moving to France the companies of the second line proceeded to Haddington under Lieut.-Colonel C. M. Cowan, T.D. Coast defence and the provision of drafts for the 1/8th were its principal functions. In May 1915 it moved to Peebles, where all Home Service men were detached and sent to Kinghorn for coast defence, the 2/8th being put under the command of Lieut.-Colonel R. W. Tweedie, T.D. From Peebles it proceeded in November to Falkirk, and in February 1916 it was posted to the Sixty-fifth Division, with which formation it was sent to Essex, where it remained till January 1917.

In January there began a spell of service in Ireland, the 2/8th being stationed at Richmond Barracks, Dublin. There were often risky jobs to perform; during Easter 1917 when information was brought of a conspiracy to blow up Kynoch's works at Arklow, the 2/8th had the honour of providing the guard which frustrated the plot. In the summer of 1917 the unit was disbanded, most of the officers and men of the 2/8th being then drafted to Scottish battalions in France.

3/8th Battalion The Royal Scots.—The 3/8th Battalion was formed at Peebles in December 1914 under Lieut.-Colonel (Hon. Colonel) The Hon. W. G. Hepburne-Scott, V.D., afterwards Lord Polwarth. With the exception of a brief period from November to December 1915, when the battalion was in billets at Prestonpans, Peebles was the home of the 3/8th Royal Scots until the summer of 1916, when they moved to Stobs. Previous to this Colonel Lord Polwarth was appointed in December 1915 to command the "A" Group Lowland

Reserve Brigade, which was then in Yorkshire, and the command of the 3/8th devolved on Lieut.-Colonel D. Ballantyne, who assumed command of the 4th (Reserve) Battalion The Royal Scots, when that battalion was formed in July by the amalgamation of third line units.

2/9th Battalion (Highlanders), The Royal Scots. — (The following account is based on a short history of the battalion contributed for publication in *The Leather Sporran*, the Journal of the 2/9th Royal Scots, by Lieut. D. A. Bannatyne).

This battalion was formed at the headquarters of the 9th Battalion (Highlanders) The Royal Scots on the 12th September 1914, and on its inception was composed of 4 officers and 473 N.C.Os. and men. It was commanded by Captain A. C. Aitken till the 21st September, when Lieut.-Colonel (Honorary Colonel) James Ferguson, who founded the 9th Volunteer Battalion (Highlanders) The Royal Scots, in 1900, was gazetted C.O. Its main duties were to take over the Home Service men of the Service Battalion, when that unit proceeded on active service, to obtain recruits, and to train and supply drafts.

After being known as the 9th (Reserve) Battalion (Highlanders) Royal Scots and later as the 9th (Home Service) Battalion (Highlanders) Royal Scots, the unit, on the 8th February 1915, was officially designated the 2/9th Battalion (Highlanders) The Royal Scots. Billeted in Edinburgh, the unit was included in the Lothian Infantry Brigade, which formed part of the Scottish Coast Defence Forces, and its first duties were to find guards for Leith Docks, Holyrood, and the Scottish Command Office. At the outset the battalion was composed both of men who attested for service overseas, and of men who enlisted only for home defence. This involved a constant interchange of men with the 1/9th Battalion, as Imperial Service men were transferred from the second to the first line and Home Service men from the first to the second line.

Originally organised in five companies, the battalion, on the 15th November 1914, was reorganised in eight companies. On the 18th December it was transferred to Kilmarnock, and while there reorganisation on a four-company basis was effected: the Imperial Service men were, from the 19th February, grouped in the right-half, and the Home Service men in the left-half, of the battalion. On the departure from Edinburgh, in February 1915, of the 1/9th Battalion to France, the 2/9th returned to Edinburgh, where it took the place of the 1/9th and became responsible for a section of the coast defences. In February Colonel Ferguson had the misfortune to sustain a broken leg through his horse slipping on ice when he was supervising training on the Braid Hills, and during his absence, until the 14th June,

when he rejoined the battalion at Peebles, Major T. G. Clark took
over the duties of C.O. Near the end of May the Home Service
group was detached from the battalion and transferred to the 5th
Scottish Provisional Battalion at Dundee; Major Clark accompanied
this group to Dundee, and the command of the 2/9th Royal Scots,
which then proceeded to the Brigade Camp at Peebles, was taken
over by Major C. T. Gordon.

Thus reduced to two companies, the battalion remained at Peebles
till the 6th October 1915. During June the 3/9th Battalion was
raised at Peebles, and the enthusiasm of the 2/9th took on a keen
edge, because it was intimated that this unit was to be brought up to
full strength and sent on active service. Colonel Ferguson was
transferred to the 3/9th as C.O., and Major Gordon, promoted Lieut.-
Colonel on the 20th May, assumed command of the 2/9th. In
October the unit proceeded to Selkirk, and near the close of
November it was included in the 195th Brigade, the other three
battalions of which were all composite ones. On the 24th November
it moved to Tillicoultry, which was the home of the battalion till
February 1916, when the 195th Brigade, which formed part of the
Sixty-fifth Division, was sent to Essex.

By this time the 2/9th had been restored to a four-company basis,
and when, on the 26th April, a considerable number of recruits joined
the battalion, the prospects of its being sent on active service seemed
far from remote. On the 11th June 1916 another change in command
took place, when, following on the retirement of Lieut.-Colonel Gordon,
Lieut.-Colonel A. F. Egerton, D.S.O., was gazetted C.O. Unfortunately all hope of the unit being employed overseas was dispelled on
the 30th July 1916, when the 2/9th was suddenly called upon to
furnish a draft of 300 N.C.Os. and men. Since its inception, drafts
amounting to about 400 men had been supplied by the battalion,
and this new demand so depleted the 2/9th that it was thereafter
relegated to garrison work and draft-finding.

In the spring of 1917 the battalion was sent to Ireland; one half
was stationed at Tralee and the remainder at Limerick. In the
following year the unit was transferred to Moore Park, County Cork,
Ireland, where it was disbanded in July 1918.

3/9th Battalion (Highlanders) The Royal Scots.—Raised at
Peebles in June 1915 as a training and draft-finding unit, this
battalion was placed under the command of Colonel Ferguson. Its
career was brief. In November 1915 it was transferred to Selkirk, and in
May 1916 to Stobs. In November 1916 the battalion went to Catterick
and remained there throughout 1917. In the spring of that year

Colonel Ferguson retired on account of age, and was succeeded as C.O. by Lieut.-Colonel C. P. Doig. Towards the end of July the battalion was amalgamated with the 4th (Reserve) Battalion The Royal Scots.

1/10th Cyclist Battalion The Royal Scots.—The mobilisation of the 1/10th Royal Scots, commanded by Lieut.-Colonel M. W. Henderson, was carried through at Linlithgow without a hitch at the beginning of August 1914. The first move of the unit was through Edinburgh to East Linton in East Lothian, and thereafter, coast defence was its principal rôle. In October 1914 Lieut.-Colonel Henderson left to command a New Army Unit, and he was succeeded by Lieut.-Colonel, subsequently Colonel, A. P. Simpson. The battalion was accepted for foreign service, but the coast defence duty, for which it had been detailed, prevented its employment abroad as a unit, though, by the end of 1916, fully 90 per cent. of the original personnel had gone abroad for service with other units. Early in 1917 Colonel Simpson left the battalion for foreign service, and the next C.O. was the Marquis of Linlithgow. In April 1918 the battalion was transferred from the Scottish coast to Ireland, first to Claremorris, then to the Curragh in August, to Port Arlington in October, and to Ballinrobe, County Mayo, in November. The Marquis of Linlithgow relinquished the command early in 1919 and was succeeded by Lieut.-Colonel R. N. Coulson, D.S.O., under whom the 1/10th moved in April to Castlebar, where Lieut.-Colonel J. J. Cameron, D.S.O., M.C., subsequently took over the command from Lieut.-Colonel Coulson. In the autumn of 1919 the battalion went to Ennistimon, County Clare, where the majority of the men were demobilised, the cadre being despatched to Linlithgow in January 1920, where demobilisation was completed on the 26th February.

4th (Reserve) Battalion The Royal Scots.—Formed at Stobs in July 1916, this battalion on its inception was composed of the 3/4th, 3/5th, 3/6th, 3/7th, and 3/8th Royal Scots, under the command of Lieut.-Colonel D. Ballantyne. It proceeded to Catterick in September, and towards the end of July 1917 the 3/9th Royal Scots were also incorporated in the battalion, the command of which was now taken over by Lieut.-Colonel C. P. Doig, D.S.O., O.B.E., of the 3/9th. On leaving Catterick in November 1917, the unit returned to Scotland, the stations occupied by it being Edinburgh, Haddington, and Cupar. During the last two years of the war it was the principal clearing-house for all the Active Service Territorial units of The Royal Scots; to it were sent on their discharge from hospital all the officers and men who had been wounded at the front and who required a spell of training at home to fit them for another bout of service overseas.

The unit was at Cupar when the armistice came into force, but demobilisation was far from being completed, when, in February 1919, strike riots in Glasgow caused it to be rushed to that city. The municipal buildings formed the H.Q. of the battalion, detachments of which were sent to occupy power stations and other places which it was essential to protect from injury. Fortunately the crisis passed over without anything occurring to bring the battalion into disfavour with the Glasgow populace, and in March it was transferred to Maryhill, where it was disbanded.

C. New Army Units.

14th (Reserve) Battalion The Royal Scots.—Formed at Weymouth in 1914 under Lieut.-Colonel A. H. Battye, the 14th Royal Scots were sent to Stobs in 1915. In October they moved to Hipswell near Catterick, and in the spring of 1916 they returned to Scotland, taking over garrison duties near Kirkcaldy. Under the command of Lieut.-Colonel J. A. Briggs the battalion, in 1917, was sent to Cromer. When the problem of man-power became acute, young boys were posted to Young Soldiers' Battalions, and the staff of the 14th Royal Scots was used for training purposes. The battalion lost its titular connection with the Royal Scots when it received the official designation of the 51st (H.L.I.) Training Reserve Battalion, but its personnel in both officers and N.C.Os. consisted principally of Royal Scots. Under Lieut.-Colonel Carr, D.S.O., from October 1917 its function was to send trained companies of young boys, as soon as they reached the age of nineteen years, to the front. The only dislocation in the procedure occurred in March 1918, when the German offensive necessitated the sending of all available troops to France, and several companies, though they had not completed their training and although the boys had not reached the age of nineteen, were at once despatched overseas. After the armistice the battalion went over as a unit to Germany; it was stationed near Solingen, where it was demobilised.

18th (Reserve) Battalion The Royal Scots.—The 18th Royal Scots were raised in June 1915 under the command of Lieut.-Colonel Sir Robert Cranston, K.C.V.O., C.B., V.D., and constituted at first a local reserve for the three Edinburgh battalions, the 15th, 16th, and 17th. From its first station in Edinburgh the battalion proceeded in October to Ripon, but returned to the Scottish Command in April 1916, when it was sent to Dundee. It was impossible, however, to maintain the battalion as a local reserve for particular units, and near the end of 1917, during which year it was at Barry, it was formed into a general reserve unit, known as the 77th Training Reserve Battalion.

APPENDIX III.

19th Battalion The Royal Scots.

This unit, organised at Blairgowrie about the middle of April 1917, was the first Labour Battalion recruited for service in France, and was composed of men below the general service standard, many of whom owed their unfitness to wounds received at the front. After a month's training it was sent to Abancourt in France, where a large artillery dump was in course of construction. Frequently the battalion was broken up into detachments, sent here and there as occasion might require, and in all its work it earned the approbation of the higher authorities. The work was often of a humdrum nature, but it was never scamped, and the men did their part so well that one of their C.Os., Lieut.-Colonel Green, wrote about them: "The battalion was particularly clean and worked so well that they helped to turn out the largest amount of work of any area in France."

In the course of its service the battalion had three C.Os., Lieut.-Colonel J. Donaldson, D.S.O., Lieut.-Colonel J. O. Kemp, and Lieut.-Colonel T. M. Green, all of whom had a long experience with front line units. The Adjutant, Captain Pugh of the Royal Scots Fusiliers, though severely crippled by shrapnel in his thigh, gave most valuable assistance to Lieut.-Colonel Green, whose own sterling worth was abundantly demonstrated by the loyal support which he received from all ranks.

Early in 1918 all Labour Battalions were transformed into large Labour Companies, and in this reorganisation the 19th Royal Scots became the 1st and 2nd Labour Companies of the 10th Labour Group, for the establishment of which Lieut.-Colonel Green was largely responsible.

1st Garrison Battalion The Royal Scots.

(This account is based upon a private diary, kindly lent by Colonel F. J. Brown.) This unit took concrete shape on the 11th August 1915, when drafts from the reserve battalions of various Scottish regiments

782

arrived at Redford Camp, near Edinburgh. Composed of officers and men the great majority of whom were unfit for active service, the battalion was raised to perform garrison duty abroad and so relieve other troops fit for the firing-line. Colonel F. J. Brown, C.B., late commanding the 2nd Battalion The Essex Regiment, arrived at Redford on the 18th August to take command of the newly-formed unit, which was organised in four companies. The site of the camp was condemned by medical officers as unhealthy, and on the 4th September the battalion was shifted to Stobs, which "was the one place that we hoped we should not be sent to as it was very unfavourably reported on by those who had had experience of it." Despite the fact that the men had no rifles, their work on parade was never slack. Near the end of September the battalion was issued with equipment, and mainly through the efforts of the officers, assisted by donations from friends and grants from other Scottish regiments, a pipe band was raised. In October Lee-Metford rifles were issued to the men.

In October, when the air was becoming uncomfortably chilly at night, orders came for the battalion to leave Stobs on the 23rd "for a secret destination." By two trains it was conveyed to Devonport, where it immediately embarked on the *Empress of Britain*. Several other units boarded the ship, and Colonel Brown was put in command of all the troops. After an uneventful voyage, broken by a stay of two days at Malta, the ship reached Mudros on the 4th November.

The Staff at Mudros, housed on the s.s. *Aragon*, at first instructed the Royal Scots to disembark at East Mudros without giving time or date, but later ordered the battalion and other two garrison units to hold themselves in readiness to proceed to Cape Helles. This could only be interpreted as a decision to employ the men on a service for which they were neither fit nor intended, and evoked a protest from Colonel Brown and the C.Os. of the other units concerned. The N.C.Os. and men of The Royal Scots were drawn from two classes : those between forty and sixty years of age, of whom several were Army pensioners and had served twenty-one years with the Colours (about 600 in all); and men under forty, many of whom had soldiered in France and had been invalided either on account of wounds or illness. There were few in the battalion capable of undergoing heavy fatigues, though all were quite fit for guards and lighter duties.

In spite of Colonel Brown's protest, a party of 400, under Major A. F. Douglas, was sent to Cape Helles on the 8th November. The remainder of the battalion was expected to follow later, but on the evening of the 8th it was ordered to land at West Mudros and encamp there. Orders, however, were altered with distracting suddenness, and the Royal Scots were instructed to land at East instead of West Mudros. At this place there were no preparations for a camp, and as the troops were not conveyed to shore till the late afternoon of the 8th November, the camp had to be pitched in darkness. The site was far from ideal, for the ground on which the Royal Scots now found themselves had been fouled by previous encampments.

First impressions of Lemnos had not been cheerful, and subsequent examination of the ground did little to elevate the spirits of the troops. Mudros was "a dirty little place," with narrow cobbled streets, and peopled mainly by Greeks and Levantines. "The women were surpassingly ugly; we heard afterwards that when the Allies' troops took up occupation of the island, all the women with any pretensions to good looks had been transported from Mudros to distant parts of the island."

A "sing-song" with the 5th Royal Scots on the 9th November was the most joyous event that the 1st Garrison Battalion had experienced since its arrival at Mudros, but a pleasant evening was followed by a tempestuous night, for a terrific sand-storm swept over the camp, and most of the officers and men had to turn out to save their tents from collapse. The Royal Scots were now employed in labour work mainly, though they had not been raised for this purpose, and the men became the helots for all units arriving at the station. The Cape Helles party was also engaged as a labour unit, and as there was no place of security there, thirty casualties were sustained from shells and bombs.

Colonel Brown, never slow to stand up for his men when he thought they were being unfairly used, wrote a spirited complaint against his unit being employed as a labour unit though it had not been formed for that purpose, but his protest was unavailing. In December the mutinous attitude of the Maltese and Egyptian Labour Corps led to the battalion furnishing an armed guard at the camp of the latter. The leaders of the disaffection were arrested and whipped, and this example cowed their comrades, who returned to work.

On the evacuation of Gallipoli the whole battalion was again concentrated under Colonel Brown, and on the 4th February 1916, having embarked on the *Empress of Britain*, it was conveyed to Alexandria, whence the men were taken to a camp (Sidi Bishr) about six miles away; on the 13th the unit was transferred by train to a less salubrious camp. One company under Captain P. Dunn was sent to Cyprus for duty on the 27th February, while the remainder proceeded to take up positions in the defence scheme of Alexandria. The first important change occurred on the 22nd October, when battalion H.Q. and one company were sent to

Cyprus as escort to 1300 Turkish prisoners of war.   Later three companies of the Royal Scots were required at Cyprus to guard prisoners, only one company remaining in Egypt.   There was a constant interchange of officers and men between Egypt and Cyprus, and on one occasion the island garrison was so depleted that there were barely sufficient officers and men to perform the necessary routine work.   Medical inspections were periodic, and as men became fit, they were transferred to service units, their places being taken by unfit men from line battalions.   Visits from hostile aeroplanes were unpleasantly frequent, and the Royal Scots were fortunate to escape without casualties.   The most interesting diversion from routine was the furnishing of escorts to Salonika.

Occasionally prisoners of war escaped, but in every case these were recaptured within a few days.   On the 14th September 1918 Famagusta, where Colonel Brown had his H.Q., welcomed eight British officers who had effected a daring escape from a Turkish prison camp in Anatolia.   After the Armistice was signed, Colonel Brown's command steadily shrank in size as demobilisation proceeded, and at the end of May 1919, the battalion, now reduced to 30 officers and 504 N.C.Os. and men, was relieved by the 1/7th Royal Welsh Fusiliers and sailed for home where it was disbanded.

During its career the 1st Garrison Battalion had more than pulled its weight; its efficient performance of necessary work had freed younger and fitter men for service in the front line, where they were most required.   Months of service, ungrudgingly and conscientiously performed, might have been gracefully recognised by the grant of a few decorations to the unit, but the 1st Garrison Battalion was content with the assurance that it had done its duty.

APPENDIX IV.

Private H. H. Robson, 2nd Battalion The Royal Scots.

For most conspicuous bravery near Kemmel on the 14th December 1914, during an attack on the German position, when he left his trench under a very heavy fire and rescued a wounded non-commissioned officer, and subsequently for making an attempt to bring another wounded man into cover, whilst exposed to a severe fire. In this attempt he was at once wounded, but persevered in his efforts, until rendered helpless by being shot a second time.

Lance-Corporal W. Angus, 8th Battalion The Royal Scots.

For most conspicuous bravery and devotion to duty at Givenchy, on the 12th June 1915, in voluntarily leaving his trench under very heavy bomb and rifle fire, and rescuing a wounded officer who was lying within a few yards of the enemy's position. Lance-Corporal Angus had no chance whatever of escaping the enemy's fire when undertaking this very gallant action, and in effecting the rescue he sustained about forty wounds from bombs, some of them being very serious.

Private R. Dunsire, 13th Battalion The Royal Scots.

For most conspicuous bravery on Hill 70 on 26th September 1915. Private Dunsire went out under very heavy fire and rescued a wounded man from between the firing-lines. Later, when another man considerably nearer the German lines was heard shouting for help, he crawled out again with utter disregard to the enemy's fire, and carried him in also. Shortly afterwards the Germans attacked over this ground.

Captain H. Reynolds, M.C., 12th Battalion The Royal Scots.

For most conspicuous bravery on the 20th September 1917. When his company, in attack and approaching their final objective, suffered heavy casualties from enemy machine-guns and from an enemy "pill-box," which had been passed by the first wave, Captain Reynolds reorganised his men, who were scattered, and then proceeded alone by rushes from shell-hole to shell-hole, all the time being under heavy machine-gun fire. When near the "pill-box" he threw a grenade, intending that it should go inside, but the enemy had blocked the entrance. He then crawled to the entrance and forced a phosphorous grenade inside. This set the place on fire and caused the death of three of the enemy, while the remaining seven or eight surrendered with two machine-guns.

Afterwards, though wounded, he continued to lead his company against another objective and captured it, taking seventy prisoners and two more machine-guns.

During the whole attack the company was under heavy machine-gun fire from the flanks, but despite this Captain Reynolds kept complete control of his men.

Private H. M'Iver, M.M., 2nd Battalion The Royal Scots.

During operations on the morning of the 23rd August 1918, Private M'Iver, while Company runner, behaved in the most gallant manner. On one occasion he pursued a German for 150 yards. The German took refuge in a machine-gun nest. Private M'Iver at once, without the slightest regard for his own personal safety, jumped into the trench, bayoneted and shot about six of the occupants, and the remainder, numbering about twenty with two machine-guns, at once surrendered. Through this man's brave action the Company was enabled to advance to their objective.

He also carried important messages continuously through extremely heavy artillery and machine-gun fire.

Corporal R. E. Elcock, M.M., 11th Battalion The Royal Scots.

For most conspicuous bravery and initiative, south-east of Cappelle St Catherine on 15th October 1918, when in charge of a Lewis gun team. Entirely on his own initiative, Corporal Elcock rushed his gun up to within ten yards of enemy guns, which were causing heavy casualties and holding up the advance. He put both guns out of action, captured five prisoners and undoubtedly saved the whole attack from being held up. Later, near the River Lys, this N.C.O. again attacked an enemy machine-gun and captured the crew. His behaviour throughout the day was absolutely fearless.

II   3 D

Lieutenant D. S. M'Gregor, 6th Battalion The Royal Scots, attached Machine-Gun Corps.

For the most conspicuous gallantry and devotion to duty near Hoogmolen on 22nd October 1918.

He was in command of a section of machine-guns attached to the right flank platoon of the assaulting battalion. In the assembly position he concealed his guns on a limber under the bank of a sunken road.

Immediately the troops advanced at zero they were subjected to intense enfilade machine-gun fire from Hill 66 on the right flank. Lieutenant M'Gregor fearlessly went forward into the open to locate the enemy guns, and having done so, realised that it was impossible to get his guns carried forward either by pack or by hand without great delay, as the ground was absolutely bare and swept by a hail of bullets. Ordering the teams to follow by a more covered route, he went to the limber, got on to it, and lying flat, told the driver to leave cover and gallop forward. This the driver did, galloping down about 600 yards of absolutely open road under the heaviest machine-gun fire into cover beyond.

The driver, horses, and limber, were all hit, but Lieutenant M'Gregor succeeded in getting his guns into action, effectively engaging the enemy, subduing their fire, and enabling the advance to be resumed. With the utmost gallantry he continued to expose himself in order to direct and control the fire of his guns, until, about one hour later, this very gallant officer was killed whilst observing fire effect for the Trench Mortar Battery.

His great gallantry and supreme devotion to duty were the admiration of all ranks, and especially of the officers and men of the 1st Border Regiment, who witnessed this extraordinary action.

Lieutenant D. S. M'GREGOR, V.C., 6th Battalion, The Royal Scots.

[To face p. 788.

APPENDIX V.

The Royal Scots Association.

Communications *re* The Royal Scots Club.

Letter issued by The Royal Scots Association.

21 St Andrew Square,
Edinburgh.

Dear Sir,—We send annexed a copy of a letter from Lord Henry Scott, for long in command of the 3rd Battalion of the Regiment and now Honorary Colonel thereof, regarding the future work of the Association, which involves, as you will observe, the creation of a Royal Scots Club in Edinburgh, open to all Officers, N.C.Os., and men serving or who have served in any of the battalions of the Regiment.

You are doubtless aware that at this time almost all Regiments are, as is only fitting, considering the advisability of erecting a Memorial in some public place to their heroes who have fallen in the war. A considerable amount of correspondence has taken place amongst leading officers of the Regiment on the subject of such a Memorial to the never-to-be-forgotten services of the old "Royals," and, so far as we have been able to ascertain, the feeling amongst them is almost unanimous that the Memorial in our case should rather be something of a useful nature than a statue or other purely monumental structure. The Memorial which has met with most approval is the creation of a Club in Edinburgh, of which all officers, soldiers, and old soldiers of all battalions of the Regiment might be members.

Many expressions of opinion have been secured on the subject, from which it would appear the wishes of those interested are that the Club should really be the centre of a powerful corporation, whose influence and existence will be felt for all time in the Capital and the military district. It will thus greatly help in asserting the right to which, by its territorial location and historic position in His Majesty's Army, the Regiment is entitled to occupy in our midst.

In this Club could be centred the whole business activities of the

789

Regiment. From there the Emergency Fund, which has already been of enormous use to dependents and disabled men, could be worked. The likelihood would be that having a publicly-known home for all the Regimental activities, many cases where assistance was required would be at once heard of and traced, where now, owing to the modesty of those honestly requiring assistance, their needs are never brought to light. Help and advice could be given to those requiring assistance in corresponding with the pension authorities, and employment-finding would occupy a prominent place in its activities. In the Club the Regimental Roll of Honour could be kept, and there could be a War Museum, a Collection of Regimental Relics, and a Library, where, among other things, copies of War Diaries of all Battalions might be preserved. The Club would provide bedrooms for country members on a visit to Edinburgh and for members passing through the city. Recreation rooms could be provided where past and present members of the Regiment could meet and keep in touch with each other.

Each battalion doubtless has commemorations sacred to themselves, and annual gatherings in memory thereof could be held in the Club much more appropriately than in the cold surroundings of a hotel.

The Regiment, as the result of its experiences in the recent war, requires to keep its name and its history ever before the people of the Lothians and Peeblesshire as the Local Regiment. In this connection a Club would catch the eye of the public and impress itself on the public mind.

Of course a Club of this sort will cost a considerable amount of money. We have no doubt that if it were taken up enthusiastically each battalion would contribute a sum down, as in the case of the Union Jack Club, which would form the nucleus round which we would gather the subscriptions of the generous people of the City and of the Lothians and Peebles. The subscriptions to our Prisoners' Fund demonstrate that once the public of this district have impressed upon it the fact that this is their local Regiment, and that other Regiments have their own districts reserved to them, there is never any fear of a want of financial support. In the past, a very large share of the energy of Edinburgh and the surrounding district has been spent upon National Schemes, while other districts have devoted their energies to their local needs or their own local Regiments. The result has been that, owing to this attempt on a National effort in this district, our own Regiment has suffered considerably, and is one of the few Scottish Regiments without a public Memorial in our streets.

The view of our Committee is that in order to make the Club thoroughly strong and representative, every battalion of the Regiment must combine together—no matter whether they are Regular, Territorial, Service, or Reserve Battalions. All ranks would be eligible for membership, and, of course, all battalions would be represented upon the management.

It is singularly appropriate that we should start off with such a scheme at this time, as we have recently had laid before us a Circular from the War Office, dated 20th January, addressed to all Territorial Associations, suggesting now the propriety of establishing Territorial Associations as the best way of keeping up and fostering local territorial spirit and *esprit de corps*. The Royal Scots Association have been the pioneers in this question, and from the very beginning of the war the Association, which has on its Committee representatives of every battalion and of all the Territorial Association, has made no distinction in its ministrations between Regular, Territorial, or Service Battalions. It is well to point out that, in connection with the supply of Comforts to the Troops, the upkeep of Prisoners of War, and in allowances to disabled men and dependents, the Association has collected and spent no less a sum than £61,623 since the beginning of the war. No distinction whatever was made between one battalion and another—they were all equally Royal Scots.

It is intended to call a meeting very shortly, to which all battalions will be asked to send a certain number of representatives, and we give you this early notice in order that you may circulate the idea amongst the officers and men with whom you may come in contact.—Yours faithfully,

E. E. DUNCAN,
CAMPBELL SMITH,
Joint Honorary Secretaries.

Letter of Lord Henry Scott.

LABOUR COMMANDANT,
MENIN AREA, B.E.F.,
29th December 1918.

DEAR MR CAMPBELL SMITH,—Many thanks for yours of 19th inst. forwarded here.

In former days The Royal Scots Association only admitted Regulars or ex-Regulars. What I aim at is an Association of Royal Scots which will comprise every man in Edinburgh and surrounding districts who has ever served in any battalion of the Regiment, the object of the Association to be a bond of comradeship whose ideal will be the future welfare of all Royal Scots, in particular to help those demobilised to employment not only now but in the future, also to give assistance to those who have been incapacitated by wounds or sickness.

The care of widows and orphans of ex-Royal Scots should also come within our scope.

I would propose that a meeting be summoned, and in particular Commanding Officers and ex-Commanding Officers of all Royal Scots Battalions be asked to attend to draw up some scheme for the future.

What I want is a powerful Corporation whose influence and existence will be felt for all time in our Capital and district. We do not desire to run counter to any other Regimental Association, but only to assert the right to which, by our territorial location and historic position in His Majesty's Army, we are entitled.

We ought to get every man to join. I prefer a shilling or sixpenny subscription for O.Rs. to any annual subscription.

The subscription to officers could be on a different scale.

We should invite the relatives and friends of the Regiment to be Associates.

We could start a club or clubs and annual gatherings. It must be on a big scale, also to be run properly, it will require financial assistance and probably a salaried clerical staff.

We would need to get into touch and get the support of all the large employers of labour.

I do not think it should be a military association, it should be entirely civil, also representatives of all ranks should be on the committee.

I feel that we have an opportunity now that can never occur again, and only wish that I was at home to carry the scheme through.

I fear some may have their own association and may stand aside.

We must try and persuade them to join in or amalgamate. Although I do not live in or near Edinburgh I am constantly there, and am quite prepared to give up part of my time for the Association.

I am afraid I have put in a rough plan of campaign, but if you are anxious to know about any other points, please let me know.

With all best wishes for 1919.—Yours faithfully,

HENRY SCOTT, Colonel,
Hon. Col. 3rd Batt. The Royal Scots.

CAMPBELL SMITH, Esq.,
Hon. Sec., The Royal Scots Association,
21 St Andrew Square, Edinburgh.

INDEX

NOTE.—*k.* indicates killed in action ; *d.w.*, died of wounds ; *w.m.*, wounded and missing ; *w.*, wounded ; *m.*, missing. Where Battalion numbers only are given, Royal Scots units are implied.

PRINTED BY OLIVER AND BOYD, EDINBURGH

Association of Lowland Scots

President
HIS GRACE THE DUKE OF BUCCLEUCH AND QUEENSBERRY, K.T.

Vice-Presidents
His Grace THE DUKE OF ROXBURGHE, K.T., M.V.O.
The Rt. Hon. THE EARL OF ROSEBERY AND MIDLOTHIAN, K.G., K.T.
The Rt. Hon. THE EARL OF STAIR, D.S.O.
The Rt. Hon. BARON NEWLANDS.
Field-Marshal THE EARL HAIG OF BEMERSYDE, K.T., G.C.B.

Chairman of Executive
The Rt. Hon. LORD SALVESEN, P.C.

Executive Committee

Lt.-Col. D. H. ABERCROMBIE-DICK, D.S.O.
Sir ANDREW N. AGNEW, Bart., of Lochnaw.
Brig.-Gen. ARTHUR BLAIR, D.S.O.
Sir ARCHIBALD BUCHAN-HEPBURN, Bart., of Smeaton-Hepburn.
G. L. CROLE, Esq., K.C., LL.D.
ALEX. COWAN, Esq., of Loganhouse.
P. J. FORD, Esq., M.P.
The Hon. LORD HUNTER.
JOHN HUTCHESON, Esq.
Col. A. MACLAINE MITCHELL, D.S.O., TD.

Col. A. C. H. MACLEAN, C.B.E.
Col. W. CARMICHAEL PEEBLES, D.S.O., D.L.
J. M. RUSK, Esq., J.P.
Col. LORD HENRY SCOTT.
The Rt. Hon. J. PARKER SMITH.
A. FRANCIS STEUART, Esq.
MICHAEL THORBURN, Esq.
Lt.-Col. C. B. VANDELEUR, D.S.O.
Col. D. G. WEMYSS.
Col. ARCH. YOUNG, C.B.E., V.D.
Sir WM. YOUNGER, Bart.

Honorary Secretary and Treasurer
C. MAITLAND SMITH, Esq., 4A York Place, Edinburgh.

Glasgow Local Committee

The Most Hon. THE MARQUIS OF AILSA.
The Most Hon. THE MARCHIONESS OF AILSA.

The Rt. Hon. THE EARL OF CASSILLIS.
R. J. DUNLOP, Esq.
The Rt. Hon. J. PARKER SMITH.
H. CARVICK WEBSTER, Esq.

Representative in London
Lt.-Col. M. M. HALDANE, United Services Club, Pall Mall, London, S W. 1.

Representative in Liverpool
T. J. WHITSON, Esq., Messrs Balfour, Williamson & Co., 25 Water St., Liverpool.

Representative in Ayrshire
Col. CLAUD L. C. HAMILTON, C.M.G., D.S.O., Rozelle, Ayr.

OFFICERS OF 1ST BATTALION, THE ROYAL SCOTS.

Back Row.—Lieut. and QM.W. G. H. Fairall, Capt. G. W. B. Clark, Lieut. E. R. H. Boyd (3rd Battn.), Lieut. G. W. J. Chree, Lieut. N. M. Young, Lieut. G. M. V. Bidie, Lieut. A. H. Rennie, Capt. H. F. M. Worthington-Wilmer, Lieut. D. R. Currie, Capt. J. A. Burke.

Middle Row.—(? ———), Capt. B. H. H. Perry, Capt. A. F. Lumsden, Capt. and Adjt. H. E. Stanley-Murray, Lieut.-Col. D. A. Callender, C.M.G., Lieut.-Gen. G. H. Moncrieff, V.D., Major G. H. F. Wingate, Capt. N. H. S. Fargus, Capt. E. J. F. Johnston, Capt. K. S. Robertson, Lieut. O. J. O'B. O'Hanlon (R.A.M.C.).

Front Row.—2nd Lieut. W. Harris, 2nd Lieut. R. J. Malcolm, 2nd Lieut. R. Appleby, 2nd Lieut. J. Hobbs, 2nd Lieut. D. Thomson.

OFFICERS OF 2ND BATTALION, THE ROYAL SCOTS.

Back Row.—2nd Lieut. A. J. L. Donaldson, 2nd Lieut. D. J. M'Dougall, Lieut. G. E. Hall, Lieut. B. de L. Cazenove, Lieut. H. D. Saward, Lieut. E. A. Godfrey, 2nd Lieut. N. R. Crockatt, 2nd Lieut. T. S. Robson-Scott, 2nd Lieut. G. H. Hay, 2nd Lieut. C. W. E. Cole-Hamilton, 2nd Lieut. R. C. Ross.

Middle Row.—2nd Lieut. Robertson, Capt. A. M. C. Hewat, Capt. and QM. A. E. Everingham, 2nd Lieut. E. P. Combe, Lieut. D. J. Montagu-Douglas-Scott, Lieut. G. C. C. Strange, Lieut. C. G. Graves, Lieut. M. Henderson, Capt. E. C. Hill-Whitson, Lieut. C. E. Scarisbrick, Capt. F. C. Tanner, 2nd Lieut. V. M. G. Menzies.

Front Row (sitting).—2nd Lieut. M. C. Bulteel, Capt. A. D. Shafto, D.S.O., Capt. A. F. S. Leggatt, Capt. C. L. Price, D.S.O., Lieut.-Col. H. M'Micking, D.S.O., Major R. C. Dundas, Major F. J. Duncan, D.S.O., Major G. S. Tweedie, Lieut. J. W. Laidlay.

OFFICERS OF 1/4TH BATTALION, THE ROYAL SCOTS.

Back Row.—Lieut. Byers, Lieut. J. M. Slater, Lieut. J. Riddell, Lieut. A. Young, Lieut. R. D. Macrorie, Lieut. T. D. Aitchison.

Middle Row.—Dr Ewing, Lieut. F. B. Mackenzie, Lieut. J. Logan, Capt. J. D. Pollock, Lieut. C. F. Allan, Capt. Tait, Capt. J. Robertson, Lieut. R. F. Mackie, Lieut. L. R. Grant, Lieut. J. Morham, Lieut. J. Gray, Capt. Pirie Watson.

Front Row.—Capt. G. M'Crae, Capt. W. C. C. Sinclair, Major J. N. Henderson, Major J. Gray, Colonel Younger, Major Simpson, Capt. J. K. M. Hamilton, Capt. A. Smith, Capt. G. A. S. Ross.

Absent.—Lieut.-Col. S. R. Dunn, Capt. R. W. G. Rutherford, Lieut. P. F. Considine, Lieut. J. Fleck, 2nd Lieut. W. J. Johnstone, Lieut. D. M. Stewart, 2nd Lieut. C. Paterson, 2nd Lieut. R. J. Gibson.

Officers of 5th Battalion, The Royal Scots.

OFFICERS OF 6TH BATTALION, THE ROYAL SCOTS.

Back Row.—Lieut. W. E. Hodgson, 2nd Lieut. J. L. B. Cuthbertson, 2nd Lieut. A. Chalmers, 2nd Lieut. H. Lord, Lieut. J. Stirling, 2nd Lieut. N. J. D. Henderson, Lieut. J. Young, 2nd Lieut. D. Rae, Lieut. J. Steele, 2nd Lieut. P. Macandrew.

Middle Row.—2nd Lieut. R. F. W. Henderson (*kneeling*), 2nd Lieut. W. Brown, 2nd Lieut. N. Barker, Capt. L. J. C. Darge, Capt. J. H. Mowat, Capt. L. Sandys-Wunsch, Lieut. F. R. Lornie, Lieut. A. M. Ballingall, Lieut. H. M. Jardine, Lieut. H. M. Morrison, 2nd Lieut. J. Grahamslaw (*between middle and back rows*).

Front Row (sitting).—Capt. J. M. Milligan, Major K. Whitton, Lieut.-Col. T. F. Turnbull, Major J. W. Adams, Capt. W. E. Douglas, 2nd Lieut. E. N. Paterson (*kneeling*).

Sitting in Front.—2nd Lieut. T. Moore, 2nd Lieut. H. Rule.

OFFICERS OF 1/7TH BATTALION, THE ROYAL SCOTS (APRIL 1915).

Back Row.—Lieut. J. A. Young, Lieut. E. J. Thomson, 2nd Lieut. D. Lyell, Lieut. J. Ballantyne, Lieut. J. C. Bell, 2nd Lieut. N. G. Salvesen, 2nd Lieut. F. W. Thomson, Lieut. W. C. M'Geachin.

Middle Row.—2nd Lieut. T. M'Clelland, Lieut. C. R. Salvesen, Lieut. A. O. Cushny, Lieut. W. R. Kermack, Capt. A. J. Wightman, Capt. J. A. Torrance, Capt. W. T. Ewing, Capt. J. M. Mitchell, Capt. J. R. Peebles, Lieut. N. C. Riddell, Capt. G. G. Weir.

Front Row.—Capt. A. M. Mitchell, Major J. D. Hamilton, Capt. J. G. P. Romanes (Adjutant), Lieut.-Col. W. Carmichael Peebles, T.D., The Right Hon. The Earl of Rosebery, K.G., K.T., V.D., Hon. Colonel, Major A. W. Sanderson, Lieut.-Col. J. Mill, V.D., R.A.M.C., Capt. J. D. Dawson, Capt. D. Clark.

Sitting.—Lieut. G. W. Hawes, Lieut. A. S. Elliot, 2nd Lieut. T. G. Clark, Lieut. R. M. Galloway.

OFFICERS OF 8TH BATTALION, THE ROYAL SCOTS.

Officers of 9th Battalion, The Royal Scots (July 1914).

Back Row.—2nd Lieut. S. Fraser, Lieut. D. Fleming (4th Gordons, attached), Lieut. A. D. Maxwell, Lieut. G. H. Green, Capt. R. J. Wallace, 2nd Lieut. R. S. Lindsay, Lieut. D. Bell, 2nd Lieut. G. S. G. Smith-Grant, Lieut. W. C. S. Lindsay, Lieut. D. A. Ross Haddon, Lieut. W. S. S. Lyon.

Middle Row.—Major J. Cumming, R.A.M.C., Capt. G. D. Cowan, Capt. J. Ferguson, Brig.-Gen. H. F. Kays, Lieut.-Col. A. S. Blair, Capt. and Adjt. R. M. Dudgeon (Camerons), Major J. Collow-Campbell, Capt. F. R. Lucas, Capt. P. A. Blair.

Front Row.—2nd Lieut. D. J. Blair, Lieut. T. W. Bennet Clark, Capt. A. Macintosh (Camerons), 2nd Lieut. W. M. Urquhart, Capt. A. C. Aitken.

Absent.—Major D. H. Huie, Major J. S. Taylor Cameron, Major and QM. A. Gordon, Capt. R. H. F. Moncreiff, Capt. J. M. Bowie, R.A.M.C., Lieut. N. Macdonald, Lieut. W. Liddle, Lieut. J. L. Robertson.

OFFICERS OF 11TH BATTALION, THE ROYAL SCOTS.

Back Row.—Lieut. C. J. Lambert, 2nd Lieut. C. Anderson, 2nd Lieut. H. C. Bellamy, 2nd Lieut. J. Smith, 2nd Lieut. I. M. K. Brown, 2nd Lieut. J. W. Brown, 2nd Lieut. D. R. Gawler, 2nd Lieut. C. C. Winchester, 2nd Lieut. G. P. Smith.

Second Row (standing).—2nd Lieut. A. C. Symons, 2nd Lieut. W. Loftus, Lieut. G. Lammie, Lieut. C. Dixon, Lieut. C. C. Pitcairn-Hill, Lieut. C. W. Grant, Lieut. J. A. Henry, Lieut. G. L. Brander, Lieut. W. S. Mullett.

Third Row (sitting).—Capt. W. Hunter, Capt. H. D. Drysdale, Capt. J. Robertson, Capt. Swindale, Major K. R. M'Cloughin, Lieut.-Col. R. C. Dundas, Capt. L. Errington, Major Evans, Capt. R. W. Campbell, Capt. J. O. Grey, Capt. A. H. Bell.

Front Row.—2nd Lieut. D. E. Calver, 2nd Lieut. J. F. G. Turner, 2nd Lieut. W. Macfadyen, 2nd Lieut. Carruthers, 2nd Lieut. Edwards, 2nd Lieut. J. S. Lockhart.

OFFICERS OF 13TH BATTALION, THE ROYAL SCOTS.

Back Row.—2nd Lieut. T. D. Burt, Lieut. J. B. Kincaid, 2nd Lieut. E. G. Mackie, 2nd Lieut. J. Elder, 2nd Lieut. W. M. Mackie, 2nd Lieut. A. H. Craig, 2nd Lieut. F. H. James, Lieut. Hay, Lieut. T. M. Tomlinson, 2nd Lieut. W. C. C. Dunlop, 2nd Lieut. A. C. Craig, 2nd Lieut. F. C. Buchanan, 2nd Lieut. E. V. Richardson, 2nd Lieut. C. K. M. Douglas.

Second Back Row.—Lieut. MacMullen, Lieut. H. J. Underwood, Capt. G. S. Robertson, 2nd Lieut. T. G. Mackenzie, 2nd Lieut. G. V. F. Davies, 2nd Lieut. G. E. Dunn, 2nd Lieut. B. C. Matthews, 2nd Lieut. A. Linton, 2nd Lieut. K. F. Balmain, Lieut. and QM. H. B. M'Donald, Lieut. C. B. Munro, Lieut. R. J. M. Christie, Lieut. R. A. M'Farlane, 2nd Lieut. H. B. Johnston, 2nd Lieut. H. G. Crowden.

Third Row (sitting).—Capt. M. Halcrow, Capt. J. H. Glover, Capt. K. G. Buchanan, Major G. D. Macpherson, Brig.-Gen. Wallerstein, Major E. H. B. Raymond, Major Beck, Capt. I. C. Penney, Capt. B. D. Bruce.

Front Row.—2nd Lieut. E. B. O. Bourchier, 2nd Lieut. J. Mitchell, Lieut. A. E. Considine, 2nd Lieut. A. M. H. Bull, 2nd Lieut. J. A. J. Cattanach, 2nd Lieut. C. W. Yule, Murray Rogers (C.F.), 2nd Lieut. H. M. Scott.

OFFICERS OF 15TH BATTALION, THE ROYAL SCOTS.

Standing.—Lieut. A. Smith, Capt. A. M. Macdonald, Capt. R. D. Bruce, Lieut. A. G. Scougal, Major H. L. Stocks, 2nd Lieut. W. C. G. Black, Col. Sir R. Cranston, K.C.V.O., C.B., Capt. G. E. Gee, Lieut.-Col. A. G. B. Urmston, 2nd Lieut. W. L. Tod, Major H. A. Rose, Major J. R. Bruce, Capt. R. B. Greig, Capt. R. R. Russell, 2nd Lieut. D. G. Shields, Lieut. W. J. Lodge, Capt. J. L. Lawrence, Capt. E. Manning.

Sitting.—2nd Lieut. A. C. Harrison, 2nd Lieut. R. K. Graham, 2nd Lieut. W. A. Hole, 2nd Lieut. G. F. Dobie, 2nd Lieut. G. P. Douglas, 2nd Lieut. W. C. Inman, 2nd Lieut. W. B. Torrance, 2nd Lieut. L. S. Robson, 2nd Lieut. J. S. Montgomery.

OFFICERS OF 16TH BATTALION, THE ROYAL SCOTS.

Back Row (standing).—Lieut. J. W. Moir, 2nd Lieut. A. Maclachlan, 2nd Lieut. N. M. L. Walker, 2nd Lieut. A. F. M'Lean, 2nd Lieut. J. Drew, 2nd Lieut. Munro, 2nd Lieut. J. M. Mackintosh, 2nd Lieut. D. M. Sutherland, 2nd Lieut. D. Strachan, 2nd Lieut. R. Armstrong, Lieut. J. Blair.

Second Row (standing).—Lieut. R. H. Husband, 2nd Lieut. M'Murray, 2nd Lieut. J. G. P. Stevenson, 2nd Lieut. L. Kitton, 2nd Lieut. J. R. M'Lennan, Lieut. R. F. Martin, 2nd Lieut. T. Grainger-Stewart, 2nd Lieut. R. C. Lodge, 2nd Lieut. H. C. Julian, Lieut. L. Coles, Lieut. J. M. Davie, 2nd Lieut. J. M'Kenzie, 2nd Lieut. J. W. Stewart, 2nd Lieut. C. W. Wood.

Third Row.—Lieut. H. Gray, Lieut. P. Ross, Capt. A. E. Warr, Capt. J. Hendry, Major R. D. Lauder, Major H. L. Warden, Lieut.-Col. Sir G. M'Crae, V.D., Capt. W. B. Robertson, Capt. J. Fowler, Capt. N. Armit, Capt. J. H. M. Sandison, Lieut. A. Whyte.

Fourth Row.—2nd Lieut. T. M. Millar, 2nd Lieut. S. M. Bryce, 2nd Lieut. H. C. Rawson, 2nd Lieut. T. R. Tod.

OFFICERS OF 17TH BATTALION, THE ROYAL SCOTS (FEBRUARY 1916).

Back Row.—Lieut. W. S. Eadie, Lieut. J. C. M‘Pake, Lieut. H. B. Kerr, 2nd Lieut. W. D. Sim, 2nd Lieut. A. D. Loch, 2nd Lieut. D. G. Ross (Sup.), Lieut. W. A. Wells, Lieut. G. B. Russell, 2nd Lieut. A. Gray Murray, 2nd Lieut. J. A. Tait (Sup.).

Second Row (standing).—Lieut. W, D. C. Knox, 2nd Lieut. H. Gladstone, 2nd Lieut. E. R. Craig, 2nd Lieut. H. Houston, 2nd Lieut. S. M‘Knight, 2nd Lieut. Wm. Spence, 2nd Lieut. A. Currie, 2nd Lieut. D. Mitchell, 2nd Lieut. D. Gellatly, 2nd Lieut. R. L. Fortune (Sup.), Lieut. W. S. Hofford, Lieut. and QM. R. S. Smeaton.

Third Row (sitting).—Lieut. A. H. Manfield, R.A.M.C., Capt. W. Graham Barnett, Capt. E. E. Ruddell, Major G. F. F. Foulkes, Major L. L. Bilton, Lieut.-Col. R. D. Cheales, Capt. A. G. Scougal (Adjt.), Capt. R. C. Barry, Capt. R. D. Edgar, Capt. A. J. Bruce, Capt. Arthur V. Ross.

Front Row.—2nd Lieut. W. R. Duff, 2nd Lieut. T. G. G. Sturrock, Lieut. E. Elliot Drysdale.

MAP 18

PASSCHENDAELE, 1917, & THE OFFENSIVE IN FLANDERS, 1918

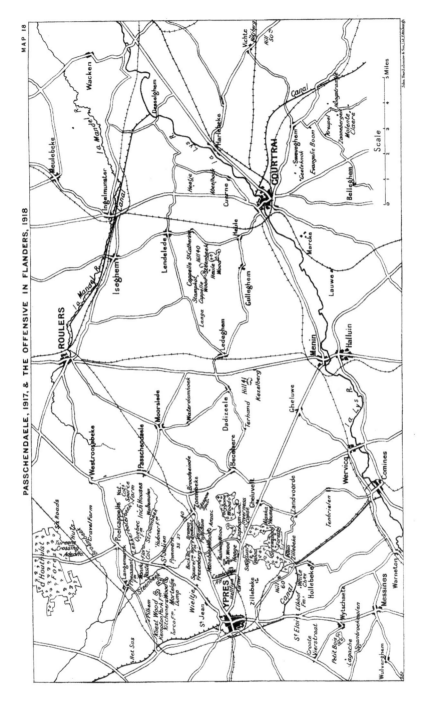

Scale

0 1 2 3 4 5 Miles

John Bartholomew & Son, Ltd. Edinburgh

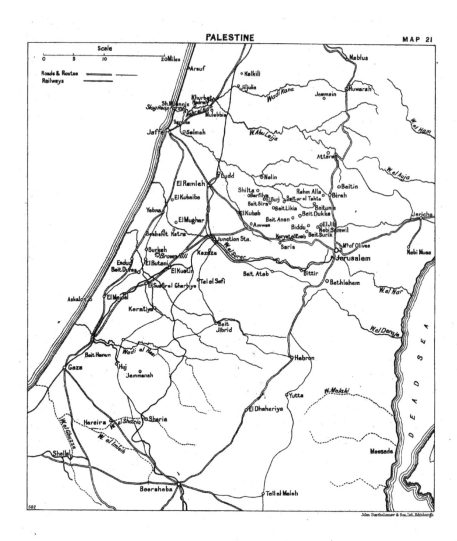

MAP 22

GERMAN OFFENSIVE AGAINST THE FIFTH ARMY (MARCH 1918) & ADVANCE OF FOURTH ARMY (AUG.- OCT. 1918.)

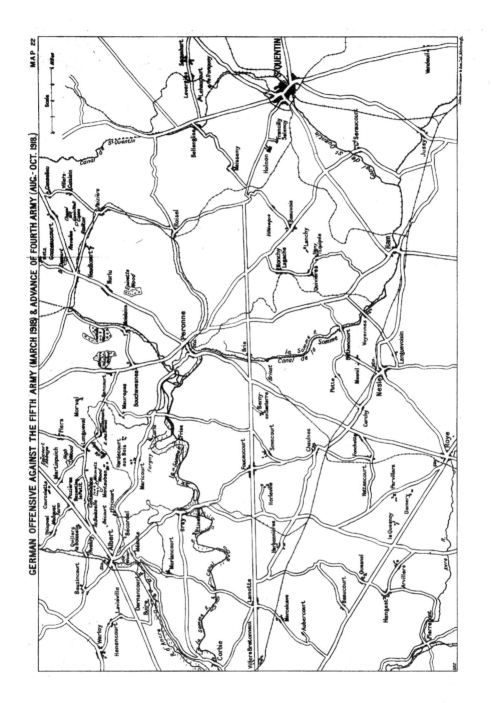

MAP 23

GERMAN OFFENSIVE AGAINST THE THIRD ARMY (MARCH 1918) & ADVANCE OF THIRD & FIRST ARMIES (AUGUST - NOVEMBER 1918.)

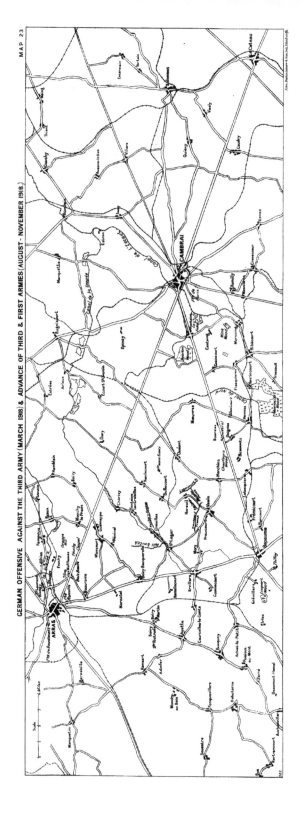

Hill 60
Klein Zillebeke
Canal
Ouderdom
Dickebusch
St Eloi
Voormezeel
Hollebeke
Zandvoorde
Reninghelst
Westoutre
La Clytte
Groote Vierstraat
Steenvoorde
Tardeghem
CASSEL
Kemmel
Wytschaete
Mt des Cats
Mt Kemmel
Spanbroekmolen
St Jans Cappel
Mt Noir
Locre
Petit Bac
Legache
Messines
Dranoutre
Warneton
Warnenton
la Lys
Meteren
Bailleul
Mont Cde Lille
Mont de l'Achelles
Ploegsteert
La Crèche
Papot
Ravelsberg
Mt Wallon Cappel
Hazebrouck
Morris
Les Trois Arbres
Nieppe
Fredlinghien
Morbecque
Vieux Berquin
Steenwerck
Pont de Nieppe
L'Épinette
Steenbecque
Forêt de Nieppe
Canal de la Nieppe
Crois du Bac
Sailly sur la Lys
la
Erquinghem
ARMENTIÈRES
Fort Rompu
St Maur
Fleurbaix
Bois Grenier
Lomme
Estaires
Merville
Canal de la Lys
St Venant
Canal de la Aire
Radinghem
Haubourdin
Beauzeleux Farm
Paradis
Vert Touquet
Fauquissart
Pacaut
Route du Bac
Rouge Croix
Neuve Chapelle
la Pilly
Meille Chapelle
Wavrin
le Cornet Malo
Mt Bernenchon
Busnes
Pont Logy
Neuve Chapelle
Croix Barbée
Legon
Lillers
Illies
Canal de Douai Lille
Oblingham
Rue Caillou
Canal de la Bassée
Essars
la Quinque Rue
Festubert
la Bassée
Allouagne
BÉTHUNE
Givenchy
Raimbert
Lozingham
Cuinchy
Auchel
Haisnes
Douvrin

Scale
0   1 Miles

MAP 28

THE FINAL ADVANCE (9ᵀᴴ 13ᵀᴴ 4ᵀᴴ & 7ᵀᴴ BATTS.) SEPT.– NOV. 1918

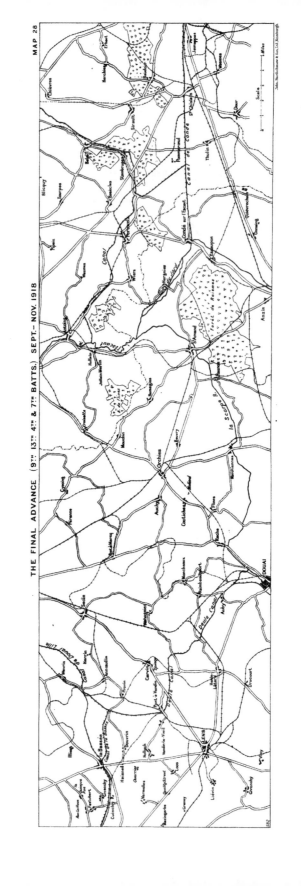